Charles Edward Moberly

The early Tudors. Henry VII.: Henry VIII

Charles Edward Moberly

The early Tudors. Henry VII.: Henry VIII

ISBN/EAN: 9783337021733

Printed in Europe, USA, Canada, Australia, Japan

Cover: Foto ©ninafisch / pixelio.de

More available books at **www.hansebooks.com**

Epochs of Modern History

EDITED BY

EDWARD E. MORRIS, M.A., J. SURTEES PHILLPOTTS, B.C.L.

AND

C. COLBECK, M.A.

THE EARLY TUDORS

REV. C. E. MOBERLY

EPOCHS OF ANCIENT HISTORY.

Edited by Rev. G. W. Cox and Charles Sankey, M.A. Eleven volumes, 16mo, with 41 Maps and Plans. Price per vol., $1.00. The set, Roxburgh style, gilt top, in box, $11.00.

Troy—Its Legend, History, and Literature. By S. G. W. Benjamin.
The Greeks and the Persians. By G. W. Cox.
The Athenian Empire. By G. W. Cox.
The Spartan and Theban Supremacies. By Charles Sankey.
The Macedonian Empire. By A. M. Curteis.
Early Rome. By W. Ihne.
Rome and Carthage. By R. Bosworth Smith.
The Gracchi, Marius and Sulla. By A. H. Beesley.
The Roman Triumvirates By Charles Merivale.
The Early Empire. By W. Wolfe Capes.
The Age of the Antonines. By W. Wolfe Capes.

EPOCHS OF MODERN HISTORY.

Edited by Edward E. Morris. Eighteen volumes, 16mo, with 77 Maps, Plans, and Tables. Price per vol., $1.00. The set, Roxburgh style, gilt top, in box, $18.00.

The Beginning of the Middle Ages. By R. W. Church.
The Normans in Europe. By A. H. Johnson.
The Crusades. By G. W. Cox.
The Early Plantagenets. By Wm. Stubbs.
Edward III. By W. Warburton.
The Houses of Lancaster and York. By James Gairdner.
The Era of the Protestant Revolution. By Frederic Seebohm.
The Early Tudors. By C. E. Moberly.
The Age of Elizabeth. By M. Creighton.
The Thirty Years' War, 1618–1648. By S. R. Gardiner.
The Puritan Revolution. By S. R. Gardiner.
The Fall of the Stuarts. By Edward Hale.
The English Restoration and Louis XIV By Osmund Airy.
The Age of Anne. By Edward E. Morris.
The Early Hanoverians. By Edward E. Morris.
Frederick the Great. By F. W. Longman.
The French Revolution and First Empire. By W. O'Connor Morris. Appendix by Andrew D. White.
The Epoch of Reform, 1830–1850. By Justin Macarthy.

EPOCHS OF MODERN HISTORY

THE EARLY TUDO

HENRY VII.: HENRY VIII.

BY THE
REV. C. E. MOBERLY, M.A.
LATE A MASTER IN RUGBY SCHOOL

WITH MAPS AND PLANS

NEW YORK
CHARLES SCRIBNER'S SONS
1889

PREFACE.

As the plan of works in this Series does not allow of systematic references at the foot of the pages to larger and more detailed histories of the period, it may be well to mention here a few of the books which are likely to be most useful to those who wish to study it more fully. So far as these are complete histories, they must be chiefly modern, as the age was not fertile in contemporary narratives. Thus for Richard III.'s time Mr. Gairdner's excellent Life of that king should be studied, with its appendix on Warbeck; for Henry VII. Lord Bacon's Life, which has been carefully edited for the Cambridge University Press by Mr. Lumby. The Stanhope Essay by Mr. Williamson on the 'Foreign Commerce of England under the Tudors' gives ample details on this subject in very small compass; and the religious movement from 1485 to 1509 is described to perfection in Mr. Seebohm's delightful work on Colet, Erasmus, and More, and in Cooper's Life of the Lady Margaret.

For Henry VIII.'s reign much has been done of late years, above all by Mr. Brewer in his celebrated Prefaces to the papers of the reign in the Rolls

Series (which have been published separately in two volumes), illustrating the years from 1509 to 1529. The history of the early Reformation is given with much detail and liveliness in Dean Hook's Lives of Archbishops Morton, Warham, and Cranmer; the Dissolution of the Monasteries and other measures of the reign have been examined with great care in Dixon's 'History of the Church of England,' a work of unusual merit. The subject of religion is admirably treated as regards Germany in Ranke's 'History of the Reformation,' which Miss Austen has translated.

It is hardly necessary to refer to Mr. Froude's history of Henry VIII., for no one can hope to know the period without reading it diligently. True it is that this industrious and most eloquent writer may probably fail in inspiring readers with his own admiration for Henry's actions, which indeed he has of late shown some disposition to reconsider. But, qualify his verdict as we will, we shall still find abundant profit as well as pleasure in reading his great work, especially if we check and perhaps correct his view of some great events by comparing with it Mr. Friedmann's recently published Life of Anne Boleyn, which is full of important information and shows the hand of a master throughout. For Scottish affairs Mr. Burton's 'History of Scotland' is all that can be desired.

Lastly, it may be permitted to refer to some very interesting papers on Henry VII. and Henry VIII.

contained in Bishop Stubbs's recently published volume of Oxford Lectures. No use has been made of these in the present work, which was in type before they appeared; its writer ventures to remark that, where he himself has praised Henry VII., he often finds with great pleasure that the Bishop does the same. It is somewhat disquieting to observe that the Lectures attribute to Henry VIII. far more innate power and ruling faculty than has been here traced in his administration, civil, military, and religious. It may perhaps serve as an excuse for differing from so high an authority that Mr. Friedmann, after taking a connected view from without of Henry's entire management of home and foreign affairs, and of the opinions with regard to him expressed by foreign sovereigns and their correspondents, is inclined to place him lower, even in mere intellect, than any English writer has yet ventured to do.

CONTENTS.

CHAPTER I.
	PAGE
National unity from despotism	1
Despotism in Spain	3
Despotism in France	7
Despotism in England	9

CHAPTER II.
Henry VII.'s claim to the throne	14
The Lady Margaret	15
Henry's invasion	16
Battle of Bosworth Field	18
Henry's title to the throne	21
The Coronation	22
Restoration of persons attainted	23
The Pestilence	25
English feeling under it	26

CHAPTER III.
Parliament of 1485	27
Rebellion of the Staffords	28
Causes of Yorkist feeling	29
Simnel. Battle of Stoke	30
Martial law	33
Affairs of Bretagne	34
French policy there	36
Northern and Scottish rebellions	38
Quasi-war with France. Peace of Etaples	39

CHAPTER IV.
Warbeck widely supported	42
Warbeck in Ireland and Scotland	45
Cornish rebellion. Blackheath Field	47

Warbeck in Devonshire 49
The Intercursus Magnus 50

CHAPTER V.

Charles VIII. in Italy 51
Royal marriages. The Italian League 54
Crusade refused 56
Prince Arthur and Katherine 57
Plan for Katherine's second marriage 59
The Archduke Philip in England 60
Empson and Dudley 63
Death of Henry VII. 64

CHAPTER VI.

State of Ireland 65
Poynings' Laws 66
Fraternity of St. George 69
Laws of Henry VII. 69
The Star Chamber 71
Navigation Law, &c. 73
Trade with the Netherlands 73
French trade 75
Voyages of discovery. Vasco de Gama. Columbus . . 76
The Cabots 77

CHAPTER VII.

Spirit of the Renaissance 79
Enthusiasm for Latin and Greek authors. Colet, More . 80
Works of Erasmus 86
Schools and colleges for the New Learning . . . 88
Printers. Wynkyn de Worde. Poetry of the time . . 91
Prose of the period. The 'Utopia' 93
Cardinal Morton and Church Reform 94
Erasmus on pilgrimages 96
Buildings, &c., of the period 98

CHAPTER VIII.

Henry VIII. fond of the navy 101
Execution of Empson and Dudley 103

	PAGE
Marriage with Katherine of Aragon	104
Death of the Lady Margaret	105
Disciplinary laws	106
Argument on Church privileges	108
James IV. of Scotland. The Bartons	108
War with France: how regarded	110

CHAPTER IX.

The League of Cambray	112
Resistance of Venice	113
Henry VIII. joins the Holy League; his failure	114
Naval operations	116
Invasion of France	117
Battle of Flodden Field	118
Home effects of the war	120

CHAPTER X.

English trade in the Netherlands	123
Cornish mining	124
Jealousy of foreigners	125
Population shifting in England	128
Depopulation of the rural districts	129
The rise in rents	129
Scotland under Queen Margaret	130
The government of Ireland	132
Vain attempts at a Crusade	132

CHAPTER XI.

The French in Italy. Battle of Marignano	133
Wolsey's administration	136
Field of the Cloth of Gold: its uselessness	139
The Duke of Buckingham executed	141
Henry's treachery to Francis	143
The War of Pavia	143
Turkish conquest of Rhodes	146
War taxation in England	147
Sack of Rome	149

CHAPTER XII.

	PAGE
Old anti-Papal laws	150
Forerunners of the Reformation. Doctrine of Luther	151
Henry VIII. Defender of the Faith	155
Beginning of the Divorce question	156
Its dangers to England	158
Commission of Campeggio	159
Fall of Wolsey	162
His arrest and death	166
The first Reforming Parliament. *Præmunire* against the clergy	167
Resistance of the clergy overruled	170

CHAPTER XIII.

Appeal to the Universities on the Divorce.	171
Cranmer's Court at Dunstable. Popular feeling towards Anne	173
Conditional excommunication of Henry	175
The Nun of Kent. Peter's Pence. The *congé d'élire*	176
Northern conspiracies. Rising in Ireland	180
Death of Fisher and More	182
Character of Sir T. More	184

CHAPTER XIV.

The Bull of Deposition drawn up	188
Execution of Anne Boleyn	189
Henry's Protestant leanings	192
State of the monasteries	193
The Universities visited	195
Visitation of the Monasteries	196
The Louth rebellion	199
The Yorkshire insurrection	201
The 'Bishops' Book'	205
Prince Edward born. Case of Lambert	206

CHAPTER XV.

Lord Exeter and the Poles. The Six Articles	209
Legislation for Wales	213

	PAGE
The alliance with Cleves. Fall of Cromwell	214
The Reformation in Scotland	217
Solway Moss. Death of James V. Attempts at Union	219
Lord Leonard Grey in Ireland	222
Katherine Howard. Death of Lady Salisbury	224

CHAPTER XVI.

Charles V. fails at Algiers	225
Henry joins Charles against Francis and the Turks	227
French attack on Portsmouth	229
The currency debased	230
Execution of Lord Surrey	231
Henry's last persecutions; his last foundations	233
Katherine Parr	234
Death of Henry	235
Henry's influence on the Church	236
Civil laws of Henry VIII.	238
Trials under Henry VIII.	240
Poetry of the period	240
The stage and prose	242
Science	243
Character of the middle classes	244
Effect of Henry VIII.'s institutions	246

INDEX 247

MAPS.

ENGLAND AND WALES, 1485-1547	*To face Title-page*
CAMPAIGN OF TEROUENNE	116
BATTLE OF FLODDEN FIELD	119
CLEVES, MARK, BERG, JULIERS	214

THE CHIEF EUROPEAN SOVEREIGNS AND MEMBERS OF ROYAL FAMILIES.

(1485–1547.)

A. EMPERORS OF GERMANY.

1. FREDERIC III. (first Emperor of the Austrian House of Hapsburg), King of the Romans 1440; crowned Emperor 1459; died 1493.
2. MAXIMILIAN I. (son of Frederic III.), King of the Romans 1486, never crowned; styles himself 'Emperor Elect' from 1503; died 1519. Married (*a*) Mary of Burgundy; (*b*) Anne of Bretagne; (by proxy—marriage dissolved); (*c*) Bianca Maria Sforza of Milan.

    Has issue—(*a*) The Archduke Philip, who inherits the Netherlands from his mother, Mary of Burgundy, 1483; marries Juana of Castile 1505; dies 1506. (*b*) Margaret of Savoy; betrothed to Charles VIII.; married to the Duke of Savoy.
3. CHARLES V. (son of Philip and Juana), King of Spain 1516; King of the Romans 1519; crowned Emperor 1531; abdicated 1558.

B. SOVEREIGNS OF SPAIN.

1. { FERDINAND King of Aragon . . 1479–1504
   { ISABELLA Queen of Castile . . 1474–1504
2. JUANA Queen of Spain . . . 1504–1516
3. CHARLES V. 1516–1558

Chief European Sovereigns.

C. KINGS OF FRANCE.

1. LOUIS XI.   . 1461–1483
2. CHARLES VIII.   . 1483–1498 ⎫ Successively married
3. LOUIS XII.   . 1498–1515 ⎭ to Anne of Bretagne.
4. FRANCIS I.   . 1515–1547

D. KINGS OF ENGLAND.

1. RICHARD III.   . 1483–1485
2. HENRY VII.   . 1485–1509
3. HENRY VIII.   . 1509–1547

E. POPES.

1. ALEXANDER VI.   . 1492–1503
2. PIUS III.   . 1503
3. JULIUS II.   . 1503–1513
4. LEO X.   . 1515–1521
5. ADRIAN VI.   . 1522–1523
6. CLEMENT VII.   . 1523–1534
7. PAUL III.   . 1534–1549

F. MEMBERS OF THE ENGLISH ROYAL FAMILY.

(*a*) The daughters of Henry VII.:—

1. Margaret, married (*a*) James IV. of Scotland; (*b*) Lord Angus; (*c*) Lord Methuen; and was mother of (*a*) James V. of Scotland; (*b*) of Lady Margaret Lennox (mother of Lord Darnley).
2. Mary, married (*a*) Louis XII.; (*b*) Charles Brandon, Duke of Suffolk; and was the grandmother of Lady Jane Grey.

(*b*) The House of Lancaster (descended from John of Gaunt through the Beauforts):—

The Lady Margaret (mother of Henry VII.).

(*c*) The House of York (descended from Lionel Duke of Clarence, the third son, and Thomas of Woodstock, the sixth son, of Edward III):—

1. Margaret Duchess of Burgundy, sister of Edward IV.
2. Elizabeth, daughter of Edward IV., married Henry VII., died 1501.
3. The Earl of Lincoln (killed at Stoke 1487) and the Earl of Suffolk (beheaded 1513), sons of Elizabeth, sister of Edward IV.
4. The Earl of Warwick, son of George Duke of Clarence (beheaded 1499), and his sister.
5. The Countess of Salisbury (beheaded 1539); had issue (*a*) Lord Montagu (beheaded 1539); (*b*) Cardinal Pole; (*c*) Sir Geoffrey Pole (and others).
6. The Marquis of Exeter (beheaded 1539); his mother was Lady Courtenay, daughter of Edward IV.
7. The Duke of Buckingham (beheaded 1521) was descended from Thomas of Woodstock, sixth son of Edward III.
8. The Earl of Surrey (beheaded 1546); had the same descent through his mother, who was daughter of the Duke of Buckingham.

G. MEMBERS OF THE SCOTTISH ROYAL FAMILY.

1. Mary (Queen of Scots), daughter of James V.
2. The Duke of Albany, son of a younger brother of James III.
3. The Earl of Arran, son of a sister of James III.
4. Margaret Lady Lennox, daughter of Queen Margaret of Scotland by Lord Angus; mother of Henry Darnley.

THE EARLY TUDORS.

CHAPTER I.

THE GROWTH OF DESPOTISM IN EUROPE DURING THE FIFTEENTH CENTURY.

FOR those who, like ourselves, are trained under free institutions, it is hard to realise that great nations are generally those which have been long under the stern discipline of a despotism at last shaken off. *Unity from despotism.* Yet it cannot be denied that this form of government, extending over the whole of a large country, and ruling all things within it, has been more able than any other to create a strong sense of nationality overpowering narrow local differences, to establish thorough internal security, and to direct the people to enterprises requiring great exertion in the general cause, and leading to strong enthusiasms, whether through defeat or victory. It has been mostly when their energies have been thus guided that nations have forgotten the jealousies of province against province, county against county, district against district, and learned that the members of one State are immeasurably nearer to one another than any foreigner can be. And when this feeling for the first time gains strength, and a great nation is brought to feel its own unity, how many important consequences spring from the change! A people which has been thus ruled, if only the despotism does not last long enough to break its spirit, is sure to feel intensely. Loyalty to the power which has made it one becomes a passion, sometimes even a madness. Bravery makes no account of its own life or of other men's. Self-devotion prevails in many of its most striking forms. High-spirited men become proud of laying down their freedom at the feet of a master who gives them in exchange for it the prospect of ruling over their fellow-men as his deputies. In such times we must not indeed expect to find justice, humanity, and peacefulness, or even truth and honour as now understood; these are plants which spring only from the soil of freedom. But we can say that the national mind, in order that it may some time feel truth and right strongly, is at any rate learning to feel *something* strongly. That something may be, and often is, perverse; indeed it is with a people as with a child, in whom we tolerate a certain violence and misdirection of will, because we know that such strength is the very seed-bed of future excellence, and that no one can be really great of whom we cannot say that 'quidquid volet valde volet.' Such, then, is on the whole the meaning of those who say that few nations become really great without having been under despotism for a time. In this sense eminent Italian politicians, even of the present day, sometimes hold to Macchiavelli's opinion, that it is the greatest of national misfortunes to their countrymen never to have been welded together by passing through this stage; and far-seeing thinkers among ourselves have considered the present constitution of Russia not unfavourable to her chance of being great at last, seeing that despotism has certainly built up her unity and inspired her with the spirit of obedience and self-sacrifice, without hitherto breaking down the energy which will some time achieve her political freedom.

Whether the history of England from the sixteenth century onwards proves the truth of this theory will be best settled when we have gone through it. It is plain enough, at any rate, that a despotism *did* establish itself under the Tudors, and that many of the qualities likely to characterise a nation thus governed did, in fact, show themselves in Englishmen. We do, as a matter of fact, see them proud of their national unity, bearing themselves haughtily towards foreigners, immoderately fond of aggressive expeditions, recklessly brave, deeply and sometimes even insanely loyal. The object of this work is to trace the rise of the autocracy which had these effects; and, as the history of England is seldom or never so cut off from that of the Continent as to have nothing in common with what goes on there at the same time, it will be well, by way of introduction, to show that increasing despotism was in the fifteenth century the law, so to speak, of advance in the countries of Western Europe. Thus we shall presently be enabled to see what changes among ourselves sprang from direct imitation of our neighbours, and what others arose from causes of a general character affecting all countries alike.

Spain, as might be expected from the mixture of Eastern blood in her people, and the military type of her civilisation, had been first to enter upon the course of absolutism which for a time raised her power to such a portentous height, and then laid it prostrate. Indeed her feuds of the Trastamare family had been as effective as our Wars of the Roses a hundred years later in clearing off the turbulent nobles, and thus enabling the Crown of Castile to strengthen

Despotism in Spain.

itself by the help of the Commons. Under the young
Henry III. (1390), the husband of Catherine of Lancaster, the Third Estate was in remarkable prosperity;
commerce and manufactures improved greatly, and the
history of the country might have been different but
for Henry's death in 1406, at the early age of twenty-
eight. He was succeeded by his son, John II., whose
reign of forty-eight years was little else than a perpetual conspiracy against his subjects' freedom. Aided
by his imperious minister Alvaro de Luna, he excluded
from the royal Council the deputies of the Commons,
raised taxes without legislative sanction, and issued
pragmaticas asserting his own right to make laws for
his subjects. When opposition to these arbitrary measures was threatened, he devised and carried out successfully a wicked scheme for dividing the popular party.
Some of the towns were induced, first to petition that
they might defray the expenses of their deputies during
the session of the Cortes; and then, with a surprising
want of political foresight, to allow them to be excused
attendance altogether, in order to save the same charges.
Thus after a while only eighteen towns sent deputies,
the rest being obliged to entrust their interests to these.
So successfully were the seeds of division thus sown, that
in 1506, when some of the excluded towns wished to have
their ancient rights back, they were vigorously opposed
by the privileged cities, which maintained that the right
of representation was theirs alone. The policy of
John II. was followed by Henry IV., Isabella of Castile's
elder brother, who also threw the trade of the country
into utter disorder by debasing the coinage, besides
demoralising society by his own bad example. Isabella
herself, on her accession in 1474, resolved to resume the
old policy of relying on the Commons, to which she was

the more inclined from her earnest desire to benefit the people which she ruled. By decrees obtained from the courts of justice she wrested from the nobles many of the estates, annuities, and other grants which they had unconstitutionally got from her predecessors. Besides this, both she and her husband, Ferdinand, King of Aragon, employed men of humble birth in posts which had been always held by nobles; above all, she adopted, and placed under the patronage of the Crown, the 'Holy Hermandad,' an association of the towns for the repression of violence; using it, in defiance of the nobles, as a national police which she could entirely trust. It must not for a moment be thought that her patronage of the people aimed in the least at restoring their ancient liberties: on the contrary, by establishing and enthusiastically supporting the Inquisition in her dominions, Isabella made any return to constitutional methods impossible, besides deeply staining her own character for honour, patriotism, and humanity. Satisfied with making the towns prosper materially, and with using their support against the grandees, she never foresaw that they would so soon be trying to wrest from her grandson by force of arms the liberty which she denied them. Few passages of history are sadder than the account of their rebellion against the young Charles V. in 1520; when, amidst a host of quite rational petitions for the better conduct of justice, for the relief of taxation, for a native administration, for the abolition of all privileges obtained at the expense of the Commons, for the reform of the Cortes, and for sessions once in three years at least, they still, short-sighted like their fathers, demanded that the estates of the nobles should be re-annexed to the Crown—as if they wished to destroy all barriers against despotism except their own. Accordingly, when their forces were beaten on the fatal field of Villalar, and their leaders sent to execution by Charles's ministers, the mainspring of popular freedom in Spain was broken, and they entered upon a long period of decay which has not closed even now, and which hardly required that Philip II. should ensure it by destroying, as he did in 1592, the last fragments of real power possessed by the Cortes both in Castile and in Aragon. These changes were the more melancholy because Spain had in her old institutions a thoroughly good foundation for rational freedom. Her Cortes dated from two hundred years before the time of Simon de Montfort, and had the completest control over state affairs. The accession of each fresh sovereign required their sanction, and they exercised most fully those powers of remonstrating against grievances and of voting supplies which have always been the two pivots of English freedom. In one point they went beyond us; for their petitions, if accepted by the King, had at once the force of law. In Aragon, where the ancient liberties were even stronger than in Castile, the 'Justicia' judged officially and of right whether the King's letters were genuine and his acts constitutional; while the acknowledged privileges of the kingdom acted as Magna Charta did among ourselves. Catalonia and Valencia again had all the free spirit which goes with maritime enterprise. Here the traders were often knights, all being held equal within the mercantile guilds, and the sons of merchants valued as high as those of noblemen if hostages were required in war. No cause less baleful than the bigotry which created the Inquisition could have destroyed such safeguards and the high hopes which might have been founded on them.

Before the end of the fifteenth century, a similar struggle with the nobles in France had also ended in favour of the Crown. Yet no sovereign could have been weaker than Louis XI. at his accession in 1461, and when, four years later, his nobles began the war of the 'Bien Public' against him, he was surrounded by great feudatories, all of whom he had offended bitterly. Charles the Bold, Duke of Burgundy, held, in France, Burgundy proper, with Artois and Franche-Comté; beyond it, Brabant, Limburg, Hainault, and the wealthy cities of Flanders; and was on the point of excluding France from all communication with the rest of Europe, except through his States, by seizing the Provençal dominions of René of Anjou. The Dukes of Bretagne and Bourbon, and the Count of Armagnac with his Gascons, were equally opposed to Louis; and there was not one of these potentates who would have scrupled for a moment to call in against him the English or any other foreigners. In spite of all this, he succeeded by unresting vigilance and craft in baffling them one by one, and in establishing his own power on the ruin of theirs. On the other hand, the Commons were with him, and favour to them was a ruling principle of his reign. He was never tired of encouraging trade (as when he founded the silk manufacture in France) or of increasing the privileges of the cities. As his reign advanced, and enemy after enemy fell before him, agriculture flourished more and more from the ever-increasing security of the country. His taxation was heavy, for he bought off such enemies as Edward IV. instead of fighting them; yet, in spite of Commines' invidious comparison between his revenue of 4,700,000 francs and the 1,800,000 paid under his father Charles VII., there is no appearance that his imposts were considered excessive in his lifetime. Such

Despotism in France.

were some of the points marking his government of the masses; he was to the best of his knowledge a supporter of the low against the high. Yet all that he tried to do on their behalf was more than counterbalanced by his masterful administration. Other kings had fitfully claimed a right to collect taxes by their sole authority; precedents to that effect had been common in the reigns of John, Charles V., Charles VI., and Charles VII. But Louis all through his long reign of twenty-two years, never raised money in any other way, and thus made his people forget the very notion of freedom. For, though isolated thinkers like Philippe de Commines still held that a king who levies money unconstitutionally is tyrannous and violent, and that, as long as he does so, he will never be really strong, the States-General had altogether forgotten such ideas when they assembled at Tours after Louis's death to provide for the regency. Although they took at first a high tone, and claimed the abolition of the 'taille' and other arbitrary taxes, they still allowed themselves to be worsted by a manœuvre of the Court, and granted the new king the right to levy the taxes of Charles VII., with an addition of twenty-five per cent. Their stipulation that this power should be treated as a concession of their own, and last for only two years, after which the States were to be assembled again, hardly looks like a serious attempt at freedom, when we remember that a French king could get his revenue from the Provincial Councils much more easily than he could from the States-General, and was therefore most unwilling to summon the latter, at the risk of remonstrances against every act of his government and every detail of his household arrangements. Thus Louis XI., from the success with which he organised a system of arbitrary taxation, and established it by means of his personal popularity, must needs be considered as one of the great overthrowers of liberty in France. As to other points of administration, it is almost superfluous to remark how absolute he was. No purely patriotic care for his subjects' welfare can be ascribed to the king who had men tried before judges who were to have their property if they were found guilty; nor can he be considered tender of their lives who ordered his guards to shoot down every one who came near his palace walls before a stated hour in the morning or of their personal freedom who enclosed them at pleasure in iron cages. We must, therefore, ascribe his care for commerce and the towns to the absolute necessity under which he lay of finding popular support against his too powerful feudatories. That this view of interest ripened into a positive sympathy with the industrious classes, which showed itself in many simple and natural acts of kindness, we are in no degree called upon to deny. But it is not the less true that he demoralised these very classes, first through the crooked contrivances by which he quelled their oppressors, and then still more completely by his resolution to allow them nothing like political as distinct from municipal freedom; and thus left them at his death prepared to submit to any tyranny which the course of time might produce.

It is not necessary to enumerate the various tyrannies which had raised themselves at the time we are considering upon the ruins of popular freedom in every great city of Italy, with the one exception of Venice; nor yet those which the weakness of emperors like Frederic III. had allowed to begin in the various States of Germany. But the last Plantagenet reigns in England are so important as paving the way for the Tudor despotism, that a few words must needs be said upon them, under the guidance of the latest and most learned of our constitutional historians.

The fifteenth century may be said to begin with the accession of the Lancastrian dynasty in 1399. As regards the points on which political writers most frequently dwell, Henry IV. and Henry V. were strongly inclined—the former from his defective title and the latter from an innate power of influencing men as he would— to a really constitutional government. Again and again did Henry IV. listen to the remonstrances of his Parliaments; as in 1401, when they claimed that he should accept no account of their proceedings except from themselves; in 1404, when he consented on their petition to remove *any* councillor distasteful to them, and in particular to dismiss all aliens from the Queen's service; in 1406, when they insisted that he should give an account of his expenditure and dismiss 'the rascally crew' which composed his household; and in 1407, when the Commons protested against any bill of supply originating with the Lords. Besides this, parliamentary grants to him were strictly appropriated to their intended purposes—a restriction which we are inclined to consider an improvement of modern times, and one to which even Cromwell as Protector was unwilling to submit. The Parliaments of Henry V. were naturally compliant, from the overflowing favour with which a war in France was regarded, where, as Commines repeatedly notes, every Englishman made sure of enriching himself by plunder and the ransom of captives; thus in 1417 and 1419 large subsidies were willingly paid. When, however, they *did* make remonstrances, he was, like his father, always ready to attend; as when they prayed in 1414 'that there be never no law made' (on their petition), 'and engrossed as statute and law, neither by addition nor diminution, by no manner of term which shall change the sentence and the intent asked'—a point which was to come out on a memorable occasion in after-time.

As to the safety for life under these sovereigns, it cannot be called unsatisfactory, except as regards, first, the exercise of martial law in war-time, and, secondly, the effect of statutes coming from Parliament itself. It has been well said that, in beheading Scrope and Mowbray in 1405, and the Southampton conspirators in 1415, Henry IV. and his son were sowing the wind that their dynasty might reap the whirlwind; inasmuch as from these precedents sprang the practice, so universal in the Wars of the Roses, of putting the captured leaders to death after each battle, either by a mere order, or by the sentence of such men as Montague or Tiptoft, who tried prisoners 'summarily and plainly, without any noise and shew of judgment,' and sometimes according to the law of some foreign State where the judge had received his university education. As for the barbarous executions which followed the statute 'de Hæretico Comburendo,' these of course are not technically acts of royal tyranny, since the authority for them was parliamentary, and grounded on a belief which, though in itself both cruel and stupid, had yet darkened all counsel ever since the days when it misled the strong intellect of Augustine. Here, accordingly, the State, the Crown, and above all the Church, had to share the terrible responsibility among them.

There was, therefore, under the early Lancastrian kings some ground for the admiration of England, as contrasted with France, which is expressed alike by Philippe de Commines and by the English Fortescue, whom Commines may have seen during his exile in France. Under these kings we really had what Fortescue calls a 'dominium regale et politicum:' they would not have ventured, as Edward III. did, to assent to a petition of Parliament, and then a few weeks later to rescind the Act by their own authority on the ground that they had 'dissimulated,' never having really intended to grant it. But a woful change came over England with the accession of the House of York. First the Privy Council began to assume the powers which made it such a terrible engine of oppression under Henry VII. and his successors. This body really had from Parliament a standing authority—to be exercised, however, under strict supervision—by which they could suspend the execution of various important statutes. In pecuniary matters they were authorised in case of emergency to pledge, up to a certain limited amount, the credit of the kingdom—a practice which Commines seems to have had in mind when he says that in his judgment such emergencies as make it really necessary for kings to collect money more quickly than by the normal processes of law hardly ever occur. As the king had long ceased to judge in person, and the Council was considered chiefly as his substitute, its members could not actually try cases. But to examine men before trial when suspected of treason, and to rack them for the purpose of extracting evidence, appears, in spite of Fortescue's declaration that torture was unknown to the English law, to have been thought within the royal prerogative, and therefore within the competence of the Council. The first registered instances of such torture are in 1468, under Edward IV., when more than one of Queen Margaret's messengers were burned in the feet or racked to make them discover their accomplices. The jurisdiction of the Constable under which Tiptoft and Montague acted (the latter even impaling prisoners after death) was part of the same bad system. Edward IV. also introduced the system of perpetual forfeitures for treason. Before his time restoration after a period of eclipse had been the understood rule ; he set this principle absolutely at nought by bestowing the Percy earldom on a Nevile and that of Pembroke on a Herbert. When we add to these changes the well-known extension in Edward's reign of the system of benevolences and forced loans, the extreme infrequency of parliaments, and the trivial character of the business which they were allowed to take in hand, together with the frequent executions of those whom the king feared—including his own brother, the Duke of Clarence—we shall readily understand what a vast breach in the Constitution this reign really made ; a breach which the reign of Richard III., inclined as he naturally was to support the weakness of his title and to put his crimes out of remembrance by popular concessions, was much too short to repair; especially as his necessities after a while drove him to collect money by methods hardly differing from the illegal ones which he had professed to abolish. Accordingly, Henry VII. on succeeding to the crown found himself very slightly fettered by constitutional precedents, and would doubtless have been a violently oppressive governor if he had not been far more inclined to the sort of chicane natural to one whose early life had been passed in avoiding dangers, and who in many things kept before his eyes the example of Louis XI. He thoroughly realised that to govern as he chose two main conditions were required ; he must need few or no subsidies, and he must avoid the foreign wars which would make subsidies indispensable, and which might also raise up competitors for the Crown. Such then was the starting-point of the prince who was to inaugurate more than a hundred years of autocratic government in England. And by keeping these two principles constantly in view, he gave a new political character to the century which followed his accession, which it will, in the following chapters, be our business to trace.

CHAPTER II.

HENRY OF RICHMOND. BOSWORTH FIELD. THE CORONATION. THE SWEATING SICKNESS, 1485, 1486.

IT is desirable first to sketch the early life and the accession of the sovereign who was in so many ways to influence the history of England.

Henry of Richmond could claim a twofold royal or quasi-royal descent. His father, Edmund Tudor, by creation Earl of Richmond, was son to Catherine of France, the widow of Henry V. Obviously no original title to the throne could be thus derived, even if it were certain that Catherine was ever married to Owen Tudor (of which unfortunately no evidence is known to exist); yet, with the ideas of succession prevalent in those times, such an origin might add force to other stronger claims. Henry's maternal descent constituted such a claim, inasmuch as his mother, Margaret Beaufort, was great-granddaughter to Edward III.'s fourth son, John of Gaunt; and, although the Beauforts were illegitimate, yet after their birth John married their mother, Catherine Roet (the sister-in-law of the poet Chaucer), and succeeded in inducing Richard II. to carry through Parliament in 1397 an Act for their legitimation, which, however, did not allow them to bear the name of Plantagenet. This Act was confirmed in 1407 by Henry IV., who seems to have thought that by introducing the words 'excepta dignitate regia' into Richard's original grant, as preserved in the Patent Rolls,

Henry's claim to the throne.

he was barring the Beauforts from succession to the throne ; although the document of confirmation, as submitted by him to Parliament, contained no such exception. As the latter was of course authoritative, Henry inherited from John of Gaunt a parliamentary title to the throne in case of failure, first of the lines of John's elder brothers, and, secondly, of heirs from his earlier marriages. Both of these contingencies had in great measure occurred. The line of the Black Prince, Edward's eldest son, had ended with the unhappy Richard II. in 1399 ; William, the next brother, died early, and the House of York, the representatives of Lionel, the third brother, had been almost exterminated. As for John's earlier marriages, the Lancastrian line, beginning with Henry IV. (whose mother was Blanche of Lancaster), had also become extinct when the young Edward, son of Henry VI., was murdered by his uncles on the field of Tewkesbury. Thus, when Henry VII. succeeded to the throne, his only rivals in title were John de la Pole, Earl of Lincoln, the son of Richard III.'s sister Elizabeth (who had been declared by Richard heir to the throne) ; his brother the Earl of Suffolk ; Edward Plantagenet, Earl of Warwick, the son of the Duke of Clarence put to death by Edward IV., his sister Margaret (afterwards Countess of Salisbury), and Elizabeth, the daughter of Edward IV.

Margaret Beaufort, Henry's mother, successively Countess of Richmond and of Derby, was, as will be shown in a subsequent chapter, one of the most remarkable women in English history. *The Lady Margaret.* Her father was John Beaufort, the first Duke of Somerset. On his death in 1444, she became the ward of William de la Pole, Duke of Suffolk, and by him was married at the age of nine to his son, who afterwards succeeded to the title. On her guardian's attainder, she was transferred to the custody of Edmund Tudor, Earl of Richmond, and his brother Jasper Tudor, Earl of Pembroke, the former of whom became her husband in 1456, her former marriage having been simply set aside. Both these noblemen had been treated as brothers by Henry VI., who bestowed great care on their education, and received from them loyal support in the civil war, Jasper Tudor having been engaged in several of the chief battles and attainted with the King and Margaret of Anjou in 1461. Edmund Tudor died five years before this last event, a few months before his son's birth. The Countess of Richmond, thus widowed at the age of sixteen, lived for awhile in her brother-in-law's castle at Pembroke, and then, in 1459, married her cousin Lord Henry Stafford, son of the Duke of Buckingham, and through him descended from Thomas of Woodstock, the sixth son of Edward III. (the Duke of Gloucester who was so foully kidnapped and murdered by Richard II.) In 1482 she was again a widow; but soon married Lord Stanley, a widower with a numerous family. There are circumstances connected with this last union which give the impression that she entered into it unwillingly, and merely in order to gain protection for her son, for whom alone she seemed really to live. For this purpose her husband was well chosen, as he was a strong Yorkist. Indeed, but for this marriage, her life would have been forfeited in 1483 for the part which she took in Buckingham's rebellion against Richard III. Soon after this she succeeded in gaining over Lord Stanley to her son's party.

In 1471, after the battle of Tewkesbury, Jasper Tudor followed Margaret's advice by sending the young Henry, his nephew, out of the country.

Henry's invasion.

Henry was now fifteen years old, and it was his mother's wish that he should take refuge with Louis XI.

of France. This plan, however, failed, for he was wrecked on the Breton coast, and had to pursue the life of imprisonment and surveillance which became so familiar to him. Indeed, he once said to Philippe de Commines 'that from the age of five years he had constantly been kept and concealed as a fugitive in prison.' Edward IV. and Richard III. made frequent attempts to recover him from Francis II., Duke of Bretagne; Richard, indeed, promised to make him his son-in-law, if surrendered. Accordingly, by the contrivance of Landois, Francis's minister, during his master's illness, Henry was sent to St. Malo to be delivered up; but, receiving a hint from his faithful supporter Bishop Morton that Landois was trying to get for his master in exchange for his surrender, the earldom of Richmond (which had formerly been held by the Dukes of Bretagne), he escaped, first into the woods, and then into French territory at Angers. Here he was well received; and the circumstances of the country soon made it highly expedient to support his claim to the English throne. For as Richard III. was sending archers to France in support of the French nobles in their attempt to raise a second 'War of the Public Good' against the young Charles VIII. (who had just succeeded his father on the French throne), the wise and politic Anne of Beaujeu, Duchess of Bourbon, who was Regent during her brother's minority, allowed Henry, in 1485, to collect about 2,000 men—'des plus méchants qu'on put trouver,' says Philippe de Commines—and also supplied a small sum of money to help the descent on England. Accordingly, on August 7 in that year Henry landed at Milford Haven, and immediately took the decided step of sending circulars calling for help against Richard as an usurper of his rights to the throne and a rebel. He then marched to Shrewsbury, where

c

he received the adhesion of Rhys ap Thomas and other Welsh chiefs. Ap Thomas had sworn that the invader should only enter England 'over his belly.' It is said to have been suggested by high authority that he might discharge himself from this vow by lying down on the ground and letting Henry step over him; or by going under a bridge while Henry crossed it above him. In making, not for Worcester and the lower Severn, but for Shrewsbury, Henry had in view his stepfather Lord Stanley's Cheshire influence. At Stafford he heard that Stanley could not immediately join him without sacrificing the life of his son, Lord Strange, whom Richard had seized as a hostage; but, going almost alone in advance of his army to his camp at Atherstone, he received from him the most encouraging promises of support. At almost the same moment he was joined by Sir Walter Hungerford and Sir Thomas Bourchier, two of Richard's trusted officers, with a body of choice troops. From Atherstone he turned eastward to meet Richard, who was encamped between Hinckley and Market Bosworth. Even with the reinforcements just acquired he had scarcely 5,000 men, barely half the number of Richard's forces; so that his chance of victory was small, unless more leaders deserted to him in the battle.

Mr. Gairdner, in his excellent History of Richard III., has stated very clearly the causes which led to Henry's decisive success. Richard had, it appears, been misled by a prediction which he had heard about his rival's landing at Milford, referring, as he imagined, to a small village of that name near Christchurch in Hampshire. Accordingly he had taken very few effective precautions to secure the fidelity of the Welsh leaders, or of Sir W. Stanley, who had the chief power in North Wales. As to Lord Stanley,

Battle of Bosworth Field.

Richard seems to have had the incapacity (not uncommon in tyrants) to reflect that those whom they injure are certain to remember the wrong when they themselves have forgotten it. His soldiers had all but murdered Lord Stanley on the day when he sent Lord Hastings to the block; yet he trusted him in a manner to the last, making, however, a breastwork in rear of his own camp, for fear of being attacked by him. As for Sir W. Stanley, he had been declared a traitor even while commanding for Richard. It is most satisfactory to find that Richard's chance of ultimate success had departed from him as soon as the murder of his nephews in the Tower became known. Indeed, revolt after revolt thenceforward made it clear that, even though he might succeed in cajoling the mother and sister of the victims, he could not silence the groans and indignation with which his atrocious act was stigmatised in every street and market-place of England. The feeling against him was like that against King John for his treatment of Arthur, or against the Emperor Sigismund during his London visit in 1416 for the murder of John Hus. Making a virtue of necessity, Richard acknowledged, as we are informed, his crime in his final address to his soldiers, but pleaded that he had 'washed it away by salt tears and strict penance.' He was however quite unable to excite the emotion which he desired.

Advancing by the road from Hinckley to Stapleton and Market Bosworth, Richard drew out his forces on Sutton Heath. His enemy's position was difficult to force, as Redmore Plain, on which the Lancastrian troops were drawn out, was covered on the left and rear by a brook hard to cross, and on the right by Sutton Ambien Wood and by a morass—an arrangement which evidently made it necessary for Henry to conquer or die, as retreat would have been most difficult. Yet, after all, Richmond made the common mistake of inexperienced soldiers, and desired his men to advance beyond the morass, thus running the risk of seeing them driven in and the whole position carried by the enemy's rush. Seeing the danger, the veteran Earl of Oxford first ordered the men not to move ten feet from the standard; and then, when he had got them well in hand, seized the right moment for hurling them on the enemy, who seemed indisposed to advance and unlikely to make much resistance. At this moment Lord Stanley deserted Richard, and with him the Earl of Northumberland; while the Duke of Norfolk, Richard's firm supporter, was slain, and his son, the Earl of Surrey, taken prisoner. Few events in English history are better known than those which immediately followed—Richard's catching sight of his rival and charging him desperately; his Plantagenet prowess in the fight; his refusal to fly; the coming up of Sir W. Stanley; Richard's shouts of 'Treason,' 'Treason,' as he struck right and left; his fall with many wounds; the finding by Reginald Bray in a thornbush of the crown which Richard had worn on his helmet, and the crowning of Henry with it by Lord Stanley. The battle may be considered typical of the period at which it occurred, combining as it did the use of such modern weapons as cannon (as proved by the balls from time to time dug up on the field) with a mediæval encounter, almost hand to hand, between the competitors for the throne. The victor followed the bad precedent of the Wars of the Roses by ordering some of his prisoners to be at once executed. As, however, his vengeance only lighted upon Catesby, the minister of Richard III., and two of his agents, he was considered to have been strangely merciful. The distribution of due honours and rewards was deferred, with some exceptions, till the meeting of Parliament in November.

It was necessary at once to settle by what title Henry should claim the throne. The right of conquest was suggested, but at once put aside from an instinctive sense of the principle (explained by a great authority of our own time in a celebrated judgment) that, 'when a country is conquered, its inhabitants retain for the time their own laws, but are under the power of the Sovereign to alter these laws in any way which to the Sovereign in Council may seem proper.' Men were as clear on this point in 1485 as they were when the 'conquest' theory was broached in 1693 in favour of King William III., and when it excited, as Lord Macaulay tells us, a complete tempest of indignation against its unlucky propounder. There was another resemblance between the two periods; namely, that Henry was as determined as William was in after days not to be a mere King Consort; if he married Elizabeth of York, the daughter of Edward IV., he would not owe his title to her. Accordingly on August 22 he assumed the crown in virtue of his Lancastrian descent, without making the least mention of Elizabeth; and in order to guard against Yorkist competition, he imprisoned in the Tower the Earl of Warwick, the son of the Duke of Clarence whom Edward IV. had murdered. This unhappy young man had for a time been treated by Richard III. as his heir, but then put aside in favour of another nephew, John de la Pole, Earl of Lincoln, the son of Richard's sister Elizabeth. The chief part of the Warwick property was dealt with in a manner characteristic of Henry. He ordered its restoration to Anne, Countess of Warwick, the widow of the 'Kingmaker,' but forced this aged lady at once to execute

Henry's title to the throne.

a 'feoffment' granting to the King and his heirs all that had been her husband's and her own. This property included the islands of Guernsey, Jersey, and Sark, the city of Worcester, the town and castle of Warwick, and a vast number of manors and lordships in nineteen counties of England. Only a moderate pension and one manor in Warwickshire were left to her who, when young, had been the greatest lady in England. Nothing was reserved for her grand-daughter Margaret, who afterwards married Sir Richard Pole, and is well known as the Countess of Salisbury executed by Henry VIII. in 1541.

On September 28, Henry made his entry into London; 'in a close chariot,' says Lord Bacon, 'in order to strike reverence into the people'; a theory of Henry's motives which has been curiously amplified by a German historian of England, who dilates on his strange conduct in thus withdrawing himself, popular and triumphant as he was, from the homage which awaited him in the streets, and yet resuming his military character in order to consecrate his standards in St. Paul's. The truth is, however, that Bernard André, the historian of Henry, really spoke of him as entering London 'lætanter'; and that Lord Bacon's 'close chariot,' as well as Pauli's longer paraphrase, is due to a misreading of this word into 'latenter.' Henry immediately announced his intention of marrying Elizabeth; she was sent for from Sheriff's Hutton, and placed under her mother's protection till the Coronation was over and Henry's first Parliament had been held. He thus guarded, with almost superfluous care, against the chance of being thought to claim the crown through her. There was some fear that the prevalence in London of the 'sweating sickness' might delay the inauguration; but as the force of the disease abated within two months, it

The Coronation.

was possible to perform it on October 31 following. The marriage did not take place till January 18 in the next year.

Henry was sparing of new creations on his accession; but his stepfather, Lord Stanley, was made Earl of Derby, his uncle Jasper Tudor Duke of Bedford, and Sir Edward Courtenay Earl of Devon. On the other hand pecuniary grants were abundant in the first months of the reign. *Restoration of persons attainted.* As a matter of course the chief sufferers in Henry's cause were reinstated in their property, often with large additions. Such were his mother, the Lady Margaret, now Countess of Derby; Sir Thomas Stafford, the son and heir of the late Duke of Buckingham; Catherine Duchess of Bedford, the same Duke's widow; and Piers Courtenay, Bishop of Exeter, who, like his brother Sir Edward, had been with Henry in exile. To John, Earl of Oxford, whose father had lost his life in the Lancastrian struggle, and who had distinguished himself in 1473 by the seizure of St. Michael's Mount, was given the office of Admiral of England, Ireland, and Aquitaine. With this grant were joined many others; among which we should not have expected to find Lord Oxford's appointment as keeper of the lions, lionesses, and leopards in the Tower, with a shilling a day for himself, and sixpence for the food of each animal. It may here be remarked, once for all, that in this reign money was about twelve times its present value.

Another highly interesting restoration at this time was that of Henry, Lord Clifford—the 'Shepherd Lord' whom Wordsworth has celebrated. His family had been attainted in 1461, and he himself concealed in a shepherd's hut to avoid the vengeance of the Yorkists for his father's murder of the child Earl of Rutland at the battle of Wakefield. In this condition he passed twenty-four years, working at shepherds' tasks, and learning to know the stars by watching them from the Cumberland fells. Some manuscripts still remain in the possession of the Clifford family which prove his fondness for alchemy—a study which, though prohibited under pain of felony by a statute of Henry IV., had flourished in the very court of Henry VI., and was destined, as we shall see in a subsequent chapter, long to retain its hold on English belief. He was also given to astrology, which was then held to be the great practical use of star-knowledge. Lord Clifford lived till the tenth year of Henry VIII., and, in spite of the 'tranquil soul' which the poet ascribes to him, distinguished himself highly at the battle of Flodden.

At the same time an immense number of minor offices, such as the wardenships of royal parks and castles, were transferred from the supporters of Richard to those of Henry. Few comparatively were bestowed on Welshmen, though Sir Rhys ap Thomas, to whom Henry owed so much, was made Constable of Brecknock, Chamberlain of South Wales, and a Commissioner of Mines. Welshmen were, however, freely admitted to the small body of guards which Henry now formed, in imitation probably of Louis XI.'s Scottish Archers. Following the same King's example, Henry at once showed himself favourable to trade. Some London merchants claimed that by old custom they were to pay no tunnage between the day of a new king's accession and that on which his first Parliament met (this indulgence being considered as counterbalancing the extra expense which they incurred in guarding their property at such times), and their claim was allowed. Several Venetian traders who wished to come to England received a special safe-conduct; and some other Italians were relieved from penalties incurred under a statute of Richard III.

The 'sweating sickness,' above alluded to, which broke out among us for the first time in 1485, was one of the most alarming of mediæval epidemics; and it recurred so often in these reigns as to deserve a brief description here. According to Dr. Hecker of Berlin, who has collected all existing notices of it, it was a violent inflammatory fever, prostrating the bodily powers as with a blow, and suffusing the whole body with a fetid perspiration. The internal heat which the patient suffered was intolerable, yet every refrigerant was certain death, and the crisis was almost always over in twenty-four hours. Shortly after the royal entry on September 28 it began its ravages in the City, two Lord Mayors and many aldermen dying in a week. From thence it ranged through the greater part of England, stopping short, however, at the Scottish Border, and not spreading to Ireland, in spite of the constant maritime intercourse with that country. It mostly attacked persons in the prime of health and strength, and not those who were weak from age, sex, or disease; and this appears to disprove the opinion that it was caused by the presence of Henry's army in London, and was a consequence of the privations which they had suffered on shipboard and on their march. The disease gained fresh terror from the impotence of medicine to grapple with it. So complete was this, that the distinguished Linacre, who afterwards founded the College of Physicians, is not known to have written on the subject. Strange to say, this failure of the profession of medicine probably led to its quicker cessation; for, as there was no scientific guidance, the people treated those attacked by the light of nature, making them go quietly to bed and stay there

The Pestilence.

till better, taking no food and only the mildest beverages. In subsequent years when the disease returned, and medical practice, as then understood, had risen to the occasion, the very opposite treatment to this was adopted in some countries. In the Netherlands, for instance, the patient was loaded with the hottest garments, and crushed, sometimes to actual suffocation, under a mass of featherbeds kept down by the weight of several men lying at the top. There is no trace of such violent remedies being ever used in England; on the present occasion the methods of common sense were blessed in their results, for the disease went on diminishing through the autumn, and was at length brought to an end most sudden and complete by the violent storm of New Year's Day, 1486.

It is always interesting to observe the moral conduct of a people during a time of terrible pestilence. In the present instance we may remark that when hardly one person recovered out of a hundred attacked, and when, moreover, the disease followed Englishmen abroad and spared foreigners resident among us, it did not rouse either the national hatreds or the superstitious terrors which might have been expected. We hear of nothing like the execution at Meissen in 1507 of 'böse Buben' suspected of having poisoned the wells; and the theological strife had not yet arisen which induced the citizens of Cologne in 1517 to burn heretics in the hope of averting a fresh eruption of the same plague. Nor can it be said of England at this time (as Mr. Burton quotes of Scotland in 1569), that 'in time of plague selfishness ruled the day, every one being so detestable to others, and especially the poor to the rich, as if they were not equal with them touching their creation; but rather without soul or spirit, as beasts degenerated from mankind.' No cases are recorded like those

English feeling under it.

during the 'Black Death,' of near kinsmen forsaking one another; nor were there any such fierce outbreaks of fanaticism as those of the Flagellants, which soon after this maddened Germany and Hungary. Superstition of many kinds was indeed rife in England in 1485; but its types were at any rate somewhat gentler and more humane than those of other countries.

CHAPTER III.

LAMBERT SIMNEL. THE BRETAGNE WAR.
1486–1492.

ON November 7, 1485, Henry VII. held his first Parliament, thus seeming to fulfil the general expectation that as a Lancastrian sovereign he would follow the example of Henry IV. and Henry V. in taking kindly to constitutional government. *Parliament of 1485.* His House of Lords contained only twenty-seven lay peers—a fact which has been supposed to prove how many families had become extinct during the Wars of the Roses. In reality, however, only two had thus failed for want of heirs; and the number of peers in this Parliament was so small because no summonses had been sent to twenty-five who were likely to be malcontent. Henry wished in the first place to have the succession settled upon his own heirs by whatever wife; this was done, and, at his strongly expressed desire, confirmed by a Papal Bull. He also wanted the attainders of his supporters to be formally reversed, and not merely cancelled by his act in employing them, as he had done in several cases. He intended to issue a general pardon of his enemies with some exceptions; yet was unwilling that Parliament should enact this, choosing rather to deal with individuals, who might be made to pay dearly for it, and thus the better enable him to do for the present without any parliamentary revenue beyond the tunnage and poundage which was granted to him for life. For the same purpose he declared invalid all alienations of property from the Crown made since 1454. He kept also a keen eye on the fines imposed upon foreign merchants for 'non-employment;' that is, for attempting to dispose of their wares in England without buying a return cargo there. As if 'born to the manner' of English royalty, he picked out for his ministers two of the ablest churchmen of the time, Morton, Bishop of Ely, his old and tried supporter, and Fox, Bishop of Exeter. The services of men like these on his Council would be invaluable, yet would cost him nothing, seeing that they might be paid by translation to richer bishoprics. After giving indemnity to all the King's partisans for any injury done to the opposite party, and enacting that Gascon wines should only be brought to England in English, Irish, or Welsh vessels, the Parliament was on the point of being prorogued when the members humbly petitioned Henry to be pleased to marry Elizabeth. With this request he complied, as we have already seen, yet her coronation was not for the present allowed.

Considering himself now fairly established on the throne, Henry resolved on a progress to the North, the great home of the Yorkist party, whence Richard III. had recently drawn his best and most faithful troops. On the way thither he kept his Easter joyously at Lincoln, but was rudely disabused of his confidence in his own fortune by an insurrection raised by Lord Lovel, Sir Humphrey Stafford, and Sir Thomas Stafford, who had been in sanctuary at Col-

Rebellion of the Staffords.

chester since Bosworth Field. The Staffords were sons of the Humphrey Stafford slain by Cade in 1450; and, like Lord Lovel, had fought for Richard at Bosworth. They made for Worcester, apparently trusting for their safety to local connexions there. These, however, failed them entirely, and their forces dispersed on Henry's first proclamation of pardon. Lord Lovel fled to Lancashire and then to Flanders, and the Staffords took sanctuary at Culham, near Abingdon, but were removed from it for trial on the ground that the place had not sufficient privileges as a sanctuary to shelter traitors. The elder brother was then executed, the younger pardoned as having acted under his influence.

This rebellion had little or no connexion with the feeling in favour of the House of York, which was still very strong in England, and attributable to two main causes. In the first place, the Lancastrians (including the present King) were hated by the violent and unreasoning part of the community for having lost, under Henry VI., the English provinces in France, the wars occasioned by which had been such perennial sources of plunder to Englishmen serving there; and the White Rose was therefore popular as more or less representing the idea of empire abroad. In the second place, traders and manufacturers held the same opinion on different grounds; for, from the very accession of Edward IV., the head of the House of York, much had been done for them by the numerous commercial treaties which he made with foreign powers, and by his personal interest in trade; especially had the greater strength of his government guaranteed our sea-coasts and trading vessels from those attacks of pirates which remained for more than a century longer the invariable mark of a weak or careless rule in England.

Causes of Yorkist feeling.

We can therefore readily understand the strength of Yorkist feeling in London and in the North, seeing that so large a part of English trade and English manufactures belonged to these districts. In Ireland the same sentiment existed, but appears to have sprung chiefly and characteristically from a remembrance of the gentle sway of Richard, Duke of York, as Lord-Deputy there in 1459; when, after the defeat of his party at Blore Heath, he crossed the Channel, seized the government of Ireland in defiance of Ormond and the Lancastrians, and proceeded to hold a Parliament there which claimed to be independent of the English Parliament and courts of law. George Duke of Clarence had also been loved in Ireland for his father's sake, and had distinguished himself by his courteous behaviour to the people between the years 1461 and 1470, and afterwards from 1472 till his death.

To arouse and stimulate all these feelings of opposition to Henry's government was the life-long purpose of Margaret of York, the sister of Edward IV., who had been second wife to Charles the Bold, Duke of Burgundy. After the death of her husband in his war with the Swiss (1477), this princess had seen the French part of his dominions absorbed by Louis XI., and the Flemish provinces passing by the marriage of Mary her stepdaughter into the hands of Maximilian of Austria, the young and chivalrous son of Frederick III., Emperor of Germany; she herself, however, retained so much independence in the districts which had been assigned to her as a dowry on her marriage, that it was vain to appeal to the Emperor when she did acts hostile to England. The marriage of her niece with Henry had by no means conciliated her; she rather hated Elizabeth as a deserter from the White Rose. Her ill-feeling found

Simnel. Battle of Stoke.

its opportunity in 1486, when Lambert Simnel was brought forward as a pretender to the English Crown. The broad facts of the imposture were that this youth was represented as being really the Earl of Warwick whom Henry had under lock and key in the Tower. When, therefore, we find that his cause was supported by the Earl of Lincoln, Richard III.'s own nephew, who had once been heir-presumptive to the Crown, it seems plain that Lincoln's hope must have been to get rid of Henry by means of this deception, and then quietly to put the puppet aside and stand up for his own right; adopting, in fact, the plan which Buckingham would probably have pursued towards Henry himself if the rebellion of 1483 had been successful. As so many people knew the true Lord Warwick by sight, and as Henry took care that all London should see him on the way to and from St. Paul's, it was thought best that Simnel should make his first appearance in Ireland. There he found men's minds fully prepared for a Yorkist insurrection. Accordingly his cause was taken up by Lord Kildare, who was then ruling Ireland as deputy for the Duke of Bedford, and he was actually crowned at Dublin (May 24, 1487) as Edward VI. without a sword being drawn. At this point Margaret struck in to aid him, showing herself as courageous as her husband, but with a feminine craft which was all her own. She helped a skilful commander named Martin Schwartz to equip nineteen vessels carrying about 2,000 veteran soldiers; and Simnel sailed for England with these and with some Irish troops commanded by Lord Kildare, besides a few Englishmen under Lord Lincoln. Landing at Fouldrey in Lancashire, he made first for York, striving hard as he went to keep his men orderly and humane, so that the impression of his being really the rightful King might strengthen. By this time, however, Henry, after making a pilgrimage to Walsingham, had fixed his headquarters at Nottingham, as Richard III. had done just before Bosworth; both Kings considering this place well situated for commanding the various roads from the North to London. He had also much to encourage him; for, popular though the Yorkist cause might be, most Englishmen disliked the thought of having a king imposed upon them by a mob of Irishmen and Flemings. Accordingly Lord Lincoln had to engage at Stoke, near Newark (June 16), with little more than the force which he brought from Ireland. The battle was obstinate, there being little thought of giving quarter to foreigners or Irish. Lord Lincoln fell with Martin Schwartz and Lord Lovel; unless, indeed, the story is true that Lovel was concealed for several years in a strong-room at Minster Lovel, in Oxfordshire, and at last died there from the negligence of a servant who failed to provide him with food. The unhappy Irish, armed as they were with nothing better than darts and knives, were of course cut in pieces. Content with the death of his chief enemies in battle, Henry pardoned the nobles who had assisted in the Dublin coronation, on their pleading that they had been misled, not only by the very governor whom the King had placed over them, but by the Archbishop of Dublin and the chief part of the clergy. He even spared Simnel himself, making him, first a turnspit in his kitchen, and then, by way of promotion, a falconer. In the course of the next year he, with not a little quiet humour, exhibited the pretender dressed in his livery to the Irish nobles who were visiting London; and enjoyed immeasurably the uncourtly execrations into which they burst at the sight.

After his victory Henry thought it prudent to conciliate Yorkist feeling by allowing the coronation of

Queen Elizabeth; this took place November 25, 1487. He could afford to comply thus far, as he had just made a Northern progress of a very different character from the one which he had designed in the preceding year. His object now had been to punish all who had adhered to the rebellion; and when we hear that for this purpose he proclaimed martial law, it is easy to judge of the terror which his presence must have caused, in spite of his generally preferring fines to bloodshed. With regard to such proclamations, it is satisfactory to learn from the highest authority that, the rebellion being at an end, they were quite illegal; indeed an Act of Indemnity was afterwards required to protect from penalties those who had used force under them. Strangely enough, one of those on whom the King's hand fell heavily was his wife's mother, who on the first report of Simnel's rebellion was imprisoned for the rest of her life in a nunnery at Bermondsey, with little allowance for her support. This was done by authority of the King in Council; the reason alleged, namely that she had placed her daughters in King Richard's hands instead of remaining with them in sanctuary, was so plainly frivolous that the object in making it must have been to suggest that there was much more behind. Lord Bacon conjectures that she may have borne a part in teaching Simnel how to make people think him a prince, from a notion that Henry was unkind to her daughter, and a consequent wish that he might be slain or deposed. Yet he appears to have been, on the whole, an affectionate husband; although we are told some years later that Margaret, Henry's mother, was somewhat tyrannical to her daughter-in-law. On this view, it must be acknowledged that the situation was strained; for the Lady Margaret, Lancastrian to

Martial law.

D

the backbone, was allowed by Henry to regulate on the most critical occasions all the details of Elizabeth's household, to the utter exclusion of her Yorkist mother, who must surely have been more or less than a woman and a mother-in-law if she could have calmly endured such exclusion. Perhaps we need go no further to account for her ruin.

Henry's second Parliament was now held (November 9, 1487). It established for the first time the Court of Star Chamber, for reasons and in a manner which will be stated in another chapter, where also its statute against carrying off women will be described. The main subject which it had to deal with was the critical state of affairs in Bretagne. Here Duke Francis, at whose court Henry had long lived, was now in extreme old age, and, as he had no son, the question was what should become of his province when he died. The determined resolution of Anne of Beaujeu to bring about the union of Bretagne to France by a marriage between Charles VIII. and its heiress Anne was creditable to her patriotism; her personal interest was all the other way, as Ferdinand and Isabella had in 1486 promised that, if she arranged a marriage between their daughter and Charles VIII., they would support her in claiming a perpetual regency in France, their hope being that she would maintain between the two countries the peace which was certain to come to an end if Charles assumed the full powers of the French Crown. England was still more strongly against the union between France and Bretagne; and not unnaturally so, considering the great danger to our navigation from the long line of coast which would thus come into French hands, instead of being hostile, as it generally had been while under the separate governments. Doubtless our

Affairs of Bretagne.

mariners knew well the fact, remarked in our own time by the Duke of Wellington, how clearly ships going along our coast may be detected at a great distance by the light on their sails from the southward sun, while French ships on the other side escape notice and pursuit from their sails being in shade. Troubles between Bretagne and France began even in Francis's life-time; for the Duke received and befriended the Duke of Orleans (afterwards Louis XII.), who, after the fashion of heirs-presumptive, had raised against the Regent's power the war of the 'Public Good' already alluded to. Accordingly in the preceding September an embassy had been sent to England by the French Government requesting Henry to remember his old obligations to France, and either to join in the attack on Bretagne, or at least to remain neutral in the war. The ambassadors reached him at Leicester, and were almost immediately asked whether it was true that Charles VIII. was planning a marriage with Anne. They professed to be scandalised at the very suggestion—it was well known, they said, that their master was affianced to Margaret, the daughter of Maximilian King of the Romans; indeed, this very young lady had for some time been residing in Paris, and receiving a French education. Besides this they declared that Charles was arranging an expedition into Italy; his views, therefore, were in a direction quite opposite to that of Bretagne. The ambassadors might have added that Maximilian himself was the only person whom Anne would at the time hear of as a husband—as indeed she afterwards married him by proxy. Henry replied by a counter-embassy, offering his mediation for the re-establishment of peace between Bretagne and France. Charles VIII. declared that such an arrangement was just what he most ardently desired; but would it not be well, he asked, that Urswick, the English ambassador, should go to Rennes on his way home, and come to an equally clear understanding with the Breton Government? This could not well be refused, and the result was just what Charles had foreseen: the answer to Urswick was really given, not by Francis II., but by the Duke of Orleans, whose interest was entirely against peace. Louis would hear of no terms of accommodation; he also urged most strongly that the union of France and Burgundy must be contrary to English interests. On this Charles asked Henry to continue his mediation till peace was brought about, but at the same time announced his own intention of at once going on with the warlike operations. He therefore invaded Bretagne and besieged Nantes (June 1487); and at this time a few English volunteers under Lord Woodvile went over to help the Bretons—a proceeding at which Henry professed himself very indignant.

This was the state of things on which the Parliament of November 1487 had to decide. They were asked pointblank by Archbishop Morton whether or no they would advise the King to ally himself with Bretagne against France. Morton told them that an honourable foreign war would be better for Henry than the domestic tumults which had given so much trouble of late. The position of England as to the Continent had, he remarked, been much altered for the worse of late by the absorption of Burgundy into the dominions of France and Austria: were they to allow Bretagne, their other trusty confederate, to be constantly joined with France against them? Besides, such a precedent of the greater being allowed to swallow up the less would be a fatal one for small countries like Scotland, Portugal, and many of the States of Germany.

<small>French policy there.</small>

These arguments seemed conclusive to the members, who would naturally also fear the loss of Breton trade (as we then obtained from thence our chief supplies of linen and canvas); and a subsidy for the war was unanimously voted. Henry would not, however, begin hostilities without another embassy; and before this came to an end, the battle of St. Aubin had been fought, the Duke of Orleans taken prisoner, and Lord Woodvile slain with most of his men (July 28, 1488). Somewhat confused at this effect of his long delay, Henry at once sent over Lord Brook, one of his companions in exile, with 8,000 men. Yet this commander could not or would not bring the French to battle; and after the death of Francis II., which occurred September 9, the English, finding that no one claimed them as allies, simply returned to England, five months after their departure for France. This of course left matters for the present in the hands of the French Government; which showed, it must be admitted, considerable tact in the management of difficult circumstances, beginning by claiming only Charles's right as suzerain to break the marriage of Anne with Maximilian, as being contrary to the interests of France. This was done; and the unlucky King of the Romans had both to lose his wife and to take back the little daughter whom he had hoped to make Queen of France. He had, however, gained more than one point by these transactions. For though Bretagne was finally lost to him, and though the Duchess Anne became the wife of Charles VIII. (December 1491), yet the lady never forgot that she had once been Queen of the Romans, and was perpetually plotting in favour of his family; indeed, on one occasion she attempted to marry her daughter to Charles of Spain, Maximilian's grandson, and thus, in defiance of the Salique law, to make France part of his overgrown dominions. Besides this the English, before the hope of Maximilian's marrying Anne was over, had supported him vigorously against his own rebellious subjects at Bruges, Ghent, Ypres, and Sluys. The popular party in the cities had invited the French to their aid; and, under pretence that the safety of the garrison of Calais was threatened by their revolt, Henry sent about 2,000 men, under Lords Morley and Daubeny, who inflicted a heavy blow upon the French besiegers of Nieuport. Thus both in Bretagne and on the north-eastern frontier of France there had been fighting between the English and French, while at the same time Henry and Charles strongly maintained that the peace between the countries was unbroken.

The subsidy for the war granted by Henry's third Parliament in 1489 was not levied without great difficulty in the North of England. It was opposed most strenuously in Yorkshire and the Bishopric of Durham; the people maintaining that the miseries which they had been suffering made such payments impossible. In fact, they seem to have been just able to tolerate a Lancastrian sovereign if he, for his part, never asked them for money. The King ordered the Duke of Northumberland to enforce the collection; but on the first attempt he was murdered by the recusants. On this the Earl of Surrey, who had been lately released from the Tower, where he had been prisoner since the beginning of the reign, was ordered to take the command against them, Henry himself leading up a reserve force in case of disaster. However, the rebels were put down before it arrived; their chief leader, Sir John Egremond, fled to the Duchess of Burgundy, while the plebeian rioters were hanged in considerable numbers. At about the same time with these events Henry heard of the death of

Northern and Scottish rebellions.

James III. of Scotland, whose friendship he had repeatedly tried to win, obtaining from him in 1487 a truce for seven years, renewable for similar periods. James died miserably in consequence of an accident which threw him from his horse and left him stunned and defenceless (1488) to be murdered by one of the rebels who had just defeated his troops at Sauchie.

There is something really amusing about Henry's pomp of preparation in 1492 for a war with France to avenge the absorption of Bretagne which he had failed in hindering. The warlike spirit of England had been strongly stimulated by the news of Ferdinand and Isabella's capture of Granada from the Moors, which arrived in the spring of that year, the city having surrendered on the 2nd of January. This, indeed, was an event of which it would be hard to exaggerate the importance. For the Mohammedan power had till then appeared irresistible: and the fall of Constantinople in 1453 had invested the Sultans with a thousand claims, as representing the empire of Constantine, which might at any moment be pressed in the most alarming manner. In 1486, Mohammed II. had made his famous descent upon Otranto; intending to use this as a base of operations, first against Rome and Italy, then against the other States of Europe—an enterprise which was hindered by nothing but his death in the following year, and the succession of the unwarlike Bajazet. The tide had now been turned by Spanish valour: Islam had lost the chief outwork of its power, and the victory had added to the territories of Castile and Aragon a country of brilliant fertility and resource, the possession of which had an effect in consolidating the Spanish monarchy superior even to that produced in France by the annexation of Burgundy. England had been represented at the

Quasi-war with France. Peace of Etaples.

siege of Granada only by one gallant volunteer, Lord Scales, who had greatly distinguished himself in the early part of the war. Nevertheless the event was celebrated by a service of triumph held in St. Paul's: and Archbishop Morton, who had now at Henry's express request been made a Cardinal, congratulated the vast assembly on the close of the 700 years of war with the unbelievers in Spain, and the certainty that numberless souls would now be gained to the Kingdom of Christ. Stirred to the emulation of such prowess, the Parliament allowed Henry (a former Act notwithstanding) to raise a benevolence for the French war; it was on this occasion that Cardinal Morton devised his celebrated 'Fork,' ordering his commissioners to press hard men who spent much, as this proved them to be rich, and also men who spent little, as it was plain that they must be saving largely. Tournaments and military exercises were held everywhere to 'stir the blood' of the people; and a striking success in Flanders excited still more enthusiasm. The Duke of Saxony, pretending a wish to arbitrate between his ally Maximilian and his rebellious subjects at Bruges, had been admitted into that city with a small force. Instead, however, of staying there and communicating with the magistrates, he passed out unchecked by the gate leading to Damm and Sluys, and seizing the former of these towns cut off Bruges from the sea, access to which was all important for its trade. On this Henry allowed his troops to help Maximilian by besieging Sluys, which commanded the embouchure of the canal leading to Bruges. This he was the more inclined to do as Ravestein, the leader of the insurgents, had made Sluys the headquarters of a vigorous system of piracy. He therefore sent Sir E. Poynings with a considerable force, which assailed the castles while the Duke of Saxony besieged the town. After much obstinate fighting the place surrendered, and the rebellion against Maximilian was practically at an end, very mainly through English help. This, however, did not overcome Henry's reluctance to plunge farther into the war. True he had assembled a force not less than 26,000 strong; but the question of ways and means constantly weighed on his mind. Maximilian was above all things impecunious; his father, the old Emperor Frederic III.—' l'homme le plus chiche qui fut jamais,' as Philippe de Commines calls him—could not be reckoned on for much; subsidies were hard to wring from the people at home, and even if collected, their value was trifling compared with the vast expense of such a war, in which the commonest archer would be paid at least sixpence a day (a sum, as we have seen, equal to six shillings of our money). Tidings also came that Ferdinand of Aragon had just made a treaty with France on most advantageous terms, receiving back Roussillon and Perpignan, which his father had pledged to France for 300,000 crowns. Accordingly, though Henry sailed for Calais (October 6), leaving orders for the army to rendezvous there, and even began the siege of Boulogne (as an instalment of the sovereignty which he claimed over all France), yet he was not insensible to the advantage of negotiating, and allowed a peace to be concluded at Etaples (November 3), receiving under the name of expenses a sum of 127,000*l*., besides a pension or tribute of 6,000*l*. a year to make good what he had spent in Bretagne. Thus the war ended, not heroically we must admit; yet how much better would it have been for England if Henry's successor had been more like him in hating useless conquests. The present King's motives were doubtless mixed enough; what his enemies called avarice had much to do with his conduct, and he also feared war in general, as tending to raise up competitors for a throne in some sense gained by conquest. Avarice, however, is hardly a fault when it takes the form of sparing the people taxes; and when we hear of so many sovereigns plunging into battle in order that their title may not be canvassed, we ought surely to have a good word for the King who thought the permanence of his reign best secured by peace. Thus much at least must be admitted, that inspiration itself would hardly have guided Henry better at this juncture than did his own mental habits and tendencies. For a danger was soon to burst upon him which required his very fullest attention; well for him that it did not find him hampered by a dangerous foreign conflict in which success was unlikely, and almost sure to be useless even if attained.

CHAPTER IV.

WARBECK. BLACKHEATH FIELD.

1492-1496.

As early as 1491, a youth named Warbeck had gone to Ireland in the service of a Breton merchant, Pregent Meno. He was strikingly handsome and well-dressed, and attracted considerable attention on his arrival at Cork. Gradually a report was spread that he was really a Plantagenet; what precise member of that illustrious family was now among them was a point on which authorities disagreed. He was first made out to be the Earl of Warwick, then a bastard of Richard III.; but, at last, all Ireland was convinced that he was no other than the Duke of York, one of the

Warbeck widely supported.

two youthful prisoners murdered in the Tower. Thus encouraged, Warbeck wrote letters to the Earls of Desmond and Kildare to enlist them in his cause. He made little progress for a time in gaining powerful adherents, and had, indeed, as yet scarcely been heard of in England; still, his Irish sojourn had given him a good opportunity for studying the part which he was to play. When the war with France was declared in 1492, the French Government thought it worth while to invite him to Paris; there he was received as a royal prince, and attended by a guard of honour. On the conclusion of the Peace of Etaples he was not surrendered to Henry, but simply ordered to leave France; upon which Margaret of Burgundy received him with enthusiasm as her nephew, and may also have done something in the way of prompting him for his part, though the stories of her having been his chief instructress are inconsistent with the comparative lateness of his visit to her. It is almost strange that Henry allowed the affair to go on thus long with so little notice. He may have thought even Margaret's genius hardly equal to such a *tour de force* as the launching of another counterfeit prince, only six years after her first failure in this line; and certainly did not know that Warbeck had many partisans in England, and had promised Margaret that, in the event of success, her long unsettled dowry should be paid, and also her expenses for him and for the earlier Yorkist rebellions. Accordingly he considered it enough for the present to send Sir Edward Poynings and Dr. Warham on an embassy to Flanders (July 1493) and remonstrate against the countenance given to the pretender, taking at the same time some steps towards having a force ready in case of need. The ambassadors received only an evasive answer from the Archduke Philip's Council. 'It was impossible,' they said, 'to interfere with the Duchess of Burgundy's actions within the districts which belonged to her.' The only method now at Henry's disposal, short of actual war, was a prohibition of trade between England and Flanders; so all Flemings were banished from England, and the mart for English cloth transferred from Antwerp to Calais. The misfortune was that this prohibition created distress in England as well as in Flanders, besides exciting a furious jealousy in London against the German merchants there, who were less affected by it. This feeling reached such a pitch that the Steelyard, which was the London centre of their trade, narrowly escaped utter destruction.

Meanwhile Henry, as a worthy pupil of Louis XI., was using many artful means for tracking out the conspiracy against him. He directed various spies to pretend loyalty to Warbeck and his party, and thus to ascertain on whose help they counted in England. At the same time they were to take every opportunity of detaching Englishmen abroad from the rebellion. It is said that he took particular care to have these spies cursed at St. Paul's, as if they were really his enemies. This, however, would happen in the natural course of things, if he kept secret their real intentions. The results of this policy soon appeared in the arrest of Lord Fitzwalter and some other men of rank, several of whom were beheaded. But the most startling revelation still remained; it was found that Sir W. Stanley, who had deserted to Henry at Bosworth Field, had now joined the conspiracy against him. Little is known about the degree of Sir William's guilt. The indictment against him only specified his having said in conversation with the informer Clifford, that 'if he were sure that the young man was King Edward's son, he would not bear arms against him.' The judges held that treason could not escape from being sheltered under such a condition; and Stanley was accordingly executed (February 16, 1495). It appears also that he had deeply offended Henry by applying for the Earldom of Chester, which was then, as it still is, an appanage of the Crown and annexed to the title of Prince of Wales.

Meantime Maximilian and his young son Philip were in rapture at the splendid chances which were now presenting themselves. Warbeck appears to have given them the additional promise, either to abdicate in favour of Philip, or to hold the kingdom in subordination to him; it seemed quite probable that Maximilian would soon be able to hurl all the forces of England at the King of France whom he hated so entirely. Henry VII. therefore became suddenly aware that England was to be at once invaded, and that Warbeck was held to be really the Duke of York, not only by those who had been maintaining him for two years, but by the Pope, by James IV. of Scotland, by Charles VIII. of France, by the Duke of Savoy, by the King of Denmark, and perhaps also by Ferdinand and Isabella. To a man habitually prudent and foreseeing there is something unbearable in the thought of having allowed danger to accumulate by sheer neglect; and Henry suffered this misery to such an extent that he became in a few days quite like an old man.

At the beginning of July 1495 Warbeck's fleet, or rather Maximilian's, was off the coast of Kent. Some of the troops on board disembarked near Deal, and were at once set upon by the country people. No attempt was made to rescue the prisoners, and the expedition passed on; its leaders little thinking that the acute Ferdinand would at once divine that one who acted so pusillanimously could not be a genuine

Warbeck in Ireland and Scotland.

Plantagenet. Warbeck made for Ireland and began the siege of Waterford, which had been always favoured as the original landing-place of Henry II., and had shown its loyalty eight years before by holding out against Simnel. Its inhabitants now resisted the attack with such spirit for eleven days that the pretender found it necessary to raise the siege; and so little was to be accomplished in Ireland that he now resolved to try his fortune with James IV., who had promised him help even before his departure for Flanders. Accordingly he landed in Scotland, was received with considerable ceremony by James at Stirling (November 26), and an invasion of England was planned, for which Scotland was to be compensated by 33,000*l*. and the cession of Berwick. Henry, now thoroughly awakened to his difficulties, was attempting the same arts which had prospered in Flanders. He was in constant correspondence with John Ramsay Lord Bothwell, who had promised, if possible, to kidnap the 'feigned boy' and despatch him to England, and also to intimidate his supporters. Bothwell traitorously pressed upon Henry that war with Scotland was always dear to Englishmen; that James's government was most unpopular; that it would be easy to send a fleet and destroy all the shipping of the country; and that Edinburgh Castle itself was only half armed. However, before Henry was prepared for such enterprises, the Scottish raid into England took place (September 17), and was carried out with a cruelty which shocked Warbeck himself; indeed he expressed his grief at it in a way which his allies considered as 'unprincely' as his cowardice at Deal had been. As the invaders numbered only 1,400, nothing was really effected; the only reliable hope had been that Warbeck would find support beyond the Border, none of which appeared during the four days which the invaders spent in England. By this time both Charles VIII. and Ferdinand had bethought themselves how important it was to compete for Henry's friendship; and each was declaring that he alone could supply undoubted evidence of Warbeck's real birth. Henry, not ill pleased at finding his alliance thus valued, and his danger from Warbeck getting less every day, nevertheless used the rebellion as an excuse for remaining neutral in the Franco-Austrian quarrel; 'how,' he asked Ferdinand and Maximilian, 'could he possibly declare against France while such a home-danger was close upon him?' Whether any of the new evidence was now communicated to James is uncertain; at any rate, Warbeck was ordered to leave Scotland and advised to land somewhere on the English coast in the hope of gaining support there. That the recommendation was serious we may judge from the fact that when he embarked at Ayr (July 1497), it was in company with the celebrated Scottish mariners Andrew and Robert Barton, of whom we shall hear more in the next reign. Instead, however, of at once carrying out James's plan, he went for the third and last time to Ireland; but, finding that the Deputy, Lord Kildare, would now oppose him vigorously, he thought it better to try his fortune in Cornwall, where a rebellion had been repressed only three months before, and might perhaps be renewed by his presence.

This Cornish dissatisfaction had originally sprung out of the old grievance of subsidies. That a trifling Scottish invasion should be held to justify such exactions all over England appeared intolerable to a sturdy race of miners who would have thought little of resisting a few hundred foreigners, if any such had landed in their counties. Being informed by Thomas Flammock, a Bodmin attorney, that taxes were illegal for such a purpose, they actually resolved to march to London in arms in order to petition against the impost, and to call for the punishment of those who advised it—that is, of Cardinal Morton and Sir Reginald Bray. In Devonshire their conduct was peaceful; but on entering Somersetshire near Taunton, they murdered a Commissioner for the subsidy, and forced Lord Audley to be their general. Under his command they marched by way of Salisbury and Winchester into Kent, where they hoped to find a population like-minded with themselves, doubtless from the memories of Cade's rebellion. In this they had no success, the Kentish men being proud rather of their recent resistance to Warbeck than of any achievements of their fathers. Henry also, fortunately for himself, had forces in hand which had been prepared for the Scottish war; these were immediately ordered to advance towards Blackheath, where the rebels were now encamped, while at the same time bodies of horse were sent to their rear to prevent their straggling in that direction. Officers were also detached to the city of London to organise resistance and check the panic which seemed impending there. Confidence having been thus restored, the commanders spread a report that they intended to attack the rebels on Monday, June 24; and, having thus thrown them off their guard, they ordered their outposts at the bridge over the Ravensbourne at Deptford to be driven in on the Saturday afternoon. This was done by Lord Daubeny; and as the Cornishmen had arranged no supports in case of repulse, he had no difficulty in making his way up Blackheath Hill, and charging the main body on the plain above. His victory was soon complete, 2,000 rebels being slain and the other 14,000 completely hemmed in by the troops in their rear. It is remarkable that although the good archery of Cornwall had cost Henry the lives of 300 men slain on the field, he yet contented himself with inflicting capital punishment on Lord Audley, Flammock, and a third leader, the Bodmin blacksmith Michael Joseph.

Escaping with difficulty from some Waterford pursuers who were overhauling his vessels, Warbeck landed at Whitsand Bay; and the Cornishmen, no whit daunted by the results of their excursion to the metropolis, joined him in such numbers that he was able, after a fashion, to besiege Exeter. Being driven from thence by the Earl of Devonshire, he led about 7,000 men as far as Taunton; then his heart failed him so miserably that he deserted his wretched followers and made for the sanctuary of Beaulieu in the New Forest. Being taken to Exeter, where Henry then was, he made a full confession of his imposture, the substance of which has been lately confirmed by the discovery of a letter from him to his mother, written at about the same time, and with family details closely corresponding to those in the confession. Strange to say, his life too was spared, even after he had made one attempt at escape; but, being afterwards imprisoned in the Tower, he was allowed to communicate with the captive Earl of Warwick. The two plotted a new evasion, and were then both executed: 'the winding-ivy of a Plantagenet,' as Lord Bacon says, 'thus killing the true tree itself.' Mr. Gairdner, from an appendix to whose work on Richard III. the newer details here given upon Warbeck have been taken, is inclined to believe that the pretender was spared only that he might entrap Lord Warwick. If Henry really contrived this, he must have been a graduate in treachery worthy to rank beside Louis XI. and Richard III. Yet it is hard to see why Warwick could not have

Warbeck in Devonshire.

been destroyed by simpler means; and we should in justice remember that Henry had let Simnel live without any such motive. Indeed, with all his faults, bloodthirstiness seems to have been foreign to his character, at any rate when he felt himself safe without capital punishments. There was a quaint kindliness, too, which sounds sincere, in his reply to his Council's condolence on his being so troubled with impostors. 'It is,' he said, 'the vexation of God himself to be vexed with idols; therefore, let not this trouble any of my friends. For myself, I have always despised them; and am only grieved that they have put my people to such great trouble and misery.'

Even before these events came to an end the prohibition had been removed against commerce with Flanders.

The 'Intercursus Magnus.' The intermediate difficulties of the country had been much lightened by the patriotic conduct of the 'Merchant Adventurers' (a corporation dating from the fourteenth century), who resolved to buy for cash goods for exportation exactly as they would have done if there had been trade as usual. This, of course, locked up much of their capital, and even hazarded their credit with foreign countries. It was, therefore, most important that restrictions should cease; and this was finally effected (April 1496) by a treaty called by the Flemings the 'Intercursus Magnus.' It guaranteed freedom of trade, without licenses or passports, and in all commodities, between England, Ireland, and Calais on the one hand, and Brabant, Flanders, Hainault, Holland, and Mecheln on the other. Each contracting nation was to be allowed to possess houses suitable for themselves and their merchandise in the dominion of the others; and while the traders were to pay all customary dues, they were also to be reinstated in all their former privileges. So welcome was the treaty to both parties, that the English merchants, on arriving at Antwerp, were escorted to their house in a kind of triumph by the whole population. It is not without regret that we find the Merchant Adventurers so far presuming on their services at a critical time as to make in 1497 a determined attempt to engross to themselves the whole foreign trade of the country, and to prevent all who did not belong to their corporation from resorting to countries abroad without its license. They made the matter worse by claiming the license-money for a 'fraternity of St. Thomas of Canterbury'—an intrusion of religious pretences which was not likely to commend their view to the general community; especially as an old claim of 3s. 4d. was now raised to no less than 5l., besides further demands for entrance money from individuals. Yet most of this outrageous claim was conceded to them (though with a proviso that 6l. 13s. 4d. should be the highest sum which they were to demand from any one for a license to trade); and the powers which they thus acquired remained for many years a source of ever-recurring controversy.

CHAPTER V.

ALLIANCES AGAINST FRANCE. DEATH OF HENRY.
1497–1509.

To trace Henry's connexions with the French wars in Italy, and his reason for joining the Italian league against Charles VIII. in 1496, it is necessary to go back to events two years earlier. Charles had carried out in August 1494 the attempt on Italy of which his ambassadors had spoken in

Charles VIII. in Italy.

England, not heeding either the dissuasions of his wise sister, or the dying advice of Louis XI. to give France at least five or six years of rest. He had in his mind a collection of the strangest and most confused motives and purposes that can be conceived. The strongest feeling of all was the vanity which made him wish to stand forth as a youthful Cæsar or Charlemagne, at the head of a France which the late annexations had made stronger than it had been for centuries. Besides this he had a fitful belief that he was divinely ordained to break the power of the Turks; but his notions of the way to accomplish this were as indirect as those of his predecessor St. Louis, who landed at Tunis in order to conquer Jerusalem. First Naples must be subdued, then the whole of Italy; after this, it would be easy to become king of Greece and to organise the whole for the conquest of the Holy City. As to the first step, he might claim Naples as being a titular possession of Réné of Anjou, who had ceded his dominions to Louis XI.; indeed Réné had been nominally king of Jerusalem as well, so that this claim too had been conveyed by the same cession. It is hardly possible to imagine a more irrational mode of opposing the victorious Turks; for Charles's plans were sure to shatter rather than consolidate the means of resistance by setting one Italian State against another. Besides this, it was necessary, before he started, to bribe other princes not to attack his own dominions during his absence; and for this purpose he surrendered, to Maximilian, Artois and Franche Comté, and to Ferdinand, Roussillon and the Cerdagne. Of these districts the first two had been given up to Louis XI. in 1481, and their retrocession now laid France open on the north-east; the latter were the keys of Catalonia, also pledged to Louis in exchange for his support at a critical juncture, and their recovery was now regarded by the Spaniards as hardly less important than the conquest of Granada. Yet, after all, Maximilian was not conciliated, for he knew that Charles hoped to make himself a kind of Eastern emperor, and therefore his rival; nor yet Ferdinand, who was sure to take the first opportunity for supporting the Aragonese dynasty of Naples which Charles intended to dethrone. In Italy itself the only ally of France was Ludovico Sforza, who had usurped Milan from his nephew Giovanni Galeazzo Visconti, and in order to retain it was delighted to throw all Italy into confusion by a French invasion.

Only the briefest summary of the French operations can be given here. Charles at once alienated Ludovico Sforza by supporting his nephew in a fit of romantic generosity, and lost the hope of Florentine friendship by insisting on entering the city as a conqueror, and on delivering Pisa from its supremacy; he also began the bad fashion of carrying off works of art to ornament his own capital. In the States of the Church he occupied the fortresses, and drove the Pope and Cardinals to take refuge in the Castle of St. Angelo. The result of all these follies was that, although the extraordinary unpopularity of Alfonso of Aragon made the conquest of Naples as rapid as one within our own memory, it was utterly impossible to hold the country. For a league against France was secretly formed by Venice, Ferdinand, Pope Alexander VI., Maximilian, and Sforza. These powers undertook to cut Charles off from France, and if possible to take him prisoner. He, however, succeeded in making his way through the opposing forces at Fornovo, near Piacenza, leaving behind him 9,000 men to hold his conquests, but appearing afterwards to forget all about these unfortunate troops, who perished almost entirely by war and disease.

The manner in which these events influenced Henry's policy was curious and characteristic. Of course it was ordinarily the interest of an English sovereign to form no very close connexions either with France or Spain, but to allow these powers to weaken themselves and each other by perpetual strife, so that neither might be able to join with Scotland in attacking him. The annexation of Bretagne had, however, caused in England a positive hatred of France, while the fact that her King was engaged in enterprises so far away made it safe to side with Spain against him. Ferdinand and Isabella on their part were willing to draw towards Henry, in order to use him as an ally in the rear of their great enemy. In fact, the Spanish sovereigns had for some time been looking for opportunities of conciliating him; and their ambassador, Don Pedro de Ayala, had been most influential in persuading James of Scotland to give up his support of Warbeck, thus freeing Henry from the great danger of his reign and raising the value of his friendship. Two marriages were now planned with the object of uniting both Scotland and Spain with England, and detaching both irrevocably from the French alliance. Henry's eldest son Arthur was to be the husband of Katherine, the younger daughter of Ferdinand and Isabella, and his daughter Margaret was to become Queen of Scotland. The consequences of these two marriages would be wide-reaching. That with Scotland might lead to the union of the two countries by the succession of a Scottish prince to the English throne; if this happened, Henry acutely remarked that Scotland would still be only an accession to England, and not

Royal marriages. The Italian League.

England to Scotland, inasmuch as the greater would necessarily draw the less. That with Spain would directly cause firmer friendship and more vigorous commercial intercourse with the Netherlands, as the Archduke Philip, Maximilian's eldest son, had married Juana, Katherine's elder sister; and this again would compel the Duchess Margaret of Burgundy to desist from any further Yorkist enterprises against Henry. Yet, with all these motives to conclude Arthur's marriage at once, the negotiations for it went on slowly. An agreement was formed about its conditions in September 1496; on August 15, 1497, the betrothal took place at Woodstock, but the marriage itself was delayed till November 1501. The same kind of caution showed itself in Henry's adhesion (September 1496) to the Italian League. He accompanied this with a stipulation that he should not, like the other members of the confederacy, be called upon to make war with Charles. Ferdinand was willing to receive him into the League even on these terms, feeling sure that circumstances would soon compel him to take a more decided part. Meantime the King of Aragon was preparing, as late historical discoveries have shown, a plan for overthrowing the peculiar liberties of the Gallican Church, as established by Charles VII., the grandfather of the present King; but for these, it was thought, no king of France would ever dare to wage war against the Pope as Charles had been doing, or to show himself so disobedient to his spiritual authority. That the marriage of Katherine should have been thus planned with the decided object of strengthening the Papacy may surely be considered as one of the most striking instances on record of the irony of fate. As having this object, it could not but be religiously dangerous to England and ominous to our liberties. Lord Bacon remarks that prosecutions for heresy were rare under Henry VII.; yet they were not unknown, for Joan Boughton, Lady Young, and several other persons had been burned as Wycliffites in 1494 and the following years, and the spirit of heresy was abroad. What then was likely to be the effect of so close an alliance with Ferdinand and Isabella, who had allowed the Inquisition to burn 500 persons annually for many years together in their dominions? Here again, we should feel some gratitude to the sovereign who, whether from timidity and indecision, or from something within him which did not love cruelty, did after all guard us from the worst risks which his policy was likely in itself to bring on.

The proposal of a Crusade by Alexander VI. in 1500, on different principles from those pursued by Charles VIII., produced a fresh indication of Henry's unwillingness to trust the Pope too far. When asked to join with Hungary, Poland, Bohemia, Venice, France, and Spain in a combined attack against the Turks, he replied with hardly concealed contempt that no prince on earth should be more forward than he to join in so holy an enterprise, but that surely the Mediterranean powers, being so much nearer than he was to the scene of action, and so much better supplied with ships and galleys, ought to take the initiative in it. Yet if these should refuse, rather than his Holiness should go alone, he would wait upon him as soon as he could be ready, 'always provided that he might first see all differences among Christian princes fully settled, and might have some good Italian ports put into his hands for the retreat and safeguard of his men.' That the envoy should be 'nothing at all discontented' with this answer seems to show that the plan was not intended to be really serious.

Crusade refused.

At the time of Katherine's betrothal, when she was only thirteen years old, and her bridegroom three years younger, the question had been raised in Spain whether she should be sent to England for education. Opinions varied on this point, some maintaining that Henry's court was morally by no means a fit place for the training of a young lady, others that, as she would have to go there at last, it would be better that she should have as little remembrance as possible of any happier home. At the end of 1500 her journey was at length to take place; and hearing that her entrance into London was to be magnificent, Isabella wrote entreating Henry to curtail such expenses, and give Katherine more, if possible, of his fatherly affection in lieu of them. She was to be endowed at once with the third part of the principality of Wales, of the dukedom of Cornwall, and of the earldom of Chester; and, in case of her becoming queen, she was to be 'as richly endowed as any former queen had ever been.' In exchange for this somewhat hazy promise, she signed a renunciation of her dowry of 200,000 ducats; the young couple were married in the following November, and sent to reside at Ludlow Castle, from which the poor young bridegroom wrote to his father after a week or two that he had never conceived the possibility of such happiness as he was then enjoying. His occupations also seem to have been truly royal; much of the town of Ludlow had been destroyed in the civil wars, and he encouraged its restoration by all possible means. Besides this, he devoted himself, with the help of the Welsh members of his Council, to the improvement of the laws by which the Principality was governed. He is praised too for the peaceable disposition which made him check at once all quarrels among

Prince Arthur and Katherine.

the members of his household. But all this genial promise was cut short by a misfortune like that which carried off at a very early age the two other sons-in-law of the Catholic sovereigns. A neglected cold settled on Arthur's lungs; and he expired within five months of his wedding-day. Before the unhappy Katherine emerged from her retirement, an ambassador came from Spain with a public commission to bring back the Princess, at the same time claiming her dowry and payment of the income guaranteed to her: yet so important did Henry's alliance appear to Ferdinand and Isabella, that they gave their envoy private instructions to arrange, if possible, that the young widow should marry the Duke of York her brother-in-law, a boy five years younger than herself. Of course such a marriage was irregular, and would require a special dispensation from the Pope; yet, considering the object proposed by the league between Ferdinand and Henry, it seemed not impossible that such a point might be conceded, especially if, as reported, Katherine had been Arthur's wife only in name. Subject to the chances of papal pliancy, the King thought it well to allow the parties to be affianced to one another; whether the marriage actually took place or not would depend on future combinations. Meantime, the Archbishop of Canterbury's country house at Croydon was appointed for Katherine's residence; and she was treated well or ill according to the ebbs and flows of Henry's good will for Spain, holding, as she did, a kind of political agency for the interests of her native country. At one time Henry VII. conceived the outrageous design of marrying her himself, but was deterred from it by Isabella's declaration that such a notion was 'too wicked to be so much as named in Christian ears.'

The conclusive reason for Ferdinand and Isabella's urgency in the affair of their daughter's second marriage must be looked for in the state of France, where Charles VIII. had been succeeded, in April, 1498, by his cousin Louis of Orleans, whom we have seen revolting against him in Bretagne. *Plan for Katherine's second marriage.* The new King's first care was to bribe Pope Alexander VI. to grant a divorce from his unloved wife Jeanne of France, the daughter of Louis XI., and to secure Bretagne to the French Crown by at once marrying Anne, the late King's widow. Immediately on ascending the throne, he assumed the titles of King of Naples and Duke of Milan, the former as heir to Charles VIII., the latter as being descended from the Visconti of Milan. Before the year of his accession ended he allied himself with Venice and the Pope, overran the Milanese, dethroned Ludovico Sforza, who had been restored to his dukedom after Charles VIII.'s retreat from Italy, and imprisoned him in the terrible castle of Loches, near Tours. He then made with Ferdinand the strange agreement that the two powers should divide Naples between them, Apulia and Calabria being assigned to Spain, and the Terra di Lavoro and Abruzzo to France. For this purpose the French invaded the country in July 1501, took Frederic King of Naples prisoner, and occupied the provinces assigned to them, while Gonzalo de Cordova, Ferdinand's general, reduced Tarento and the southern districts. The natural consequences of this preposterous contract were not long in appearing; the two Kings differed as to the division of the central provinces, each claiming them as belonging to his own portion. This quarrel was rising to a height at the beginning of the year 1502; so that just at the time of Arthur's death the Catholic sovereigns had the strongest motives to hold fast to the English alliance. Indeed their ardent desire for

this made them, as it would appear, overlook many of
the difficulties in the way of Katherine's re-marriage.
Henry, on his part, was not without scruples, which were
strengthened by the decided opinion expressed by Warham, Bishop-elect of London, against the Pope's power
to sanction it. However Bishop Fox and other high
authorities were of the contrary opinion; indeed, considering what the Pope had already done in the way of
allowing divorces, Henry might think it hard to assign
any limits to his power in this direction. At any rate, the
magnificent victories of Gonzalo de Cordova in Naples
soon made him think no more of his doubts; and he gave
full assent to the future marriage, yet by a refinement of
caution made his son execute privately a formal protest
against it.

The latter days of Henry were once more embit-
tered by the fear of a Yorkist insurrection. The Duke
of Suffolk was a still surviving brother of
Lord Lincoln, and had commanded for the
King at Blackheath Field. This nobleman,
having committed manslaughter in a brawl, was forced
by Henry to appear personally in court, and there to sue
out his pardon. Affronted at being thus treated like
a common person, he fled to his aunt the Duchess of
Burgundy in Flanders. Finding little encouragement
there, he made his peace with Henry and returned home.
But just before Prince Arthur's marriage, for which he
had incurred large debts, he once more retreated to
Flanders, in the hope that new discontents at home might
afford him an opportunity. On this Henry resorted to
his former arts. Sir Robert Curzon was instructed to go
over to Flanders, pretend to join Suffolk, and gain information as to his confederates at home. This led to
the arrest of the King's brother-in-law the Earl of

The Arch-duke Philip in England.

Devonshire (husband of Elizabeth's sister Katherine), and of Lord Abergavenny; others of meaner rank, such as Sir James Tirrel, the murderer of the Princes in the Tower, were at the same time executed. The plans of Suffolk were thus deranged, and he was reduced to live in hopeless exile, receiving, however, protection in Flanders from the Archduke Philip, who by the death of Isabella was now King of Castile in right of Juana his wife. Suffolk was, however, driven from this refuge by a singular accident. In January 1506 Philip and Juana were on the way to Spain in order to take possession of their heritage. Their fleet ran down the English Channel, firing guns by way of bravado when they were near the land; but in the midst of this amusement they were surprised by a storm which shattered and dispersed their vessels, driving the sovereigns themselves into the harbour of Melcombe. No accident could possibly be more delightful to Henry; for he thus got into his power the prince who had been his most determined adversary, launching Warbeck's expedition against him, and agreeing to receive the Crown of England in the event of its success. He eagerly invited Philip and Juana to visit him at Windsor; where, under cover of an honourable reception, they would be still more completely in his power. Amid a thousand courtesies, he still held firmly to one main point; Suffolk must be surrendered. This was at last agreed to, though with extreme unwillingness; Henry on his part promising not to punish him for his rebellion, and consenting that the matter should be so arranged that the exile might seem to return by his own free will. At the same time Philip was compelled to make a new commercial treaty, which was so unpopular among his subjects that they called it the 'Intercursus Malus' (by way of contrast with the great treaty of 1496), complaining that it sacrificed their interests by allowing English cloth to be sold in Flemish towns generally, instead of only at the two emporia of Bruges and Antwerp, and thus taking out of their hands the profits of local trade in their own country.

Henry was now a widower of some years' standing; the fair and good Queen Elizabeth having died in 1501. Anxious at the thought that the succession to the throne now depended on the life of one son, he began to think of marrying again. He was not too old to hope for fresh offspring, though his weak constitution gave him an appearance of age. Several ladies were at different times proposed; and he has been deservedly ridiculed for the catalogue of enquiries which he directed to be made about the personal charms of some of them. He urgently pressed for a portrait of the widowed Queen of Naples, Isabella's niece; but met with a blank refusal—the lady would not allow her beauty to be sent about on approval. Maximilian's daughter Margaret, after being first Queen-elect of France, then wife to the heir-apparent of Spain, then Duchess of Savoy, seemed at one time likely to end with being Queen of England. Besides this, Henry had been more than suspected of ardently admiring Queen Juana on the Windsor visit, when the evident ill-health of her husband gave a prospect of his death, which happened a few months after. All these schemes having failed, the King made a virtue of necessity, and remained for the rest of his life unmarried.

A curious attempt was made in 1508 to procure from Pope Julius II. (who had succeeded Alexander VI. in 1503) the canonisation of King Henry VI. Lord Bacon hints that the fees payable to the Roman Court on such occasions were unreasonably high, amounting as they did to nearly 1,000 ducats. He inclines, however, to the view that Julius was too sensible so to honour one who was 'little better than a natural.' That the expense would not have deterred Henry is proved by his having willingly paid similar fees for the canonisation of Anselm, which took place at this time.

As there were no regular parliamentary subsidies in the last thirteen years of Henry's reign, he had to provide for the expenses of government otherwise, and did so by means which have stained his memory deeply. He made money out of every office in his Court, received bribes for conferring bishoprics, and sold pardons to those concerned in the Cornish rebellion, the sums paid varying from 1*l.* to 200*l.* But far the most discreditable exactions were those which are connected with the names of Richard Empson and Edmund Dudley—the former a Towcester tradesman's son, employed by Henry in imitation of Louis XI.'s love for low-born ministers; the latter the founder, at least, of a great family, as his son John played a considerable part in English history under his successive titles of Lisle, Warwick, and Northumberland. These men enriched Henry by a course of the most odious chicane directed against wealthy men all over England. We hear of their prosecuting Sir William Capel for being remiss in enquiring about base coin when Lord Mayor of London, and fining him 2,000*l.* As this was the second time Sir William had been thus treated, he firmly refused to pay, and remained a prisoner in the Tower till the end of the reign. Other persons were indicted of crimes before magistrates, and then left in prison untried, in defiance of Magna Charta, till they consented to pay fines or ransoms for their freedom. Sometimes, as Lord Bacon tells us, Empson and Dudley even dispensed with the help of magistrates, and committed accused persons to

Empson and Dudley.

prison by their own authority, the pecuniary object in each case being the same. They got enormous sums for restoration in cases of technical outlawry, and even tried to establish the principle that such a composition should never be less than half a man's income for two years after the outlawry began. Endless vexations were also practised at times when new heirs were succeeding to landed property, by maintaining and aggravating every feudal exaction applicable to such occasions. Especially was this the case with royal wards, whose lands were given up to them only after paying extravagant fines. Empson and Dudley had also agents everywhere employed in the detestable task of hunting out defects in the title of landholders, and trying to revive obsolete rights of the Crown. This practice, a return to which had in after years so much to do with the ruin of Charles I., would almost certainly have overthrown both Henry himself and his dynasty if it had been carried on long; as it was, his feeling of his approaching end made him inclined to listen to remonstrances, some of which were urged, as we are glad to hear, by the honourable boldness of the Court preachers. Yet the abuses were not restrained till the King had amassed treasure to the surprising amount of 1,800,000*l.*; while his agents had laid up for themselves a store of public hatred which only waited for their master's death to discharge itself.

Henry's last public act was the conclusion of a project of marriage between his daughter Mary and Charles Prince of Castile, the son of Philip and Juana.

Death of Henry VII. He thus hoped that he had built round his kingdom the long hoped-for 'wall of brass;' since he was to have for his son-in-law the King of Scotland on the one side and the future Lord of Spain and Burgundy on the other. When he perceived his end approaching, he proclaimed a general pardon for State offences, and also showed some desire that unjust acquisitions of the Crown should be restored. Soon after this he died calmly at Richmond (April 22, 1509), at the age of only fifty-two, and after a reign of twenty-three years and eight months, the troubles of which had long ago brought on him infirmities far beyond his years.

CHAPTER VI.

LEGISLATION FOR IRELAND. ENGLISH LAWS OF HENRY VII. FOREIGN TRADE. MARITIME DISCOVERY. 1485–1509.

THE administration of Ireland in this reign (as indeed in most reigns) stood on such a different footing from that of England, that it is well to speak of it separately; if, indeed, we ought not rather to say that all administration there had come to an end since the days when the popular government of Richard Duke of York had drawn away so much of the country's strength to perish in the battle of Wakefield. Of course, as the Wars of the Roses got fiercer and fiercer, it became more and more out of the question to send either men or money there, or even to forbear from recalling its English colonists. Thus the purely Irish families recovered much of their lost ground, especially in Ulster; in the South and West the few remaining English were content to assimilate themselves to the native Irish. So the Geraldines, as Spenser tells us, were so enraged at the death of the Earl of Desmond in 1467 that they rose in arms against Edward IV. and renounced all obedience to the Crown of England, carrying with them the greater part of the English in Munster; while the

State of Ireland.

F

Norman families of Butler and De Burgh became as Irish as the O'Neils or O'Donnells, living according to Brehon law, and making private war at their pleasure. Many of them took Irish names, adopted the Irish language, dressed in Irish fashion, contracted marriage and fosterage with the natives, formed their retainers into bastard septs, and instead of regular rents and services, learned to practise the irregular exactions called by the English Coyne and Livery. 'These renegades to Irishry,' says Mr. Goldwin Smith, ' seem to have imbibed even the peculiarities of Irish intellect; for the Earl of Kildare, the head of the Geraldines, being summoned to answer for an act of sacrilege in burning down the Cathedral of Cashel, pleaded in his defence that he "thought the Archbishop was in it."' · To the strange attraction which thus acted upon the English settlers must be ascribed many of the sternest and most repressive Irish laws of the Plantagenets. Thus if the Statute of Kilkenny (passed under Lionel Duke of Clarence in 1367) forbade the English to let the Irish graze cattle on their lands, its object was not so much to hinder Irishmen from prospering as to keep Englishmen aloof from the companionship which tempted them so strongly to forswear their country. The 'unchartered freedom' of Irish life carried with it so strange an allurement that it was all which law could do to contend against it.

If Ireland had any preference for either of the great contending parties in England, it was, as we have seen, for the House of York; and from this cause chiefly sprang the change of Henry VII.'s mode of governing the dependency which on ascending the throne he had found all but severed from his dominions. At first he had thought it best to employ the native nobility for this purpose, and had chosen for

Poynings' Laws.

Deputy the Earl of Kildare—setting him, as the story ran, to rule all Ireland, because all Ireland could not rule him. When, however, he had time to reflect on the dangers springing from the Irish support of Simnel and Warbeck, from which he and his dynasty had escaped so narrowly, he perceived the necessity of bringing the country under a more regular government. Accordingly he sent over in 1494 (at the time when Warbeck was preparing for his descent on England) Sir Edward Poynings as Lord Deputy, a statesman and commander well experienced in the most important affairs of the time. Poynings soon found that his military enterprises against Warbeck's wild Irish supporters in Ulster were always foiled 'in respect of the mountains and fastnesses' in which the enemy found refuge; on this he accused his predecessor Lord Kildare of correspondence with the rebels, procured his attainder by the Irish Parliament, and ordered him to be arrested and sent to England. Meanwhile he summoned a Parliament at Drogheda, and there carried, among other Acts, the two most commonly associated with his name. By the first of these it was provided that 'all statutes lately made in England should be deemed good and effectual in Ireland.' It had been common, as Mr. Hallam remarks, to extend to Ireland the operation of English statutes, even when that country was not particularly named, if the judges thought that the subject was sufficiently general to require it; and a majority of them had held in Richard III.'s reign that borough towns in Ireland were bound by statutes made in England. From the date of Poynings' Law all doubt was held to be cleared away as regards any English statutes passed before it (though it is hard to see how the expression 'statutes *lately* passed' could be so all-embracing); those subsequent to that date were not binding on the people of Ireland, unless specially named or included under general words (such as 'all his Majesty's dominions'). It may be well here to remark that a declaratory Act of Parliament was passed in comparatively recent times (1719) making it still more clear that the Crown, with the consent of the Lords and Commons of Great Britain in Parliament, had power to make laws to bind the people of Ireland. It was the repeal of this law which in 1782 led to that independence of the Irish Parliament which lasted up to the Union of 1800.

Still more important was the provision, in another section of the same statute, that no parliament should be held in Ireland without the bills intended to pass at it being submitted to the King in Council; these were then to be returned to Ireland under the Great Seal, and either passed or rejected as seemed good to the Irish Parliament, but not altered or amended. Thus the Irish colonists, in spite of the status of Ireland as a separate kingdom, were debarred from the privilege of independent legislation; yet when we consider how small a portion of the population of Ireland they formed, and by what oppressive means they habitually aimed at securing the ascendency, it can hardly be seriously denied that some such control was really imperative. This, in fact, is clear enough from other parts of the same statute which were aimed at curbing the lawlessness of the settlers. In case of one of their number being murdered, they were forbidden by it from pillaging or exacting a fine from the sept of the slayer, though this had been expressly allowed by the Dublin Parliament in 1475. Noblemen were restrained from private war, and from making the citizens of towns their retainers for this purpose; and 'coyne' and 'livery' were again forbidden under stronger penalties.

In the same year Henry suppressed the so-called

'Fraternity of St. George' in Ireland, which had been established to meet the anarchy caused there by the Wars of the Roses, and bore some resemblance to the Spanish 'Hermandad' described in Chapter I. It consisted of thirteen deputies sent up by the counties of Kildare, Dublin, Meath, and Louth, who bound themselves to maintain a small and quickly moving force of 120 archers and 40 horsemen, always ready to arrest rebels and those for whose apprehension warrants had been issued. Every year on St. George's day the members met at Dublin and elected a captain for the ensuing year; to defray their expenses, the government had assigned to them the proceeds of a tax of one shilling in the pound on merchandise landed at Dublin. Doubtless the mode in which such a body acted would have too much of the appearance of private war to find much favour in Henry's eyes. After the recall of Sir Edward Poynings, the country was governed in an irregular way; sometimes under Lord Kildare (whose attainder was reversed by the English Parliament in 1495), sometimes under English governors, one of whom was Henry Dean, Bishop of Bangor, and afterwards Archbishop of Canterbury, whose power of persuasion had done much to secure the passing of Poynings' laws by the Irish Parliament.

Fraternity of St. George.

The mention just made of Henry's legislation in Ireland may properly introduce some account of his English enactments, which are most important and practical, founded as they are mainly on the admirable principle that obedience to existing laws and a general feeling of responsibility are what a good government should chiefly aim at securing. In fact, in spite of the many faults of Henry's administration, Lord Bacon seems quite justified in stating that in legislation

Laws of Henry VII.

he deserves a place among our early kings next to that of
Edward I. With regard to the power of the Crown he
carried two highly important statutes. The first is that
which exempts from the penalties of treason all who do
service to a *de facto* king. Lord Bacon's view of this
law is that it was 'rather just than legal, rather mag-
nanimous than provident,' as it made rebellion easy by
securing from punishment those who served any pretender to the Crown who might be strong enough to
establish his power for a time. Yet, on the other hand,
it would make rebels begin sooner to think of an accommodation, instead of fighting on as men do whose life is
certain to be forfeited in case of defeat; and was, therefore, so far in favour of a king *de jure*. And when we think
how manifestly just it was that the same law which made
it treason (as in Sir W. Stanley's case) to express the
slightest and most hypothetical doubt as to the title of
an actual sovereign should also protect those who upheld
it, we may be inclined to recur once more to Burke's
admirable dictum, that in political matters magnanimity
is always the truest wisdom. This law, passed in 1496,
was in a manner counterpoised by an earlier one (1488)
which made it a capital crime to conspire the death of
any of the King's Council, or of any lord of the realm.
That of 1496 did not protect persons serving a possible
Republic or possible Protector of England. Had it done
so, Sir Henry Vane could not have been executed at the
Restoration for the one crime of having been an energetic
minister under the Republic.

Another class of laws was aimed at the repression of
acts of violence. Thus it was made in 1488 a capital
crime to carry off heiresses or women of property in order
to marry them by force; an instance had occurred in
which a widow named Margaret had been so treated by

a band of men a hundred in number, who had been pursued by forty others 'modo guerrino armati' (armed in warlike manner) into another county, and there overcome and arrested. In the same year it was ordained that trials for murder should follow while the memory of the deed was fresh and evidence easily attainable, instead of being delayed, as they often were, for a year and a day, in order that the friends of the deceased might have a chance of first proceeding by the private and vindictive mode of action called 'Appeal of Murder,' which Lord Macaulay has described in its application to the case of Spencer Compton. Another Act of 1488 allowed justices to determine without a jury all offences against unrepealed statutes, except treason, murder, and felony; it was on this statute that Empson and Dudley relied in trying men privately in financial cases.

But far the most important of the laws passed by Henry in favour of public order was that which in 1488 established the celebrated Court of Star Chamber. Its preamble states that 'the King, remembering how by unlawful maintenances, giving of liveries, . . . untrue demeanings of sheriffs in the making of panels, by taking of money by juries, and by great riots and unlawful assemblies the policy and good order of this realm is almost subdued, and that for punishing these inconveniences little or nothing may be found by enquiry' (that is by an ordinary trial before a jury), 'ordains that the Chancellor, Treasurer, and Privy Seal, with a Bishop and a temporal Lord of the Council and two Judges . . . shall have authority to call before them offenders and witnesses, and to examine and punish them according to statute.' This was held to be not so much a novelty as a parliamentary recognition of an ancient authority inherent in the Privy Council. At any

The Star Chamber.

rate it furnished the Crown with a most powerful instrument for checking abuses, and was soon held to apply to forgery, fraud, perjury, contempt of court, and many other crimes; nay, even occasionally to civil causes. Hardly a term passed without juries being fined by it for acquitting felons or murderers contrary to the evidence. Sir John Hussey, a member of the Privy Council, was prosecuted in the Star Chamber in 1492 by Alice Fordman, as accessory to the murder of her husband; noblemen were indicted before it for sheltering outlaws or for interfering with the election of sheriffs, and justices of the peace punished for neglecting their duties. The fines imposed at this time by it, though mostly less ruinous than those of after days, when prosecutor and judges were alike enriched by them, were still such as thoroughly to daunt evil-doers; sometimes also men of rank had to appear almost naked and sue for pardon. Above all, the Court of Star Chamber aimed at enforcing the statute of Livery, which prohibited under heavy penalties the maintenance by noblemen of large bodies of retainers wearing their livery and ready to wage private war in their behalf. All histories mention the enormous fine of 15,000 marks (equivalent to more than 100,000*l.* of our money) which Henry inflicted on his staunch supporter the Earl of Oxford, for breaking this statute in order to entertain him more splendidly; it appears to be a close imitation of the conduct of Louis XI. in vindicating his sole right of chase by burning all the nets and other implements collected by the Sire de Montmorency for his use on a visit. It was, however, far more justifiable than this act of the French King; for it is evident that the Earl of Oxford's conduct, if established as a precedent, would at any time have justified noblemen in surrounding themselves with large bodies of warlike supporters just when the King was going to receive their hospitality, and thus to place himself most completely in their power if they had any treasonable intentions.

Other laws of this period were aimed at benefiting the people according to the ideas then current. Henry, following the example of Ferdinand and Isabella, endeavoured to regulate the weights and measures throughout England. He introduced the first Navigation Act, providing that wine and woad from Saxony and Languedoc should be conveyed only in English vessels, and thus sacrificing cheapness in these commodities to the hope of creating a navy. He ordered that the byelaws of trade guilds should not be binding till they had been sanctioned by the great officers of State. With a notion of humanity much in advance of his time, he got Parliament to enact that gaolerships should not be patent offices, but should be always under the control and responsibility of the sheriffs. Abuses in prisons were, however, too deeply rooted to be thus abolished. And he provided the order for suits *in forma pauperis*, in which attorneys and counsel are assigned free of all charges to very poor men—a fact on which Lord Campbell has made the interesting remark that in our day counsel are always anxious to do their very best on such occasions; as also in defending persons accused of treason, when fees are illegal. *Navigation Law, &c.*

Another important part of Henry's legislation was that which had to do with foreign trade. This occupied much of his attention, as we might expect from a King who had watched Louis XI.'s exertions in this line. The chief exports of England at this time were wool, cloth, and hides; our lead mines roofed nearly all the cathedrals and large buildings of Europe, and of tin we had a monopoly. The chief *Trade with the Netherlands.*

foreign market for wool was afforded by the Netherlands. Accordingly one of the main objects of our commercial policy was to foster this trade, and also, if possible, to force English cloth into sale in Flanders, in spite of the jealousy felt there against the rising manufactures of England, which were bidding fair to supersede their own. As we have seen, the risks from this cause were much aggravated by Margaret of Burgundy's vehement hatred to the Lancastrian King, which had once caused the transference to Calais of the English staple. When this cause of difference had at length ceased, the 'Intercursus Magnus' of 1496 replaced the Flemish trade on a sufficiently liberal basis. Besides its already mentioned provisions, it ordained that custom-house officers were to be polite, and not to break up packages needlessly; and that on no account were they to force sales to themselves. In case of injury, the aggrieved party was not to make reprisals, but to appeal to the offender's sovereign; and, to avoid piracy, each owner was to deposit double the value of his ship and cargo, to be forfeited if his mariners could be proved guilty of that crime. Neither party was to allow foreign vessels to be attacked in its ports by any hostile power, or their plunder to be sold there: in case of shipwreck, the cargo might be reclaimed within a year and a day on payment of salvage expenses. Care was also taken to foster the Mediterranean trade, which subsequently lost much of its importance through Vasco de Gama's discovery of the sea route to the east by the Cape of Good Hope (1497) but was still considerable in Henry VII.'s time. It was conducted almost entirely through the republic of Venice, whose galleys used to come in flotillas to the English Channel, and unload at Sandwich, Southampton, or London. Their cargo consisted of spices (including pepper), Malmsey wine from the Morea and Crete; sugar from Cyprus, Crete, and Alexandria; silk from Persia, Syria, Greece, and Sicily; cotton from Egypt and India; glass from the East and from the Murano factories at Venice, together with paper, illuminated books, and other articles. The Venetians exported in return the standard English commodities of wool, cloth, hides, lead, and tin; being liable, like other merchants, to a suit for 'non-use' if they did not take return cargoes of English goods.

The trade with France was chiefly for Gascon wines, woad from Toulouse, and salt, linen, and canvas from Bretagne. When Louis XII., in 1504, avenged some injuries done to his subjects in England by forbidding the export of wines in French bottoms, this naturally compelled the English to use their own vessels for this purpose—a tendency much strengthened by the Navigation Act already alluded to. From Spain came large quantities of sweet wines, fruit, and fine Cordovan leather manufactured from goat and kid skins, with the iron of Bilbao, which was much used for agricultural purposes because of its flexibility. The Spanish horses were also of a particularly fine breed and much prized as hacks and chargers. Accordingly the commercial intercourse with Spain was considerable, and our merchants in Spain and Andalusia obtained in 1530 the privilege of meeting at Seville, Cadiz, or St. Lucar, and there electing their own governors, with 'twelve ancient and expert persons to be their assistants;' so that they might be defended from Spanish exactions and the tyranny of the Inquisition.

French trade.

It is remarkable that an unadventurous reign like that of Henry VII. should have been one of such extensive maritime discovery. The lead in this direction was of course taken by other nations, especially the Portuguese, who were the first to apply the astrolabe to navigation (using it, as we do the sextant, for observations of latitude) and also the first to trust the mariner's compass for ocean voyages. They thus succeeded in reaching Cape Verde in 1443, Cape Sierra Leon in 1462, Cape Lopez in 1469, and the Cape of Good Hope in 1486; the right of discovery along the African coast was yielded to them by Spain in a treaty of 1479, in spite of the prior claims of the latter country as having colonised the Canaries in 1393. The establishment of a Portuguese monopoly in this direction naturally turned the thoughts of mariners in another; and as the hour had come when new discovery was almost imperative, so the man inspired to make it was not long wanting. In the year 1482, Christoval Colon (whose name was Latinised into 'Columbus') vainly laid his projects for reaching Asia by sailing westward before the authorities of his native Genoa, who thought them beyond their means; and then before the Portuguese government, which tried to steal a march on him by privately despatching a vessel in the direction indicated by him. Deeply resenting this ungenerous conduct, he went to Spain in 1484, and, finding the delays there intolerable, despatched his brother Bartolommeo to England in the next year. Bartolommeo was however taken by pirates, and remained long in captivity; thus it was only on February 13, 1488, that he was able to present to Henry VII. a map of the world drawn by himself, and to ask his patronage for his brother. The King liked the scheme so well that his offers actually preceded those made in Spain to Columbus: yet by a new series of cross accidents Bartolommeo reached Spain only after his brother's departure from Palos in 1492, and in fact after he had discovered the West Indies. Never surely since the world began was the fate of nations and continents decided by such a succession of strange casualties as those which on the one hand produced Columbus's success, and on the other ordained that Spain, not England, should be the power under whose flag it was achieved, and that the energy of our country should not be frittered away, as that of Spain was, upon a vast system of gold and silver mining by slave-labour. Meantime a healthier though less romantic series of discoveries was giving England the first claim to a western empire of far superior ultimate value to all that even Mexico or Peru had to offer.

As early as 1496 Henry VII. issued to John Cabot (Gaboto), a Genoese mariner long resident at Bristol, a patent of leave to discover unknown lands, and to conquer and settle them. The King was to receive a fifth of the profits without paying any part of the charges ; instead of money, he gave a monopoly of trade with the countries to be discovered, and their government subject to the English Crown. Like Columbus, Cabot hoped to find a passage to the Indies, only his aim was a north-western instead of a due westward route. One ship alone could be chartered ; this sailed from Bristol on June 24, 1497, and Cabot was soon rewarded by the discovery of Newfoundland, whose fog-banks must have been the strangest contrast to the sunny lands discovered by Columbus five years before. He then reached Cape Breton (which he called Prima Vista) and probably also Nova Scotia; thus seeing the mainland of America before Columbus, who only in his last voyage in 1498 coasted along the Isthmus of Panama. There is infinite reason to regret that Sebastian Cabot, John's son and successor, had not more of Columbus's enthusiasm and literary power, so as to put his memoirs in a shape which would have preserved them. We only know

The Cabots.

that he made, almost immediately after his father's death, one or more voyages on the original track, going as far north as the Arctic Circle, but being hindered from pressing beyond it or into Hudson's Bay by a mutiny of his crews, who were naturally alarmed at the masses of ice surrounding them. After this he entered the service of Spain, and in 1525 was commissioned to make a voyage to the Moluccas by the newly-discovered Strait of Magellan. The discontent of his officers was, however, so threatening that he turned up the Rio de la Plata, and spent some years in exploring the countries near it, ascending in boats the rivers Parana and Paraguay, and asking in vain for help to colonise these fine plains. In the course of one of his voyages, it is hard to say which, he ran along the American coast as far south as Florida, thus surveying not less than 1800 miles of low and featureless shore. During his absence the Bristol merchants sent light vessels westward almost every year in quest of new lands, and had he been in England in 1509, there is at least a possible chance that Henry's VIII.'s ambition might have been turned to discovery rather than war. Under Edward VI. he came here again, receiving a pension of 250 marks, and the title of 'Grand Pilot' —an office which appears to have been created for him. Curiously enough, the only personal glimpse of the great navigator which we can obtain is an account of his deathbed. Few men have ever lived a more active life; nor were his efforts without immediate effect on the national welfare, considering the wealth ever since derived from the Newfoundland fisheries. But his chief glory will ever be that he provided against the time to come a reserved space practically inexhaustible for the swarming thousands of Northern Europe, where every nerve would be strung by hardship and peril, where, in spite of the vast scale of obstacles, nature might still be subdued to men's needs, and where freedom would have a natural home. Such was the noble region discovered for England by this Italian mariner. Nor ought we to ignore the mental effect of such additions to knowledge, and the extraordinary stimulus which they gave to thought. Just as learned Romans felt that the world became grander to them when the mystery of Britain was at length revealed by Cæsar's invasion, so thinking men at the close of the fifteenth century saw with a kind of rapture creation thus 'broadening on their view.' 'Before these days,' says Peter Martyr in a letter to Cardinal Sforza, 'hardly half of the world's circumference was known to geographers; of the rest, only the feeblest and most uncertain mention had ever been made. But now, glorious to relate, light has under the auspices of our sovereigns been thrown on the secret of the ages. I feel my heart elated with real blessedness when I confer with intelligent men who have been in those countries. Let others delight in avarice or the lusts of the flesh; but let us be filled with rapture in thinking of God, who has revealed such wonders in our day.'

CHAPTER VII.

THE REVIVAL OF CLASSICAL LEARNING.
1390–1509.

WHEN the great masterpieces of ancient literature were first rediscovered and then spread far and wide by means of manuscript and printed copies, the effect on intellectual minds was not a little like that described at the end of the last chapter. A wide and grand America of inward thought was restored

Spirit of the Renaissance.

after centuries of oblivion, and that with the effect not merely of increasing knowledge, but of revolutionising all methods of reasoning, placing all opinions in a different point of view, and awakening a new and energetic trust in the future. There could be no doubt whatever that life was worth living when any day might restore to students some new treasure of lost wisdom, and when, moreover, each new discovery threw ever-increasing light upon those already made, and brought nearer and nearer the final victory over the old learning, which not seldom employed its crabbed and debased Latin in investigating by hopeless logical methods a variety of questions which had better have been left alone. Knowledge now showed herself once more enrobed in beauty; accordingly the time was one of progress such as it is hard for us even to imagine.

Of course the knowledge of *Latin* writers had never thoroughly died out in mediæval Europe. Monks had cultivated their domains according to the precepts of the Roman writers on agriculture. At a very early date Vergil and Horace, with Statius and Ovid, were read in German schools; and at home we have only to look through a few pages of Chaucer to see his familiarity with these poets. Infinite pains were every now and then employed in ransacking libraries for manuscripts of the great Latin authors; in this way the celebrated Poggio Bracciolini, while attending the Council of Constance in 1415, discovered at the monastery of St. Gall, covered with filth and rubbish and on the point of perishing from age and neglect, what turned out to be a complete copy of Quintilian and another of the greater part of Valerius Flaccus's 'Argonautica.' The same distinguished book-finder afterwards lighted upon the last twelve comedies of

*Enthusiasm for Latin and Greek authors. Colet, More.

Plautus, and Cicero's Verrine orations, De Oratore, and Brutus; others of Cicero's orations had been discovered about a century before. After adding a MS. of Lucretius to his discoveries, Poggio sought with the utmost anxiety, but in vain, for the works of Tacitus. These were not discovered till nearly a hundred years later, when a copy of the 'Histories' came to hand in Germany, and was presented to Pope Leo X. Most passionate of all was the longing to discover the lost works of Livy. A monk assured Poggio that he had seen a copy in the Cistercian monastery of Sora; but all enquiries for it were in vain, and the blank still remains unsupplied, except as regards about thirty books. The enthusiasm for classical works was in proportion to their rarity. Alfonso of Aragon, King of Naples, refused, even when engaged in a campaign, to miss his daily lecture on Livy, and is said to have been cured of a severe illness by the delight of hearing Quintus Curtius read. Even at an earlier date Giovanni di Ravenna, a pupil of Petrarca, knew by heart all the classics which had been discovered up to his time. Nor had Petrarca himself been far behind on this point; for he tells us that in the course of a walk he went over in his own mind the whole works of Vergil, Orosius, Pliny, Mela, and Claudian, in order to remember all that these authors had said about the position of 'Ultima Thule.' Indeed this great man, who is reverenced as the father of Italian patriotism, may also be said to have done more than any other single person in restoring scholarship, and that more than a century before the times of the great Renaissance. From him the enthusiasm for these pursuits spread very widely in Italy, and even strongly affected politics, inasmuch as Rienzi's rebellion against the Papal power in 1347 was an attempt to set up once more in Rome the authority of the 'Senatus Populusque Romanus, and was entirely founded on classical ideas, thus gaining Petrarca's strongest sympathy. Yet even the enthusiasm of this period was slight in comparison with that of the later time when Greek teachers and Greek books came at last to exhibit ancient thought, not in the form which Roman eclecticism had given it, but in its simple and native beauty. The more advanced knowledge of Greek began with Manuel Chrysoloras. This eminent man came to Venice about 1390 to entreat help against the Turks who were already threatening Constantinople; when his embassy was over, he was persuaded to return and settle at Florence as professor of his native language. In 1422 Francesco Filelfo, Chrysoloras' son-in-law, and two other Italians, Guarino and Aurispa, were despatched to Constantinople to collect books. Guarino was shipwrecked on his return, and one of two valuable cases of MSS. went down with the vessel—a disaster which is said to have turned his hair completely white, though he was hardly twenty years old. Aurispa, more fortunate, arrived at Venice in the next year, bringing 238 precious volumes, among which were the works of Plato, Lucian, Xenophon, Diodorus, Arrian, Strabo, Callimachus, and Pindar. Filelfo himself remained abroad till 1427, and then returned to become the master of Greek learning in his native country. After him a succession of magnificent scholars maintained in this new field the honour of Italy. When Henry VII. came to the throne, the celebrated Politian (so named from his birth-place, the Tuscan Montepulciano—his family name being Ambrogini) was thirty years old, and had greatly distinguished himself by his knowledge of the classical authors and of Roman laws. Contemporary with him were Marsilio Ficino the translator of Plato, and Pico di Mirandola, who before his death at the age of thirty-one had studied

Jewish literature with the most unwearied industry, was planning a gigantic 'Defence of Christianity' to be founded upon it, and lived in hope of being allowed to preach this doctrine, going from town to town barefooted with crucifix in hand. At this point began the connection of English scholars with Italian learning, inasmuch as William Grocyn, after having been for some time Greek professor at Oxford, spent two years (somewhere between 1485 and 1491) at Florence, attending the lectures of Politian and Chalcondylas; and about the same time the celebrated Linacre, afterwards founder of the College of Physicians, was selected because of the elegance and modesty of his manners as the associate in study of Lorenzo de' Medici's children. On their return, these heroes of learning communicated their own ardour to kindred spirits in England, above all to Colet, afterwards Dean of St. Paul's (who himself spent some time in Italy), and to Sir Thomas More. What rank was held by these last in the republic of letters we can in some degree judge from the account of them given by Erasmus, who on coming to Oxford in 1498 to study Greek there, declares that 'to be in company with such men as Colet he would not refuse to live even in Scythia.' 'When I hear my friend Colet,' he says on another occasion, 'it is like listening to Plato himself. In Grocyn who does not admire the wide range of his knowledge? What could be more searching, deep, and refined than the judgment of Linacre? And when did nature ever mould a character more gentle, endearing, and happy than Thomas More?' We may judge, too, of the boldness with which literary research was then pursued by the recorded fact that Grocyn, after giving at St. Paul's the one or two first lectures of a course on the 'Celestial Hierarchies,' which were supposed till then to have been written by Dionysius the Areopagite, the disciple of St. Paul, suddenly announced to the astonished audience that continued study had made him absolutely disbelieve the genuineness of this book, and that the course was therefore at an end. No such bold assertion had been made since Lorenzo Valla had dared to prove the letter of Abgarus to our Lord and the 'Donation of Constantine' to be forgeries; and in uttering it Grocyn may be said to have inaugurated that English love of truth in matters of knowledge and science which has borne ever since then such noble fruits among us. Thus classical literature soon became in England a pursuit most generous and inspiring; never getting pedantic as in Italy, where men quarrelled almost to the death on the smallest matters of philology, and on such questions as whether Lucius and Arruntius were sons or grandsons of Tarquinius Priscus. Still less was there ever in England any of the strange longing for heathenism which appeared every now and then in Italy; as when Pomponius Lætus raised an altar to Romulus, and imitated in private the worship described by Ovid. Nor were Englishmen ever inclined to heathenise Christianity by classicising the language of the Bible, as when an Italian expressed 'God the Father' by 'nimborum Pater imbripotens,' the Holy Ghost by 'cælestis Zephyrus,' and the Eucharist by 'sinceram Cererem.' Far different were the thoughts which occupied such men as More, Colet, Grocyn, and Erasmus. We find More, for instance, lecturing at St. Lawrence Church in the Old Jewry on the 'Civitate Dei' of Augustine (that is, on the ways of God to man)—'a very singular occupation,' remarks Sir James Mackintosh, 'for a young lawyer.' His house was, according to Erasmus, 'a school and exercise of the Christian religion; all its inhabitants, male and female, applied their leisure to liberal studies and profitable reading, though piety was their principal care.' From purely classical work More was debarred in later life both by his civil employments and by the practical turn of his mind; what his taste in such matters was we may guess from his sending to his imaginary Utopia 'a pretty fardel of books' containing 'the most part of Plato's works, some of Aristotle's, and Theophrastus on Plants.' 'Of the poets,' he continues, 'they have Aristophanes, Homer, Euripides, and Sophocles, in Aldus small print; of the historians Thucydides, Herodotus, and Herodian. They set great store by Plutarch's books, and are delighted with Lucian's merry conceits and jests.' Learning like this had been thoroughly transfused into More's mind, and had in a manner become his very self; instead of merely quoting Plato, he tried to think as Plato would have thought if placed among the exigencies of modern life. In the same manner Colet, Dean of St. Paul's, looked upon all classical acquirement as valuable mainly from its power of ordering the mind for thought-purposes, and raising it to the noblest objects. A theologian above all things, he loved chiefly to dwell on St. Paul's Epistles, the Gospel history, the Apostles' Creed, and the Lord's Prayer. But all these subjects were animated by him with the new spirit which springs from a liberal education. He delighted, as Mr. Seebohm says, to trace in St. Paul's Epistles the marks of the Apostle's character; the 'vehemence of speaking' which would not allow him to perfect his sentences; the rare prudence with which he would temper his speech to meet the needs of the different classes by whom his epistle would be read; his eager expectation soon to visit Spain, which, however, did not make him impatient when it was disappointed. Like Dr. Arnold in our own time, Colet would illustrate St. Paul by reference to the state of Roman society as described by Suetonius. In all these and many other ways the choicest results of scholarship were as thoroughly employed by him for religious purposes as they were by More to bring about reforms in state administration.

Unlike his two cherished friends, Erasmus was the scholar pure and simple, the man who had no occupation apart from his books; moreover he was a thorough cosmopolite. Born in 1467 at Rotterdam, he had as little of the typical Dutchman in him as can well be imagined; indeed, nothing was ever so intolerable to him (except, indeed, the monastic life at Stein, from which he had escaped in order to study at Paris) as the interminable feasts of his native country, and the utter disesteem in which learning was held there. From the terrible wretchedness to which his poverty condemned him at Paris he was rescued by Lord Mountjoy, who brought him for the first time to England in 1498, settling on him a small life pension. With this and the presents which he soon began to receive Erasmus contented himself; refusing the offer of a semi-royal pupil, James Stanley the King's stepbrother, who was to be equipped with sufficient learning to allow of his being made Bishop of Ely when just out of his teens. Before the time of Erasmus's second visit to England in 1505 he had become confessedly the first classical scholar in Europe, and was well received by Archbishop Warham and by Bishop Fisher, who were both patrons of the new learning. Utterly rejecting any use whatever of modern languages, he had formed for himself a Latin style of surpassing excellence, which seemed able, without departing from the old forms and structure, to express all the ten thousand objects and circumstances of modern life. He had in 1500 taken the

Works of Erasmus.

world by storm with his 'Adagia,' a work in which, after the fashion of Italian politicians, he grouped round a number of proverbs all the associated thoughts which he could remember in ancient writings. As specimens of these may be mentioned two on which he was for ever harping—'nil monacho indoctius' and 'dulce bellum inexpertis;' his bitter hatred for the old life at Stein was brought out in the first, his deep grief at the devastation of Italy in the second. It is striking to find that, amid the manifold hardships of his third journey to England (which immediately followed the accession of Henry VIII.), the terrible weather through which he rode, and the filth and rudeness of the roadside inns, he could quietly occupy himself in planning his wonderfully witty 'Encomium Moriæ' (the Praise of Folly), in which he most impartially satirizes bookworms, grammarians, rhetoricians, lawyers, schoolmen, pilgrims, pardoners, schoolmasters, sportsmen, monks, courtiers, princes, kings, and even the Pope himself. His 'Colloquia' are still more admirable from the brightness of their style and their beautiful description of religion working amidst all the various circumstances and accidents of common life. In reading them we are perpetually reminded of Socrates's gentle and kindly persuasiveness as described by Xenophon; for, like the Athenian philosopher, he is occupied in showing how youth can be delightful and gracious, how old age and death may be disarmed of all their terrors, and how a simple heart void of superstition is able to bear up against even the extremest hardship and danger. Above all, there stands out in this, as in all his writings, a heartfelt admiration for the simple life of a kindly household; like Luther, he is never weary of contrasting this with the so-called religious life of monasteries. Even apart from the corruptions found in the cloister, he is firmly persuaded that those who adopt such a life choose not the better but the worse part. Strongly, indeed, were these admirable works calculated to influence England, where, indeed, more than one of them were written; in point of fact, their author seemed at one time likely to stamp the age with the mark of his own moderation, thoughtfulness, and humanity. In the course of the subsequent history we shall see what he thought of the wars which were soon to disappoint his best hopes, and what farther contributions he was in spite of them to make to the welfare of both Church and State in England.

The question now occurred to thinking minds by what educational institutions there would be the best chance of giving the rising generation a firm hold on the new learning; and new and noble foundations for this purpose soon came into existence. Richard Fox, who had distinguished himself while Bishop of Durham in repelling Scottish invasions, afterwards, when Bishop of Winchester, founded the grammar schools of Grantham and Taunton. At Oxford he had thought of erecting a monastery, but was dissuaded by Oldham Bishop of Exeter, who with remarkable foresight enquired, ' Would it not be better for us to provide for the increase of learning, and for such as shall do good to the Church and Commonwealth, rather than build houses and provide livelihood for monks, *whose end and fall we may live to see?*' Accordingly Bishop Fox founded Corpus Christi College, the statutes of which strongly enjoined the Fellows to pursue the new learning. The professor of Latin then was particularly ordered to extirpate barbarism—that is, monkish Latin ('ut barbariem a nostro alveario exstirpet'), and the Greek professor was to read and explain

[margin: Schools and Colleges for the New Learning.]

all the best writers in that language. Benefits of the same kind had been conferred on Cambridge by the munificence of the Lady Margaret. Herself a person of simple and uncritical piety, and as disinclined as possible to go in search of new things, she was nevertheless so thoroughly under the influence of Bishop Fisher, her chaplain and confessor, that she was induced to erect Christ's and St. John's Colleges in that university, in the interest of the newer studies. Both of these were old institutions much decayed ; she gave them suitable buildings, and provided for the Masters, Fellows, and Scholars incomes, not splendid according to our notions, but such as would supply the low living which was then thought to lead to high thinking. Of Christ's College, which alone was completed in her lifetime, she made Fisher the Visitor, thus securing that its members should live up to their founder's idea. The Fellows were to have an annual stipend of 13s. 4d. to 16s. 8d., according to their degrees ; with one shilling a week for commons, and 13s. 4d. a year for their 'livery,' which was to be of cloth of one colour bought at the celebrated national emporium of Stourbridge Fair. In all elections the poorer candidate was to be preferred; any one who had a private income of 10l. was ineligible for a fellowship. Dogs or hawks were forbidden in college; cards and dice were to be played only in hall at Christmas-time, when other jurisdictions were for the time superseded by that of the 'Rex Natalitius' or King of Nowell. What precisely was meant by secular (that is non-monastic) education in those days we are quite clearly informed in the detailed accounts which remain of the foundation of St. Paul's School in 1510 by Dean Colet. This was to contain 153 boys (the number being taken from that of the fish in St. John xxi.), and to be taught 'the old Latin speech, the very Roman tongue

used in the time of Tully and Sallust and Vergil and
Terence; the Latin adulterate, which blind fools brought
into the world, being absolutely banished.' They were
also to learn Greek, 'if such can be gotten'—a cautiously
worded injunction, and probably meant to avoid exciting
suspicion against the school as teaching the language of
heresy. Colet commissioned the learned Linacre to draw
up a Latin grammar to be used at St. Paul's; but when
it was done thought it too long and involved for his
'little beginners.' The first Headmaster was William
Lilly, the godson of Grocyn and friend of More; he had
learned Latin in Italy and had lived for years at Rhodes
to perfect himself in Greek. In the opinion of Erasmus
(who thought a teacher as important to the commonwealth as a bishop), Lilly was a thorough master in
the art of educating youth; which meant, as another
letter of Erasmus shows, that, among other qualifications, he had studied Plato and Aristotle among philo-
sophers; among poets, Homer and Ovid; in geography,
Mela, Ptolemy, Pliny, Strabo. 'The teacher,' Erasmus
continues, 'should be able to trace the origin of words,
and their gradual corruption in the languages of Constantinople, Italy, Spain, and France. He should know the
ancient names of trees, animals, instruments, clothes,
and gems, with regard to which it is incredible how
ignorant even educated men are. . . . I want the teacher
to have traversed the whole field of knowledge, that he
may spare each of his scholars doing it.' The good Dean
of St. Paul's, though unwilling to give up the stimulus
to learning which corporal punishment affords, was yet
vehement against the tyrants who thought that only by
flogging could boys' unruly spirits be tamed. Doubtless
there was room for change in this point, when it was

undergraduate of Christ's College, Cambridge, under the Lady Margaret's window—she not interfering except by calling 'Lente, lente;' and when little boys used to be whipped in the presence of guests during dinner, not because they had done anything wrong, but because they might. Finally, instead of appointing ecclesiastics as Visitors of St. Paul's School, Colet placed it under 'the most honest and faithful fellowship of the Mercers of London'—'under married citizens of established reputation,' as Erasmus puts it. Among all men to whom life had introduced him, the Dean had found he said, least corruption in these.

Few people at this time contributed more to the spread of literature than the printers; whose business was then held to include the correction of the press, as it was not usual to send proof-sheets to the author or editor. Hence the heads of such establishments as that of the Frobens at Basle, the Aldi at Venice, the Etiennes at Paris, required to be, and actually were, men of great learning, who took care to have their sons specially educated in Latin, Greek, and Hebrew for the purposes of their business. In the workshop of the Frobens it is said that every one, compositors and all, used Greek as their daily language. Though not quite up, as regards printing, to the standard of Italy, France, or Switzerland, England still was faithful to the noble tradition of Caxton; Wynkyn de Worde, who had been Caxton's assistant, having printed not less than sixty-six works between 1510 and 1520. This is not to be taken as indicating that English writers were then numerous; on the contrary, hardly any time in our history has added so little to our literature as that of Henry VII. and his son. England was then going to school and gathering materials for future effort. Our polite

Printers. Wynkyn de Worde. Poetry of the time.

literature for this period is represented almost entirely by Barklay's 'Ship of Fooles,' printed by Wynkyn de Worde in 1508. Even this was an adapted translation from a German work; the author, however, has some personal touches, as when he confesses that he himself is like other clerks, who so 'frowardly them guide,' that when once they have got promotion they give up all study. To be made 'parson of Honington or Clist,' it is required, he intimates, to be skilful rather in flattery and field-sports than in divinity. Yet he seems to show this self-blame is more or less ironical, as in another place he speaks of the delight of having many books always in hand, and binding them handsomely in 'damas, satten, or else in velvet pure.' Hawes's 'Pastime of Pleasure' came from the same press in 1517, having been finished in 1506. In contrast to its title this poem, which is dedicated to Henry VII., is a moral and learned allegory, in which the seven sciences and a host of virtues are personified, something in Bunyan's manner, though without his raciness. It is characteristic of the time that Hawes's 'Pilgrim' chooses the way of active rather than of contemplative life, while he also equips himself with all known sciences as the right preparation for a chivalrous career, especially with that lore of the stars 'in which God himself is chief astronomer.' For it is precisely this mixture of learning with energetic action which made the best men of the period what they were.

A few shorter poems belong to this time, and were more influential by far than anything in Barklay or Hawes. Among these was the ballad of the 'Nut-brown Maid,' which appeared for the first time in 1502 in Arnold's book on London customs. 'A Lytel Geste of Robin Hood' was published by Wynkyn de Worde in 1489, and established on a firm basis the reputation of this popular hero, ever ready to support the weak against the strong. Above all should it be remarked that the oldest known copy of the noble 'Chevy Chase' is thought to date from the year 1500, and is self-evidently much nearer the original than the later forms of the ballad.

The native prose works most honourable to England at this time are, of course, those of Sir Thomas More; whose style has indeed the fault (common to him with Erasmus) of inordinately long paragraphs, yet leaves little to be desired in the way of clearness. His ' History of Edward V.' was written about 1506 (though not published till 1513). It is in the classical style, with speeches for the principal characters. But his reputation will always rest on his ' Utopia,' published in its Latin form in 1515. Indeed, this deserves to rank as a masterpiece beside the works of Philippe de Commines and of More's contemporary Macchiavelli, but far beyond either in right-mindedness and reforming enthusiasm. Its arguments are supposed to be those of a companion of the traveller Amerigo Vespucci, named Raphael Hythloday, who has discovered and describes at Cardinal Morton's table the notable island of ' Nowhere,' whose inhabitants are models of practical wisdom. Strong in the experience thence derived, the travelled man finds fault with many things in England. A good specimen of his charges against our institutions is his declaration that in other countries of Europe there is trouble from disbanded soldiers who like robbery better than work, but that English thieves are not generally soldiers. The high price of wool tempts landlords to throw into large walks for sheep, inhabited only by the shepherd and his dog, those estates which had maintained many small farm-houses; thus the old tenants are driven

Prose of the period. The 'Utopia.'

away, and when their small means are spent, they can but steal and be hanged for it. We shall see in a subsequent chapter that the English Parliament had already made one law to remedy this state of things, and was to make many more; nor can it be doubted that the country benefited much by the changes thus introduced.

In this and many other ways the rule of common sense had now begun in England, and found support and encouragement in more than one influential quarter. Cardinal Morton cast his weight into this scale; indeed, his life had been so full of accident and change, that it would have been strange if he had not had a practical turn. Narrowly escaping from the rout of Towton in 1461, he had weathered—Lancastrian as he was—the dangerous reigns of Edward IV. and Richard III.; his persuasive power had induced the Duke of Buckingham to rebel in 1483, and, as we have seen, he had warned Henry Tudor of Landois's plots against him. After Bosworth Field his attainder was reversed, and in March 1486 he became Chancellor of England. A few days after this Archbishop Bouchier died, and it soon appeared that Morton was to succeed him. If the new Archbishop could have simply followed his own tendencies, reform in the Church might have gone far in his hands. As it was, he was overanxious to conciliate the Popes of his time, and thus to obtain their help in establishing the despotic power of the Crown. The consequence was that his reforms, though in the right direction, were far less vigorous than they should have been. He insisted that all rectors should reside in their benefices, and in each benefice in turn if they were pluralists; and procured an Act of Parliament to punish 'incontinent' clergy, that is, those who lived in quasi-marriage. With a naïve reliance on the

Cardinal Morton and Church Reform.

effect of strictness in externals, he expresses great dismay at the clergy having given up the tonsure and the clerical dress; insists that they shall be shorn so as to show their ears and wear coats 'clausas a parte anteriori'; that only graduates of the university shall have fur on their garments, and that no swords or daggers shall be carried by priests. As to the monasteries, which required even more correction, though he procured from Pope Innocent VIII. a bill authorising him to carry out reforms there, he still exercised this power with preposterous lenity, as the celebrated case of the Abbey of St. Albans is enough to show. Here the Abbot was charged with offences enough to fill a 'chronique scandaleuse'; in particular with promoting ladies to high conventual offices for reasons as opposite as possible to those which should have guided his choice. Yet this libertine was not degraded from his post of responsibility; it was held sufficient to warn him that the Rule of St. Benedict must be restored at St. Albans within thirty days under pain of severer animadversion. Probably the moral and religious effect of the Cardinal's visitations would have been greater if he had not sometimes been attended by Royal Commissioners for the purpose of raising benevolences; whose zeal he was unlikely, as we have already seen, to think of mitigating. In his judgments as Chancellor he occasionally carried the notion of common sense and equity somewhat beyond the ideas of Westminster Hall; now and then maintaining that what the law of God ordains must be the law of England, and still more extra-legally threatening a dishonest executor 'qu'il serait dampné en helle.'

At any rate, no reserve, no love of despotism or fear of touching abuses in Church or State, hindered Erasmus from the loudest and most unmistakable remonstrances

against religious corruption. The superstitions connected
with pilgrimages, relics, and alleged miracles
appeared to him in a very different light
from that in which even Sir Thomas More
viewed them at a later time, when he maintained that
no one who had the ordinary intelligence required for
a juryman could doubt the working of miracles at the
great centres of devotion. By way of sapping such beliefs
at their base, Erasmus wrote his celebrated 'Colloquy on
Pilgrimages;' in which, with ultra-Aristophanic humour,
he makes the saints in heaven address a letter to Luther,
thanking him for teaching that they are not to be invoked,
and thus freeing them from a thousand importunities. He
then goes on quaintly to describe the old-fashioned
Ogygius making toilsome expeditions to Compostella and
elsewhere, ' to fulfil a vow made by his mother-in-law ' in
view of a happy event in his family. Next he tells of the
little postern at the Abbey of Walsingham to which a
knight once fled, but finding it shut, prayed to the Virgin
Mary, and was instantly on the other side of it, horse and
all; and of the authentic tablet guaranteeing the genuineness of all the relics in the place, but put up much too high
to be read. The 'Colloquy' proceeds to describe a visit
to the shrine of St. Thomas at Canterbury, which the
author made in company with Dean Colet. As the friends
brought a recommendation from Archbishop Warham,
they could ask a few sceptical questions with less danger
of being considered sacrilegious heretics than they would
have incurred elsewhere. Erasmus describes the beauty
of the two towers, which seem to salute pilgrims from
afar; the sculptured figures of Becket's murderers (who,
he says, are locally called Tuscus, Fuscus, and Berrius);
the apocryphal gospel of Nicodemus fastened to one of
the pillars; the disgusting relics which they had to kiss,

till Colet's patience failed him at the sight of an arm to which the flesh was still adhering. Presently Colet began questioning the sacristan. 'Was not St. Thomas in his lifetime a very charitable person?' 'Certainly.' 'And whatever virtues he had in this world, ought we not to suppose that he now has the same in a much higher degree?' 'Of course.' 'Well then, if he was as liberal as you say towards the poor, may I ask your opinion on this point? Suppose he saw a poor widow with starving children, or with daughters whose modesty is in danger because they cannot be married for want of a dowry, do you not think that he might perhaps wish some of the immense mass of wealth collected in his shrine to be expended for the relief of such necessities?' To this sacrilegious question no answer was made except looks of horror; and the friends were handed over to the guidance of the Prior himself, who showed them first the jewels sent by various crowned heads to the shrine, and then some personal relics of the saint of a kind perhaps hardly describable. Here Colet's disgust became so manifest, that the Prior thought it better to change the current of his reflections by ordering some wine for the highly-recommended visitors. It certainly is a striking proof of the respect for learning in these times that Erasmus should have been able with impunity to write such scathing satires on the practices of the Church. Had he not been the best Latin scholar in the world, he would not have dared on other occasions to treat the notion of Indulgences for forty days as an absurdity, on the ground that there are no days and nights in the other world, or to fling continued charges of immorality at the monastic bodies, or to declare that the man who looks after his workmen and cares for the welfare of his wife and daughters is doing better than if he visited all the 'stations' at

H

Rome and made a prayer at each. And when we consider the immense popularity of his works, we see clearly how much doubt as to the doctrines and practices of the Church must have lived on from Lollard days, to gain force and cohesion from the utterances of his genius. Had he done no more than to give this doubt words, his work would have still been important. As it was, it rose much higher, and tended to simplify and ennoble religion far beyond what his contemporaries could conceive as possible. For he deprecated the practice of developing doctrines into all their logical consequences and thus turning religion into dogma; he explained Christian faith as one with the Christian life in a way which Luther would have thought half heathen; and he was by no means anxious for rapid and violent reforms, believing as he did that false notions of religion would be more wholesomely corrected by the slow advance of sound knowledge. 'The Reformation that has been,' says an eminent writer, 'is Luther's monument; perhaps the Reformation that is to be will trace itself back to Erasmus.'

This chapter may properly end by noticing the architecture of Henry VII.'s reign. The time produced several great constructors. Cardinal Morton nearly rebuilt his residences at Maidstone, Addington, and Charing, as well as what is now the old part of Hatfield House.

Buildings &c. of the period. His arms appear several times on the fine tower of Wisbeach Church, which he probably restored. He promoted the building of Rochester Bridge, obtaining for this and for other works which he was executing the power of impressing stonemasons; and also proclaiming that those who gave money for it should have forty days' remission of Purgatory. At Oxford he contributed to the restoration of the Divinity

School and of St. Mary's Church. At Canterbury the building of the 'Angel Steeple' is ascribed to him. While Bishop of Ely, Morton had also distinguished himself as an engineer by executing the great cut or drain through the fens from Wisbeach to Peterborough which is still called ' Morton's Leame.' The people in the neighbourhood of these towns had complained that the river Nene and the ancient works connected with it were no longer able to carry the fen waters to the sea, and that after rain the flood destroyed its banks and drowned the fields. The Bishop, having long lived in the Netherlands, had thoroughly observed the management of waters there, and had no need to call in Dutch professional men—in fact, the Leame was executed under his own superintendence, and it justified his claim to be called the ' earliest of modern engineers ' in England by at once bringing more than 4,000 acres into cultivation, and by serving up to the year 1725 as the great outlet to the river.

Henry VII. himself left several stately monuments of his reign. One of these was the Palace of Sheen, a small fragment of which still remains at Richmond in Surrey. It contained a noble hall one hundred feet long by forty wide ; and its very appearance, with its numerous towers and fronts all pierced with large windows, must have told clearly of a positive delight in the feeling that security was at length established—' fair houses,' says Lord Bacon, ' being so full of glass that one cannot tell where to come to be out of the sun or cold.' An important feature of this building was that, besides the great hall, it contained a private dining-room for the King, and another for the Queen. This was a new and growing fashion ; in large mansions of this period the lord's dining-room was often separated by a partition from the hall, or in some cases built over it; in smaller houses the hall was dispensed with altogether. The change was not made without admonitions against it from high quarters; even down to Elizabeth's time government used every now and then to renew Grostete's old exhortation, which said, 'As much as ye can without peril of sickness or weariness, eat ye in the hall before your meyny; for that shall be for your profit and worship.' Now, however, nobles and gentry were getting too fastidious for this, ' much delighting and using to dine in corners and secret places ;' such retreats also contributed much to the growth of luxury by being furnished better than rooms were in earlier times, and more after the fashion long established in the Netherlands.

Henry VII.'s Chapel in Westminster Abbey is the chief ecclesiastical monument of the period. It was built under the King's personal superintendence, the first stone being laid in 1503. His intention was to honour the burial-place of his ancestress Katherine of France and of Henry VI., and also to provide a splendid tomb in it for himself and Elizabeth. Externally the chapel is remarkable for the beauty of its octagonal turret-buttresses, and of the carved flying buttresses which pass from them to support the clerestory. Every stone in the building, except those of the few lowest courses, is profusely ornamented either with foliage of great beauty or with heraldic devices. The roof within is a magnificent specimen of the later English fan-tracery vaulting; many of the fans form unsupported pendants from the roof, and the whole is most richly ornamented. This kind of work has been sometimes spoken of as 'debased' by its fondness for superfluous ornament; it is therefore satisfactory to find that it has been most heartily admired by Viollet le Duc, the chief of modern French architects, who considers it both richer and more scientific than any kind of vaulting known to the builders of his own country. To the right of the south aisle stands the magnificent tomb of Henry and Elizabeth, the work of the celebrated Pietro Torregiano; and also that of the Lady Margaret. Here Henry ordered that prayers for his soul and for the remission of his sins should go on 'as long as the world lasted.' To ensure their maintenance, he gave the Dean more than 5,000$l.$ for the purchase of manors, besides advowsons producing more than 450$l.$ a year; the uses, however, to which this income was to be applied were so strictly defined as not to leave much margin of profit. The new building was on the site of the old Lady-chapel; besides which, the ground was cleared of St. Erasmus Chapel (the work of Elizabeth Wydvile), of a tavern called the 'White Rose,' and probably of a house once inhabited by the poet Chaucer. The stone, like that of the modern houses of Parliament, was brought from Yorkshire at great expense; yet it did not justify the selection, as, unlike that of some great mediæval cathedrals, which is as fresh now as when put up, it required to be renewed after about 300 years.

CHAPTER VIII.

THE PEACEFUL BEGINNINGS OF THE NEW REIGN.

1509–1511.

WITH the accession of Henry VIII. new prospects began for England. The country, which had been scantly grateful for the economy and homely ways by which the late King had gone far to repair the waste of the Civil Wars, now felt a bounding joy at seeing its own mental power, hearti-

Henry VIII. fond of the navy.

ness, bravery, and magnificence visibly presented in the person of an eighteen-years-old sovereign. What a change from the timorous invalid whom they had just lost to the splendid youth now before them, with his glowing complexion and short-cropped golden hair, whose beauty grave ambassadors described in their despatches home, who could speak French, Italian, and Spanish, played and sang to admiration, and composed music which a high authority describes as 'not too clear or masterly to have been really the work of a royal dilettante!' And this accomplished person could also overthrow knight after knight in the lists, and tire out half-a-dozen 'second horses' carefully stationed for him along the probable line of the hunt; he also liked well to stake his hundreds like a man at the gaming-table, and his bonhomie was such that he would on great holidays every now and then encourage the lieges to scramble for the ornaments on his own dress and that of his courtiers. It seemed little that he had not been trained in political or economic knowledge: this would come in time, and meanwhile he was not worse off than many of his brother sovereigns. For the master interests of the period he might probably do much; the classicists might expect everything from one who at nine years old had written good Latin uncorrected by tutors, the Church reformers from a prince with so strong a turn for theology. Was there danger that the fatal passion for war and glory might some time engross his mind and overthrow all this fair promise? This was of course possible: yet so far as the beginnings of such feeling could yet be discerned, it took the form which has always been most justly popular in England, that of naval rather than military enterprise. Instead of schemes for reconquering the French dominion lost by Henry VI., and thus letting loose among his people the frantic passion for plunder which would be the bane of industry, he was mainly bent on making his fleet effective for the defence of his own shores. He would himself show foreigners over the 'Great Harry,' his new and magnificent man-of-war, with her seven tiers of guns one over another. His admirals never feared that he would weary over the details in their letters—how 'for the whole of Palm Sunday we stirred not, for the wind was E by S, which was the course we should draw; but on Monday it came W.S.W., which was very good for us, and that night we slept it not, for at the beginning of the flood we were all under sail, when the Katherine Fortaliza sailed very well. Your good ship the Sovereign is the flower of all vessels that ever sailed. My letter is long, but your Highness did command me to send word how every ship worked.' When the days of war began, the same writer, Lord Edward Howard, tells his master, with the cheerfulness of a Nelson or Collingwood, that he 'expects a fight within five or six days, as he hears that a hundred sail are coming towards them;' or bids him by no means doubt that 'the first wind that ever cometh, the enemy shall have broken heads that all the world shall hear of it.' Thus protected, England could have nothing to fear from without, and might therefore have continued to isolate herself, without loss or damage of any kind, from the imbroglios of foreign politics, with quite sufficient occupation for all her energies in the problems of internal government and the enterprises which belong to peace.

Even before Henry VII. was buried, his tyrannical ministers Empson and Dudley were dealt with much as Olivier le Dain had been on the accession of Charles VIII. of France. In order to hinder their being included in the general pardon

Execution of Empson and Dudley.

at the accession, they were summoned to appear before the Privy Council, and articles were at once prepared against them stating in general terms the financial oppressions of which they had been guilty. Their plea of having acted according to existing laws was summarily put aside on the ground that they had misapplied the laws to which they appealed. While in the Tower they were farther accused of having plotted to seize and put to death the young King immediately on his father's decease. It was on this charge, for which no evidence exists, and which appears simply incredible, that Dudley was tried and condemned at the Guildhall and Empson at Northampton. Both remained in prison till August 1510, when a report that Katherine was interceding for them produced a shower of petitions that they might be executed. This Henry therefore ordered, acting, as Lord Bacon says, 'more like a good king than a good master.' Several of their inferior agents were either torn to pieces by the mob, or first pilloried in Cornhill and then thrown into Newgate to die of harsh treatment. We are told by Lord Herbert of Cherbury that Dudley sent a request to the Privy Council that 'my indictment may be entered on no record, nor divulged to foreign nations, lest if they hear in my condemnation all that may argue a final dissolution in government, they invade and overcome you.' Such a mode of pleading was not likely to mollify Henry, yet Dudley's attainder was reversed some years after his death, and his family afterwards rose, as we have seen, to the highest rank and importance.

Marriage with Katherine of Aragon.

Thus sternly was one great keynote of the reign struck at its very outset; on June 7, 1509, took place Henry's long-delayed wedding with his sister-in-law, in virtue of the dispensation obtained from Pope Julius II. in 1503. Marriages between persons thus related were so completely understood to be forbidden by the actual words of the Bible, that under ordinary circumstances it would have been held that even the Pope would not grant dispensation for it. It had, however, been declared that Katherine had been Arthur's wife only in name ; and, as a visible symbol of this, Katherine was now married with her hair loose, after the fashion of virgin brides. The Privy Council, with the exception of Warham, were strongly in favour of the marriage, such objections as were raised having been answered by King Ferdinand's argument that the King of Portugal had married two sisters successively without bringing on himself any mark of divine anger. On her wedding day Katherine again signed away her dowry of 200,000 crowns (the difficulty of repaying which had been one of the arguments for the original dispensation), receiving in exchange for it lands and rents at Bristol, Bedford, Norwich, Ipswich, and about 150 other towns and parishes, with the right of receiving felons' goods, fines, waifs and strays, and treasure-trove on all manors granted her.

On June 20 Margaret, Countess of Richmond and Derby died, full of years and honours, in the precincts of Westminster Abbey; one of her last public acts was advising her grandson in his choice of privy-councillors. Of her two foundations at Cambridge already mentioned, she left Christ's College complete ; St. John's was erected some years later according to her plans. A small but graceful memorial of her taste still remains in the little Gothic canopy over St. Winifred's spring at Holywell in Flintshire, which is even now a place of Roman Catholic pilgrimage. Her divinity professorships at Oxford and Cambridge continue to bear her name ; yet her chief and best memorial will always

Death of the Lady Margaret.

be the record of her simplicity and nobleness, of the care she took that justice should be done to all her dependents, of her patronage of all kinds of learning, and of her deep and humble-minded affection to her son as King. 'To all the learned men of England,' says Bishop Fisher in her funeral sermon, ' she was a mother; to all virtuous and devout persons a loving sister; and to all the common people of the realm she was in their causes a common mediatrice, and took right great displeasure for them.' The dream of her life had been a Crusade against the all-conquering Turks, in which she would have been content to join the defenders of the truth, and 'to help them by washing of their clothes.' This may be considered one of the last flashes of the genuine crusading spirit in England: henceforward our kings, though they did not, like those of France, ally themselves with the Porte, were not inclined to do more for Christianity in the East than was implied in a casual present to the monks of Mount Athos or an aid towards the redemption of illustrious prisoners at Constantinople.

Henry's government at this time was not less determined than his father's in preserving order at home, and repressing according to its lights some of the chief influences against it. The Star Chamber was encouraged by him to strike at even the first nobles in the land; in 1510 we find the Duke of Buckingham, in spite of his royal blood, pleading in vain before it for restoration to the office of High Constable. Men of less quality were heavily fined for taking part in riots, as were also juries who acquitted them on such charges contrary to the evidence. Indeed the procedure in this court had now become so peremptory, that men of rank who knew themselves innocent still sometimes found it safer to submit and pray for pardon. As a farther effort in

Disciplinary laws.

behalf of public morality, the growing passion for games of chance was opposed in 1511 by a tolerably strict statute, which reserved the pernicious pleasure of gambling for gentlemen only, the commons being forbidden to play at dice or cards, and even at tennis or bowls, except at Christmas and under the eye of their superiors. When this law was re-enacted and completed in 1542, it gave power to justices to make raids on gambling-houses and imprison their proprietors; it has remained in force till our own time, and recently enabled the police to break up the 'hells' in St. James Street. Even ball-play in public places was prohibited by the earlier statute; this appears to have been a stroke aimed at the London apprentices and their games in Cheapside, alarming to staid citizens (the rudeness of which may have given the sting to Shakespeare's epithet, 'base foot-ball player'). As a substitute for such games, archery was to be zealously pursued, every man or boy between the age of seven and sixty being bound to practice the longbow, with its formidable range of 220 yards (which the law did not allow to be diminished), and to discard all such new-fangled weapons as crossbows and hand-guns. Archery, in fact, was considered to supply just the mixture of exertion, courage, and intelligence which was good for Englishmen. It was also, as Ascham maintained a few years later, the kind of exercise most profitable for scholars; and all the more so, as he quaintly says, 'because it was invented by Apollo the god of learning, whereas dice and such games were brought in by an ungracious god called Theuth, which for his naughtiness came never into other gods' company, so that Homer doth despise once to mention him in all his works.'

The subject of 'benefit of clergy' was now resumed, and with a clearer insight than in the preceding reign.

It was seen not only that the power of reading a verse
from the Latin psalms (and thus proving
clerkly learning) ought not to free men from
the penalties of their crimes, but that even
ordained priests ought to have no exemption. Seeing
Church rules thus assailed, Bishops not only adhered
strongly to the law as it was, but even ventured on
a prosecution of Dr. Standish who was advising change;
this, however, they had to drop upon a threat of *præmunire*. On the general question they argued that our
Lord himself had said 'nolite tangere Christos meos'—
an unfortunate quotation which laid them open to the
retort that these words were spoken, not by our Lord,
but by David more than 1,000 years before his time,
and moreover that the 'anointed' of the Psalm meant
all true believers and not exclusively the clergy. In
spite, however, of this foil in reasoning, the clergy were
for the time successful; a temporary Act upon the subject was allowed to expire, and it was only after Henry's
breach with the Pope that the Parliament ventured again
to abridge these particular privileges of the Church.

Argument on Church privileges.

By a remarkable coincidence the throne of Scotland
was now occupied by a brother-in-law who had the same
naval tastes as Henry himself. James IV.,
the husband of Margaret Tudor, had built
under his personal superintendence a vessel
called the 'Michael,' which was a worthy rival
of the largest ships in the English navy. She was 240 feet
long; her hull of solid oak was ten feet thick, so that the
artillery of the time had no effect upon her; and she carried nearly 1,500 men. Yet she never did any such ex-
ploits as those of the smaller vessels commanded by
Sir Andrew Wood of Largs and the Bartons. Sir
Andrew, with the 'Caravel' and the 'Flower,' suc-

James IV. of Scotland. The Bartons.

ceeded in bringing into Leith five English pirate ships; when Stephen Bull, a celebrated English seaman, was sent to encounter him, he carried on a running fight from the Forth to the Tay, and at last took the Englishman into Dundee. The other great naval captain, Andrew Barton, had been aggrieved by the Portuguese government, and held a letter of reprisal from James III. against them; after a while he began to extend his violences to English vessels also. On this the Earl of Surrey declared in 1512 that the narrow seas should not be so infested while he had estate enough to furnish a ship, or a son to command her; and no less a person than Sir Edward Howard, the Lord Admiral, took charge of the vessels he prepared. Sir Thomas, the admiral's elder brother, who was serving under him, parted company in a storm, and came up alone with Andrew Barton in the 'Lion;' a desperate engagement ensued, Barton cheering his men to his last breath, and they refusing to submit as long as he lived. Meanwhile Sir Edward himself had taken the sister vessel, and all who remained alive of the crews were carried to London as prisoners. Yet they were afterwards allowed to return to Scotland—a plain proof that they were not considered as absolutely foes to mankind, although Henry replied to the Scottish remonstrances that 'punishing pirates had never been held to be a breach of peace among princes.' The question where the wrong lay thus remained unsettled; and in the depression following the battle of Flodden the principal Scottish men-of-war were sold to France, and Scotland's short period of naval glory came to an end.

Early in 1511 it became too clear that the young King intended to plunge into the Continental wars arising out of the French invasions of Italy, and thus to disappoint the thinking men who had looked for an era of kindness and improvement. Erasmus, the unfailing spokesman of sound opinion at the time, was in despair at the prospect for the future. Folly, it seemed to him, was resuming her ancient reign under the auspices of the tyrants who ruled Europe; and trade, learning, humanity, religion would all go to wreck. 'O that God,' he says, 'would deign to still the tempest of war! What madness is it! The wars of Christian princes begin for the most part out of ambition, hatred, or lust, or like diseases of the mind. You may see even decrepit old men display all the vigour of youth, sparing no cost, shrinking from no toil, stopped by nothing, if only they can turn law, religion, peace, and all human affairs upside down. Think, too, of the crimes which are committed under the pretext of war, for among the din of arms good laws are silent: what rapine, what sacrilege, what other crimes which decency forbids to mention! The demoralisation, too, goes on for years after the war is over.' 'Let any physiognomist,' he says on another occasion, 'consider the look and features of an eagle—those rapacious and cruel eyes, that threatening curve of the beak, those wicked jaws, that stern front—will he not recognise at once the image of a king? Add to this that threatening scream at which every animal trembles. At this scream of the eagle the people quake, the senate yields, the nobility cringes, the judges concur, laws and constitutions give way; neither right nor religion, neither justice nor humanity, avails. Of all birds, the eagle alone has seemed to wise men the type of royalty—carnivorous, greedy, hateful to all, the curse of all, and surpassing even its great powers of doing harm by its desire for doing it.' Nor did Erasmus's friend Colet shrink from expressing quite clearly his hatred for a warlike policy even before

War with France: how regarded.

Henry himself. We are told that 'he preached wonderfully, on the victory of Christ, exhorting all men to fight and conquer under the banner of this their King.' He showed that when wicked men destroy one another out of hatred and ambition, they fight under the banner not of Christ, but of the devil. 'How difficult a thing it is,' said he, 'to die a Christian death on a field of battle! how few undertake a war except from hatred and ambition! how hardly possible is it for those who have brotherly love, without which no one can see the Lord, to thrust their sword into their brother's blood!' The King, after hearing this sermon, was anxious lest it should stand in the way of volunteering, and sent for the preacher to Greenwich; after an hour and a half of conversation he still remained persuaded that his war was exceptionally just, but those who hoped for Colet's disgrace were disappointed by Henry's declaring that this was the kind of doctor for him. This incident happened after the first campaign of the war was over; before it began Henry had been strongly dissuaded from it by his Council, who warned him that the use of firearms had destroyed the advantage which England had hitherto derived from her archery, that islands should not make conquests on the Continent, that England alone was quite sufficient as a kingdom, and that voyages of discovery were the one means of extending it profitably. It was perhaps unfortunate that Sebastian Cabot was now away, and that there was no one in the country equally capable of turning Henry's thoughts in the latter direction. As it was, all expostulation was in vain, and the fancy of a youth of one-and-twenty had its own way. There was to be a war, which was in its turn to originate many others; its causes and conduct belong to the next chapter.

CHAPTER IX.

THE WAR OF TOURNAY.

1511-1514.

IN 1511 Henry VIII. began his attack on France in defence of Pope Julius II.; and the causes of the war in which he was about to mingle require to be clearly stated as illustrating the political feeling of the time, and as accounting for things farther on. It sprang originally from the jealousy of Venetian power felt alike by the Emperor Maximilian, by Ferdinand of Aragon, by Louis XII. of France, and above all by the Pope. Between these powers was formed in 1508 the League of Cambray, so called from the secret negotiations at that place between Margaret of Savoy, Maximilian's daughter, and Cardinal d'Amboise as French plenipotentiary. Venice had of late been losing territory in the East, Lepanto, St. Maura, and others of her possessions having been taken by the Turks; accordingly she had wished to extend her dominions in Italy itself, and had seized Rimini and Faenza amid the confusion which followed the death by poison of Pope Alexander VI. in 1503, thus controlling much of the seaboard of the Papal States. Her territories now included Ravenna, Treviso, Padua, Verona, Crema, and Brescia; and in ruling these she showed such a liberal spirit as to be able in time of trial to rely on them implicitly. She had even made the beginnings of a settlement on Neapolitan soil by lending Ferdinand of Aragon 200,000 crowns, and receiving in pledge the ports of Trani, Brindisi, Gallipoli, Pulignano, and Otranto. Besides this wide do-

The League of Cambray.

minion, she was still the queen of maritime enterprise and trade, her supremacy not having been yet destroyed, in spite of the discoveries of Columbus and Vasco de Gama. Her factories still extended to the mouth of the Don, and her linen, gilt leather, silks, and glass were, as we have seen, the best in the world. Moreover, printing had been established there within fifteen years of its first invention, and carried to high perfection by the Aldi. All this magnificence excited the utmost envy in the poverty-stricken monarchies of Western Europe; the theory being, as Bayard puts it, that 'God was certainly angry with the Venetians for living so gloriously and gorgeously, and making such small account of the other princes of Christendom.' Under these circumstances a plan of spoliation was easily settled beforehand; the Pope was to recover Rimini, Faenza, and Ravenna, Ferdinand his Neapolitan harbours (without paying the sum for which they had been pledged), and Maximilian the noble cities of Padua, Verona, and Vicenza, with several others. For the conquest of these last the King of the Romans was promised help from the native nobles, who hoped that the Austrian power would re-establish against their fellow-citizens the feudal privileges of which the Venetian rule favoured by the middle and lower classes had deprived them.

The war began disastrously for Venice, as her troops were terribly defeated (May 14, 1509) at Agnadello, a village near Crema where they had proposed to stop the French after their passage of the Adda; and so little were they able to recover themselves, that the enemy advanced as far as Mestre and Fusina in the environs of Venice, and even threw some hundreds of cannon-shot across the lagoon into the city. In the midst of this confusion the Venetians resolved upon

Resistance of Venice.

I

a stroke of that magnanimity which seldom fails in political
affairs; they released from their allegiance the cities on
the mainland, and allowed them to make the best terms
they could with the victors. This created such an enthusiasm in their favour, that Treviso, Padua, and other
places took the earliest opportunity of rising against
Maximilian and returning to the Venetian rule; and
when the King of the Romans tried to punish Padua
for this, its stern resistance made him glad to raise the
siege. Very soon the usual vices of a coalition had begun
to show themselves; the French, too, offended Julius by
taking Bologna from him, and were also promoting a
Church Council at Pisa in opposition to his power. Ferdinand's natural jealousy of France had reappeared with
her victories, while the Pope had already recovered
Reggio, Mirandola, and Parma, and was ready to listen
to the Venetian offer of restoring Ravenna to him. As,
therefore, Julius had only wished to use the League of
Cambray for his own purposes, he now contrived (October
15, 1511) a new treaty, under the name of the Holy
League, by which he himself, the Venetians, and Ferdinand were to expel the French from Italy. Against this
coalition the French fought bravely under Gaston de Foix,
taking by storm the city of Brescia, which was one of
those most devoted to Venice, and utterly defeating the
Spaniards at Ravenna (April 11, 1512). Here, however,
Gaston was slain, and the loss of the victors was so enormous that their power in Italy collapsed, and they found
difficulty even in holding on at a few scattered points.

<small>Henry VIII. joins the Holy League. His failure.</small> At this point Henry VIII. resolved to strike in with his fresh and unimpaired forces. He professed to be scandalised at the impiety of waging war with the Pope, who, he main-
tained, had no superior on earth, and must be borne

with, however froward; but at the same time had the preposterous hope that he might reconquer France, though its population and revenue were four times those of England. On his marriage he had professed that he and Katherine would thenceforward be subjects of Ferdinand I. Now his astute father-in-law took him at his word by inducing him to send a force to the Spanish frontier and invade France from thence, while he himself, thus sheltered from attack, was adding Navarre to his dominions. From the English point of view there may have been an idea of waking up old feelings of attachment to our rule at Bordeaux; at any rate, attempts to conquer the Garonne country were sure to be popular, as, if successful, they would make wine cheaper by half in England. Accordingly an army of 10,000 men was organised by the genius of Wolsey, who had lately entered the King's service, and despatched under the Marquis of Dorset to Fuentarabia, where they landed June 7, 1512. Ferdinand had promised that an army of his under the Duke of Alva should join them in the invasion of Guienne; but, instead of making this good, he continued his operations in Navarre, while all kinds of misfortunes befel his unhappy allies. They found no tents provided for them, though the season was most rainy, and no sufficient provisions, though their own had been plundered by the mariners while they were seasick; the hot Spanish wines produced fever, and beer there was none. The officers were almost useless from inexperience, and discontent became rife in the camp, many of the men refusing to serve unless their pay was raised from sixpence to eightpence a day, as on the lower sum they were in danger of starvation. On August 28 a council of war was held at St. Sebastian, and the army took the strange resolution of returning home without orders. In vain did Henry write to Ferdinand desiring him to detain it by force; by October 7 they were on the way home, and a shower of epigrams from all Europe was preparing for the warriors so soon weary of the field. Unable, however, to fix the responsibility on any one in particular, Henry resolved by the advice of his Council to let the matter drop—with the satisfaction of knowing that the influence of France had been increased by the failure of his attack thus far. Soon,

CAMPAIGN OF TEROUENNE.

however, an act of peculiar, though unsuccessful, daring came to restore both King and nation to better humour.

In March 1513 Sir Edward Howard with forty-three vessels sailed for the Breton coast as the forerunner of the larger expedition planned for the year, and longing to avenge the loss of the 'Sovereign,' which had been burned in the preceding August. He soon drove the French fleet opposed to him to shelter under the guns of Brest, where they fortified themselves in order to wait for six of their galleys from

Naval operations.

the Mediterranean. Hearing that these were near, and had anchored between two forts in water too shallow for his ships to approach, Sir Edward resolved to attack all six with the only two galleys which he had; being, it is said, stung by a hint from the Council at home that in inviting Henry to command in person at the destruction of the French fleet he had wished to evade his duty. He laid his own galley close to a hostile one, and had already boarded her in person, when the vessels happened to part, and he was left almost unsupported on the enemy's deck. Unwilling that they should have the spoils of an English admiral, he threw his gold chain and whistle into the sea, and next moment was thrust overboard and perished. In recognition of his splendid services, Henry restored his father to the Dukedom of Norfolk, and made his brother Sir Thomas Earl of Surrey just in time to command at Flodden.

On July 26, 1513, Henry advanced in person from his city of Calais to join Maximilian at Are; and was hardly less beguiled by him than he had been by Ferdinand. For not only did the poverty-stricken Emperor obtain pay as Henry's soldier, but he induced him to attack two places not really important to his interests, but very much so to those of his confederate. These were Terouenne and Tournay. The former of these was a French frontier town just outside Maximilian's province of Artois. He had vainly striven to conquer it in 1479; and it had lately been a constant annoyance to his Artois subjects, who ardently desired to see it reduced and its fortifications levelled with the ground. Tournay, though in the rear of Maximilian's advanced dominions, had remained as a French outlier in his territory, and was therefore a thorn in his side. Both places were quite beyond the true line of an Eng-

Invasion of France.

lish invasion, which should naturally have been straight towards Paris. However, the siege of Terouenne was formed. On August 16, a French force under the Duc de Longueville tried to relieve it, but was defeated by a charge of Maximilian's men-at-arms, supported by the English army, an exploit which gained for the Emperor in England the title of 'the second Mavors,' and which the French, with a satire which did not spare themselves, called the 'Battle of the Spurs.' The French general La Palice and the celebrated Bayard remained prisoners. On August 22 Terouenne surrendered, and on the 28th Tournay, in spite of the strength of its walls and gates.

On leaving home, Henry had made Katherine Regent, and, in order to secure her position, had ordered the execution of Edmund de la Pole, whose life had been promised in 1506 to the Archduke Philip. It is said that Henry VII. had charged his son on his death-bed to regard the pledge as made for the reign only. During the French campaign, in fact on the same day as the Battle of the Spurs, James IV. of Scotland, who had thrown in his lot with France, was defeated and slain by Lord Surrey. This disaster to Scotland is so well known that it is only necessary to notice its salient points. After capturing the castles of Norham, Wark, and Ford, James took up his position on the defensible ridge of Flodden, an offshoot of the Cheviots between the Till on the east and the Tweed, near Coldstream, on the north—a proceeding which Surrey regarded as shabby in one who had accepted his challenge to fight the matter out on equal ground. James's camp had the Till on its left and an impassable marsh on the right, and was defended in front by the whole of the splendid Scottish artillery. It was therefore unassailable, and Surrey could only turn it; this he did splendidly by

Battle of Flodden Field.

carrying his 30,000 men first by Weetwood Bridge to the right bank of the Till (as if he were retreating to Berwick), and then back by Twisel Bridge, near the junction of the rivers—thus placing himself between James and Scotland. Borthwick, the commander of the Scottish artillery, entreated permission to cannonade the

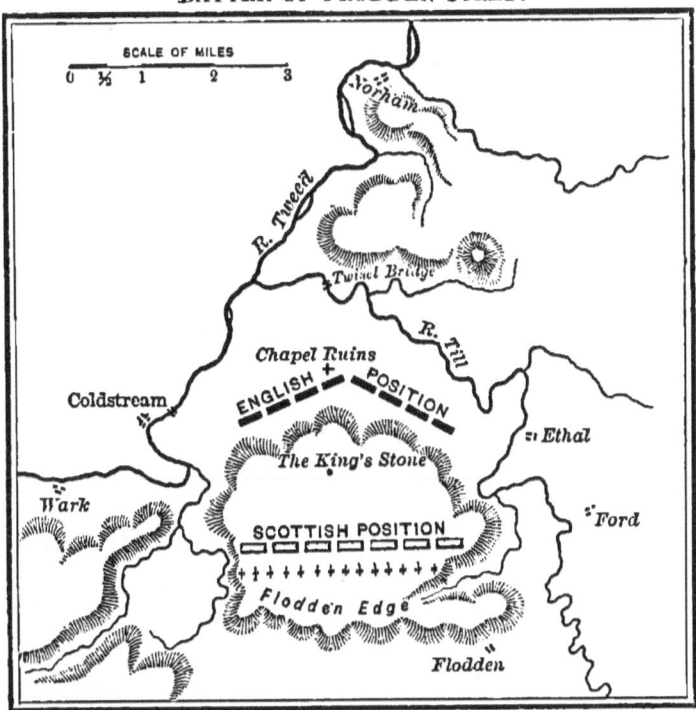

BATTLE OF FLODDEN FIELD.

enemy while recrossing the river; but the distance from Flodden, which was six miles, would not allow of the guns being properly supported, even if they could be brought up in time. Surrey was therefore allowed to get clear over and form on the left bank before James was near enough to attack. Even when he did so, everything was mismanaged. The Highlanders, who for the first time in recent warfare were then fighting beside a Lowland force, were not allowed to rush on in the peculiar manner which made them formidable; the Scottish guns did little, while Surrey's were most effective; and, worst of all, James himself, instead of acting as a general should, plunged into the fight as soon as his centre was engaged, in hope of meeting Surrey in single combat, and fell when he had all but reached his enemy, the chief men of his army being slain around him. His body was discovered among a heap of slain, and wrapped in lead, but not buried, as he had died under excommunication. There is a sad story of its being shamefully misused some years after at the monastery of Sheen; a still sadder one, that the Scots believed that he had escaped from the field and gone on a pilgrimage to the Holy Land. Nearly the whole of the Scottish peerage were among the 10,000 who fell; and of the gentry almost every family had lost one or more of its members. Well might the graceful and pathetic ballad which records the calamity say that 'the flowers of the forest were a' wede away.'

Yet this overthrow of the ally of France did little to strengthen the confederacy against Louis XII., which was by this time dying of inanition. Julius II. had died in 1513, and had been succeeded by the pacific Leo X., one of Linacre's young fellow-scholars at Florence. Maximilian had been bribed off by the promise of Louis' daughter Renée for his grandson Charles, with the French claims on Milan for her dowry, and Ferdinand was content with his acquisition of Navarre and the Neapolitan ports. In a frenzy of anger at being deserted when Maximilian and Francis made peace at Noyon, Henry meditated the wildest schemes of vengeance. He grasped eagerly at the offer

Home effects of the war.

of a French alliance, and was ready even to stultify himself by helping Louis to recover Navarre. A marriage was to cement this new friendship; the French king having just become a widower by the death of Anne of Bretagne, and Henry's young and lovely sister Mary being still undisposed of, though she had thought of marrying the Duke of Suffolk. The poor girl was therefore sacrificed to the new alliance, Henry engaging that she should be allowed to please herself next time, and the bridegroom's age and state of health affording a pleasing hope that this time was not far off. In fact, indigestion and late hours soon ended the ill-assorted union, and Mary, resolved not to be again a victim to her brother's policy, married Suffolk privately on the earliest opportunity, and managed, though with difficulty, to disarm the royal anger by agreeing to pay a large sum yearly towards the expenses of her first marriage. Louis was succeeded (January 1, 1515) by his cousin and son-in-law, the Duc d'Angoulême, under the name of Francis I.; and from Mary's second and happier marriage ultimately sprang the great family of the Greys.

We cannot but see that these campaigns left Henry and England politically where they were; except indeed that no one would now deny that the islanders were stout men of their hands and good backers for Emperor or King in a struggle. The sum spent must have been prodigious, for each archer was paid what would now be six to eight shillings a day; indeed the war devoured the income of twelve years. Public order was for the time at an end: in 1514 the royal treasure-waggons were robbed by a bold gang of whom eighty were captured and executed, the rest escaping to sanctuary. Taxation rose to an astonishing height; twice over in twelve months an income-tax of sixpence in the pound exacted from the very day-labourers between two and three weeks' wages. At the same time an Act was passed (1515) to restrain the rise in the cost of labour naturally resulting from the drain of men for the army, of which the first draught is, as Mr. Brewer remarks, in Wolsey's own hand. The want of labourers in turn converted more fallows into sheep-farms, still farther decreasing the rural population. Nor did the war deal more tenderly with traders ; for, besides the preposterous taxation which crippled them, their business was liable to interruption even by the quarrels of confederates, as when Henry in 1515 stopped the export of wool to Holland and Zealand on some notion that Maximilian's grandson Charles had affronted him. Well had the war justified its dissuaders, and, what was worse still, the notion that we ought to reconquer France might revive and renew it at any moment. It had also fostered in Henry the ruthlessness which his portraits alone would prove to have been natural to him, and which afterwards made his times of peace, like those of Alexander the Great, more dangerous to those about him than many battles would have been. Such is ever the bitter fruit of wars like his, alike causeless, ill-managed, cruel, and inconclusive as they almost always were.

CHAPTER X.

DOMESTIC AFFAIRS AFTER THE PEACE WITH FRANCE.

1515–1518.

PEACE was now restored to England; the question was whether or no the government would restore national prosperity after the trials which it had sustained. The task was not hopeless ; for, though sorely burthened at home, our commerce had been extended abroad at the expense of Venice, ships from London and Southampton having found their way to Sicily, Crete, Chios, and even to Tripoli and Beyrout; English merchants had also been profitably employing vessels hired at Ragusa and other Mediterranean ports. Indeed neither Henry nor his great minister Wolsey could be charged with general indifference to trade interests; for they founded the Corporation of the Trinity House for the management of pilotage and lighthouses, spent not less than 65,000*l.* on the pier at Dover, and improved the harbours of Hull, Southampton, Newcastle, Scarborough, and Calais. The inland communications of the country were also by degrees made better, and the navy-yards and storehouses of Woolwich and Deptford founded. In order to increase trade with the Netherlands, Wolsey obtained a congress at Antwerp in 1515 (where England was represented by Bishop Tunstal, Sir E. Poynings, and the young Thomas More), in the hope of replacing England on the footing of the 'Intercursus Malus' described in Chapter V. The Flemings strongly maintained that this had been a personal arrangement of the Archduke Philip's, and had fallen through with his death. To this the English replied that he had expressly agreed for his heirs after him, that no other agreement had been substituted for it, and that no documents could be quoted to prove that it had ever stopped. From this subject the Congress passed to the discussion of grievances, Tunstal complaining that his countrymen had been forced to pay illegal tolls even when driven in by storms, and that embargoes were sometimes laid on their vessels for years, after which they had to pay 'anchor money' for the time of detention. The quarrels on points like these rose so

English trade in the Netherlands.

high that one of the commissioners was excommunicated in the Antwerp churches, and the others were 'calumniated frightfully.' Fortunately for them, political circumstances just then made Charles's advisers more anxious than ever for an English alliance, and therefore all difficulties solved themselves. The question of the 'Intercursus Malus' was adjourned for five years; but meantime it was to remain in force. As to other grievances, our merchants must have been hard to please if they were not satisfied. All English privileges were extended: they might choose their own brokers and porters; all legal remedies should be freely open to them; their cases should take precedence of all others, and be always decided within six days; quarrels of Englishmen among themselves were to be settled in their own consular courts, which would be supported by the magistrates in case of resistance; and the factory at Antwerp was to remain theirs in full property.

About this time a curious incident arose out of Henry's anxiety for the welfare of seaports. A Cornish member named Strode had promoted an Act of Parliament hindering Cornish mine-owners from throwing rubbish into the rivers and thus forming bars below. He had overlooked the fact that the Cornish and Devonshire miners lived under a constitution of their own, holding a small district parliament under the Warden of the Stannaries, the enactments of which had the force of local laws. This body had passed an ordinance in 1510 that every one might dig for tin where he could find it, and 'carry the waters to his works according to old custom,' all hinderers being liable to a fine of 40*l.* This they proceeded coolly to inflict on Strode for his doings at Westminster; and, as he would not pay, they threw him into irons in a damp dungeon, and fed

Cornish mining.

him there for three weeks on bread and water. Fortunately he was wanted at the end of that time to do his duty as a collector of taxes, and a royal order set him free. But before he was released his captors added insult to injury by making him give a bond of 100*l.* for costs ! The sentence and the bond were of course cancelled by Parliament, which also asserted that no one could be punished either for bringing or procuring a bill to be brought into Parliament, or for any opinion delivered in speaking to a motion. Nothing was at that time done to remedy the damage to the rivers; but twenty years later, when Plymouth, Falmouth, Dartmouth, Teignmouth, and Fowey were all suffering from the same cause, and a ship of 100 tons could hardly get up where there had been water enough for one of 800, a law was passed forbidding the use for mining purposes of any river flowing into a harbour; even in this it was thought necessary to guard by an express clause againt Parliament being set at nought by the Court of Stannaries. In the latter part of the reign parliamentary privileges were farther established by the decision of the judges in 1542 that the Commons had acted legally in setting free by their own authority, and without any legal process, Ferrars the member for Plymouth, who had been imprisoned for debt by the City authorities. The quarrel was not settled until the sheriffs and all parties concerned in the arrest had been sent to prison, and the King himself had expressed strong approbation of the vigour displayed by the House of Commons in the maintenance of its time-honoured exemption.

As our traders were anxious to sell their cloths by retail in as many Flemish towns as possible, it might be supposed that they would have been ready to admit the idea of reciprocity. *Jealousy of foreigners.*
But fairness in such claims is not always thought of where

great interests are at stake; and our merchants were in point of fact not less anxious to keep foreigners' goods out of England than to sell their own elsewhere. Good reasons for restricting imports were of course ready; it was argued in the first place that foreigners made their profits by tempting people to buy 'fancies and tryfulles' such as England might well do without, and in the second (with doubtful consistency) that foreign competition was destroying all wholesome English trade. Dutchmen were bringing over timber ready cut, and leather ready manufactured, with nails, locks, baskets, cupboards, stools, tables, chests, girdles, saddles, and printed cloths. 'The Merchant Strangers,' men querulously said, 'are importing silk, wine, oil, and iron, and moreover carrying away so much wool, tin, and lead, that Englishmen can have no living.' By thus taking imports and exports separately, and not as balancing one another, and by showing to their own satisfaction that England was parting with what she most wanted in exchange either for superfluities or for what should be made by English hands, the grumblers raised the jealousy against foreigners to a white heat; and, on May-day, 1517, it burst out with great violence, through a protectionist sermon preached by Dr. John Bell at the Spital Church a few days before. Taking for his text 'Terram dedit filiis hominum,' the orator proceeded to descant on the public grievances. 'The land,' he said, ' was given to Englishmen, and as birds defend their nests, so ought Englishmen to cherish and defend themselves, and to hurt and grieve aliens, for respect of their commonwealth.' As it began to be rumoured that May-day would be chosen for an attack upon the Steelyard, which was the London centre of German trade, Wolsey took care to send for the Lord Mayor on April 30, and commanded him by all means to preserve the peace. Accordingly a meeting of the Aldermen was held, and they were ordered to proclaim in their several wards that every house-owner must stay at home and keep in all his household from nine o'clock that evening till the same hour of the following morning. The announcement, however, produced in the notoriously turbulent ward of Cheap the very disturbance which it was intended to prevent. The cry of 'clubs' was at once raised, and hundreds of apprentices came pouring from the precincts of St. Paul's. The rioters broke open the Compter and Newgate, and released some prisoners who had been committed in the last few days for attacks on foreigners. After this they proceeded, in defiance of the magistrates, to plunder private houses, especially those of strangers, the masters of which they announced their intention of beheading by lynch-law. In the midst of the tumult the Lieutenant of the Tower actually opened fire upon the city from his batteries, creating immense terror, but doing little real damage. Not finding any foreigners at home, the mob began to disperse; but the last who retreated, to the number of 300, were intercepted and sent to prison. In order to strike more terror, the government prepared ten moveable gibbets as if to execute the prisoners at all parts of the town; but, whether from the influence of bribes judiciously applied, or from a certain sympathy with the rioters felt by men in power, the only person finally executed was a broker named Lincoln, by whose persuasion the unlucky sermon had been preached. The day was long remembered in London as the 'Evil May-day,' and it is said that the gaieties proper to the season were never again celebrated as freely as before this untoward event. That foreign trade after this was thought to require some restriction we may infer from the Act of 1525 which forbade alien merchants to take any foreigners as apprentices or to have more than two foreign journeymen—a blow evidently aimed at the peculiar constitution of the German factory of the Steelyard in London, whose managers with their employés, all foreigners alike, lived in a half-monastic fashion within their fortified buildings, unmarried, and avoiding connections with their neighbours. A still unkinder stroke was that the same Act placed every alien exercising a handicraft in London under the 'search and reformation' of the fellowship of his particular craft there.

The population of England (which had been about 2,500,000 at the time of the poll-tax of 1377) had now increased to about 3,500,000. Yet, curiously enough, there was a general impression that the number of people in the country was diminishing. It was evident that the larger corporate towns, such as Norwich, were getting less populous; there being obviously little inclination to rebuild decayed houses or to restore them after a fire. But the cause of this phenomenon quite escaped the notice of political thinkers. This was, in fact, the pressure of the guild regulations in the large borough towns, which people were glad to escape by living beyond their limits. Thus an employer might be comparatively free as to his mode and hours of working, the number of his apprentices and hands, and the wages which he paid. Accordingly manufactures now spread themselves over several new districts; amongst others the towns of Birmingham and Manchester increased much at this time. As even accurate observers could not see the whole country at once, they were naturally misled by the appearances of decay in the older and more celebrated towns, and thought that the same process was going on everywhere.

Population shifting in England.

A far less imaginary depopulation of the country districts, such as the 'Utopia' had lamented, had excited alarm as early as 1489, when it was remarked that the Isle of Wight, which, as being particularly exposed to French attack, required to be well peopled, was becoming 'desolate and not inhabited, but occupied by beasts and cattle.' It was therefore enacted in that year that no one of any rank whatever should hold more than one farm there of the maximum value of 6*l.* 13*s.* 4*d.* a year, and that those who occupied several such should elect which they would retain, and their leases be void as regarded the remainder. This restored the population of the island, and enabled it, as Mr. Froude has remarked, to foil the French invasion of 1546. In the present reign the same principle was carried out more broadly by an Act of 1515, which ordered that, if the holder of any estate in England destroyed farmhouses upon it, the superior lord should resume possession of half of it until they were rebuilt; and by another twenty years after, which gave the same power to the King, if no intermediate lord had exercised it.

Depopulation of the rural districts.

The change in the hands of new proprietors from customary to competition rents was also bitterly complained of. It produced, as Bishop Latimer shows in a well-known passage, a fatal change in the position of the smaller tenants. 'My father,' he says, 'was a yeoman, and had no lands of his own; only he had a farm of three or four pounds by year, and hereupon tilled so much as kept half-a-dozen men; he had walk for a hundred sheep, and my mother milked thirty kine. He was able and did find the King a harness, with himself and his horse until he came to the place where he should receive the King's wages. I can remember that I buckled his harness when he went into Blackheath Field. He kept me to school, or else I had not

The rise in rents.

J

been able to have preached before the King's majesty now. He married my sisters with five pound or twenty nobles a piece. He kept hospitality for his poor neighbours, and some alms he gave to the poor. And all this he did off the said farm, where he that now hath it payeth sixteen pounds by year or more, and is not able to do anything for his prince, for himself, nor for his children, or give a cup of drink to the poor.' This agrees with More's declaration in the 'Utopia' that tenants were 'pilled and polled' by their landlords, who not only drove off their tenants to make sheep-walks, but constantly managed either by fraud or violence to make small freeholders sell their lands. And the trouble continued through Henry VIII.'s reign into that of his son, when the Protector Somerset's ill-planned endeavour to remedy it was one of the great causes of his fall.

In the miserable state of Scotland after the battle of Flodden two courses had been open to Henry; he might either have ordered Surrey to advance and conquer the country once for all, or he might have answered Queen Margaret's appeal for brotherly help and supported the infant King by all means in his power. Yet he took neither, but allowed his victorious army to be disbanded, and Scottish affairs to fall into hopeless confusion without interference. A Parliament was at once held at Edinburgh which appointed Margaret Regent and guardian of the King; but in August 1514 she forfeited all public confidence by marrying Lord Angus, who was considered as the head of the English party in Scotland, and a rebellion at once arose against her. Her opponents entreated Francis I. to send over to their help the Duke of Albany, the younger brother of James III., who had lived all his life in France and held the rank of Lord High Admiral there.

Scotland under Queen Margaret.

Escaping with some difficulty from the English cruisers off St. Malo, Albany reached Dumbarton in May 1515 with a considerable train of Frenchmen, whom he proceeded to raise to positions of authority, thus exciting a jealousy second only to that against England. Yet he was appointed Protector till James V. reached the age of eighteen, and at once besieged Stirling Castle in order to get possession of the royal children. All this time Lord Dacre, who commanded on the Border, was trying various means to support the English interest in Scotland. He aided as strongly as possible the resistance to Albany, received all those who were exiled for rebelling against him, tried to carry off the princes by the help of Angus, and, failing in this, at last persuaded Margaret herself to take refuge in England. The Queen escaped to Berwick in September 1515, and was immediately after this delivered of a 'fair young lady,' afterwards well known as Lady Lennox, the mother of Henry Darnley, and considered nearer the English succession from having been born on our soil. Ill and miserable, Margaret was carried on men's shoulders to Morpeth, and soon heard that her husband and his partisans had been defeated by the Protector. Angus himself was sent prisoner to France; but he soon escaped to join his wife, and Henry was glad to welcome both as instruments for any future plan against Scotland. Meanwhile Albany was getting so weary of his position as Regent, that to escape from it he would, as he said, 'gladly have walked on foot all the way to London'; and in 1516 he returned to France on business of his own, leaving French garrisons in the chief fortresses, but with little idea of returning at the time fixed. In 1517 the treaty of Noyon allowed Margaret to return to Scotland; where she found that her friends had been put to death for favouring her escape, and that she would not be allowed to take any part in the administration.

Great and various also were the Irish troubles at this time, though they did not burst into actual war. Only five half-counties were really under English law, and in these the vexations of the courts were compelling landholders to sell the smaller estates. The power of the colonists had been also weakened by a pestilence which had raged among them, by the death of several eminent leaders without heirs, and by their disuse of English weapons. The only possible remedy seemed to be to call for more colonists—if possible one from each parish in England—to civilise Irish chieftains perforce by making them Lords of Parliament if they had 1,000 marks a year, and to induce them to send their sons to Dublin or Drogheda to be taught reading and writing, with the English manners and language. But at this time Henry had not sufficient interest in their country to make him carry through reforms of such importance; consequently things went from bad to worse, and the Reformation was soon to make every difficulty tenfold.

The government of Ireland.

In 1517 the Pope produced a fresh scheme for a Crusade; as well he might, having himself been all but taken prisoner by a Turkish fleet which was sweeping the coast of Italy from Pisa to Terracina. The plan was, as usual, all too vast, including as it did the enlistment as allies of 'the Sophi of Persia, Prester John of the Indies, and the Kings of Nubia, Ethiopia, and Georgia.' It was hoped that by these strong measures it would be possible in three years, and at the cost of 12,000,000 ducats, to seize and fortify Mount Zion and several other points in Palestine, to invade Turkey from the side of Hungary and Poland, to

Vain attempts at a Crusade.

support Fez and Morocco against the Turks, to reconquer Philippopolis and Adrianople, and then, after securing Eubœa or Chalcedon for a seaport, to crown the enterprise by the seizure of Cairo, Alexandria, and Constantinople. To arrange these matters Cardinal Campeggio was sent to England as legate *a latere*, and, after some doubt whether English law would recognise him in that capacity, was welcomed with much pomp. But Papal Crusades were not believed in, and neither clergy nor laity would vote money for any such purposes; thus the progress of the Turks remained unchecked, and the risk was from time to time most imminent that the nations of Europe might be subdued by them. Indeed, though such dangers gradually diminished, they were brought absolutely to an end only by two much later events, the great sea-fight at Lepanto in 1571 and Prince Eugene's land victory over the Turks at Peterwardein in 1716.

CHAPTER XI.

THE WAR OF PAVIA.

1515-1527.

ON succeeding Louis XII. in 1515, Francis I. had instantly resolved on a career of military enterprise, feeling quite unable to endure the loss of Milan and the exclusion of French influence from Italy which had followed the death of Gaston de Foix in 1512. An application from Venice for aid against the tyranny of the Spaniards, Maximilian, and the Pope served as a plea for a new Italian expedition. As the usual descent into Italy by the Mont Cenis and Susa was strongly guarded by the Swiss mercenaries

The French in Italy. Battle of Marignano.

of Spain, Francis, after collecting his army at Lyons, was persuaded to cross the Alps by the Val Vraita, leading from Barcelonnette to Saluzzo, the head of which is even now a trackless ridge covered with loose rocks. Forcing its way thus, in spite of great perils and losses, to the junction of the Vraita with the Po, the French army appeared in Italy as if it had dropped from the skies; and the Swiss, who formed the greater part of the Spanish and Papal army, retreated in some confusion on Milan. Francis was prudently trying to bribe off their opposition when his plan was frustrated by the arrival of 20,000 more Swiss from the St. Gothard under Scheiner, the Cardinal of Sion, a bitter enemy of the French. This leader immediately harangued his men, reminding them that ever since the fall of Charles the Bold in 1477 they had been the arbiters of Europe; that no sovereign could either move or stand without their help; and that if they did but stretch out their hands, there was money enough in Francis's military chest to enrich them all for life, and glory enough in defeating his forces to prove them the most redoubtable nation in the world. With these and other persuasions he induced them to make a hurried attack on the French, who were ten miles from Milan, at the village of Marignano. The battle began late in the evening, and before dark the Swiss had gained the superiority, and even taken fifteen French guns; but Francis employed the night in posting his forces afresh, and supported them so ably with his remaining artillery that on the next day the enemy, with all their valour, could not break his lines, and were themselves crushed by charges of the men-at-arms. At least 10,000 Swiss were slain, and, what was more, their prestige of victory was broken. The survivors fell grimly back on Milan, and then retreated to their own country in consideration of a payment from Francis. The victory was decisive; for the Spanish and Papal commanders both asked for peace, leaving Milan to Francis as the prize of his few days' campaign,

Every sovereign of Europe envied the young King of France the glory so quickly won; Henry, above all, could not hide his chagrin at the victory which had so far outdone his own prowess. 'His eyes were so red,' says the French ambassador Bapaume, 'that it seemed as if the tears would come.' His chagrin was the greater because both he and the Emperor had assumed that Francis would certainly come to grief in Italy. In vain did the nobles around him urge that 'he ought to be glad that Francis, his good brother and ally, had defeated the Swiss, who were so fierce and haughty that they presumed to call themselves the rulers and correctors of princes.' Henry confessed that he ought to be glad, for that the Swiss 'were indeed mere villains, and he had ever known them as such.' However, this did not hinder him from sending to Switzerland some clever agents charged to subsidise both Maximilian and the Swiss and to excite them againt France. Money never came amiss to the Emperor; indeed, in this case, he tried to possess himself of the Swiss subsidy as well as his own, and, after leading his army up to the gates of Milan, crowned all by accepting 200,000 crowns from the French, selling Verona to the Venetians, and withdrawing by the Valteline to Trent in the Tyrol. As the bargain with France leaked out, it is no wonder that the English envoys, Tunstal and Knight, exhort Henry to 'close his purse for the future, and entertain Maximilian with words devised, thus treating the Emperor as the Emperor treated him.'

In the following February (1516) occurred the death of Ferdinand of Aragon. His grandson Charles was

now King of all Spain, having been before this the pos-
sessor of the Netherlands, Flanders, Naples,
Sicily, Artois, and Franche Comté. Thus
the chief states of Europe were in the hands
of three young sovereigns, Charles being sixteen years
old, Francis twenty-four, and Henry twenty-five; and the
rest of Henry's reign, so far as it was concerned with
foreign politics, was chiefly occupied in hindering alter-
nately Francis and Charles from becoming supreme in
Europe. For the present he was in a manner friendly
to both. He lent Charles the sum necessary for his
voyage to Spain, and when he was thus out of the way
gradually made overtures to Francis, disarming suspicion
by pretending to hate him beyond measure. One strong
inducement to this was Francis's offer to pay 400,000
crowns for the restoration of Tournay. Hence Henry
was willing in 1518 to go so far as to marry his two-years-
old daughter Mary to the new-born Dauphin of France.
Accordingly the Admiral Bonnivet was sent over to
represent the Prince, and in that capacity placed a
splendid wedding-ring on Mary's tiny finger. Little appears to have been thought of the risk that England
might thus become a province of France; probably it
was assumed that Henry and Katherine would still have
sons. Thus Wolsey had succeeded, for the time, in
placing England in a very unassailable position as regarded
the two sovereigns. The time-honoured requirement of
English trade was peace with Charles and the Netherlands; but the engagements with Francis were too elastic
and too easily repudiated to be inconsistent with this
main purpose. At the same time we had gained the power
of calling France to our help, and thus secured an object
still higher, that of freedom from Spanish control. In any
case England might make her own terms for aiding either

Wolsey's administration.

of the great rivals. And how valuable this power was appeared when, on Maximilian's death in 1519, Charles of Spain was elected Emperor against the competition of both France and Henry, and immediately began trying to enlist England on his side. For Wolsey's private ambition also, the quasi-friendship with both the great Powers was very desirable, as the circumstances might put it in the power of either Charles or Francis singly to make him Pope if a vacancy occurred during a war; and both might agree to do this if no war was going on at the time. Meanwhile the Cardinal toiled on as usual in London. Business had always been his forte from the time when he had been first recommended to Henry by his speedy return from a mission to France, and by the boldness with which he had faced the responsibility of filling up a gap in his instructions. All matters of organisation during the late wars had been carried out by him. Now he was at the height of his power, the whole direction of home and foreign affairs being absolutely in his hands. As Chancellor he was constantly at Westminster Hall or the Star Chamber, judging causes in a manner which even his rivals could not help admiring. After this came a daily multitude of State affairs, whose pressure was so great that his friends entreated him, though in vain, to do no business after six in the evening for his health's sake. He kept a strong hand over the accounts of the country, so that even Henry's wastefulness was in a measure controlled; and therefore was of course unpopular with those who, like Lord Mountjoy, had congratulated themselves at the beginning of the reign because 'avarice was now at an end, and wealth flowed like water.' To these tasks were added his duties as Cardinal and as Papal Legate *a latere*. Both these dignities had been conferred upon him by Henry's express desire—the former as the price of the King's joining the League against Francis in 1515, the latter as the only condition on which Campeggio would be received in 1517. As Legate, his rule over the Church in England had a terrible completeness; for his jurisdiction extended over all bishops, superseded all privileges, and was final for all appeals. His enemies declared that he gained his influence over Henry by witchcraft, so completely did he eclipse Warham, Fox, Norfolk, Suffolk, and the other members of the Council. His taste for splendour was intuitive; it seemed rather a part of his general greatness than a sign of vanity that he should like to see the tapestries of his ante-chambers changed every week, to have round him curious clocks or pictures by Quentin Matsys, and to be followed by many attendants mounted on beautiful and well-trained horses. His choir was held to surpass the King's, although Sagudino says that the voices in the Chapel Royal were more divine than human; indeed in all such things he seemed to aim at absolute perfection. Of course this demanded vast wealth, and he was not precisely scrupulous how he obtained it. But he was still more eager to obtain money for the King; curious proofs of this are his standing out for an unusual proportion of the proceeds of Indulgences in England in 1517, and his declaration in 1525 that he considered it a minister's duty to enrich his master at the expense of the people, ' as Joseph did Pharaoh.'

Hastening back from Spain for the purpose in the spring of 1520, the young Emperor visited England—thus performing, in the eyes of all genuine lovers of etiquette, an act of extraordinary condescension to Henry, who by Papal ordinance ranked only ninth among sovereigns. But Charles was anxious to forestall the effect of the personal interview between Henry and Francis which had been already planned for the ensuing summer. Accordingly he landed at Dover on May 25, was visited by Henry there, and, like a dutiful nephew, returned with him to Canterbury to visit Katherine, who was on her part wild with delight at seeing the head of her own family and hearing her native language spoken. The two monarchs held much secret conference, the purport of which was unknown : but the presence of the Emperor, with his small and plainly-dressed suite, was clearly exercising a powerful influence, and we shall soon see that the heartless splendours of the Field of the Cloth of Gold were quite unable to counterbalance it.

When the Emperor was gone, Henry sailed for Calais (May 31), Wolsey having obtained a promise that no French war-vessel should leave any Channel port as long as the interview lasted. The forlorn town of Guisnes was appointed for the meeting, but the English architects had during the preceding weeks raised on the Castle green there a splendid summer palace 328 feet square, pierced after the fashion of the day with many oriel windows. Its entrance was adorned with olive-crowned statues of antique appearance, and a secret passage led from it to the castle. Francis, on his part, had imitated in a distant kind of way the English magnificence, having in vain asked that costly tents should be forbidden on either side; he had also proclaimed, in order to limit his suite, that none of his subjects should come unbidden within two leagues of the royal procession. When the signal for starting was fired from Guisnes and answered from the French headquarters at Ardres, there was a moment's anxiety, Lord Abergavenny declaring that Francis had brought with him twice the stipulated number of soldiers ; Henry, however, readily believed that his men were frightening

Field of the Cloth of Gold: its uselessness.

the French quite as much, and did not hesitate to advance. The sovereigns embraced first on horseback, then on foot, while the English made the best use possible of their few words of French, the main part of which seems to have been 'bon amis.' At the next meeting Henry laughed outright at hearing a herald describe him as King of France, and jovially declared this to be 'a very great lie indeed.' On June 11 the jousts began and were continued for a week; during them two notable events occurred, the death of a French knight by a too royal thrust of Henry's lance, and Francis's chivalrous act in coming to the English palace at breakfast-time with only four attendants, and thus deriding the precautions which had hitherto guarded their interviews. Such was in outward seeming the Field of the Cloth of Gold: of the inward heart-burnings which attended it no record has been kept, but we can easily imagine the feelings of those who, like the Duke of Buckingham and Lord Abergavenny, hated the whole thing as Wolsey's work, and would have been thankful if some quarrel had sprung from it to shake his power. There was no need for anxiety as to its effect in strengthening the French alliance; for it was hardly over when Henry betook himself straight to the Emperor at Gravelines to renew the Canterbury conference, not vouchsafing to Francis the slightest hint of what the two were planning together. His next step was to send an ominous remonstrance against the French repairs of the Ardres fortifications: 'was his good brother intending to disquiet the English subjects of the Pale?' Of course Francis's right was clear on his own side of the boundary: still he thought it better to yield, in the hope of at least delaying Henry's enmity. Meanwhile Charles's motives for conciliating Henry became stronger every day; the cities of Spain were engaging in the struggle for liberty mentioned in Chapter I., and neither from thence nor from the Netherlands could he get any supplies of money. He had pledged himself to hold a Diet at Worms in the course of the year, and to settle there, not only the Luther affair, but all the outstanding feuds and disputes of Germany; and it was most desirable for him to be in Italy and hinder the consolidation of French influence there. To accomplish even a part of these objects, the alliance of England was indispensable; and negotiations to strengthen it were therefore going on apace, when the attention, not of England only, but of the foreign powers, was distracted by the striking episode of the trial and execution of the Duke of Buckingham in May 1521.

As this nobleman was descended from Thomas of Woodstock, the sixth son of Edward III., his royal blood made him constantly fret against Wolsey's domination. His anger too was dangerous from his powerful connections; for he had married the daughter of the Earl of Northumberland, Lord Surrey was his son-in-law, and Ursula the daughter of Lady Salisbury his daughter-in-law. He had offended the King as early as 1509 by inducing Sir W. Bulmer to leave the royal service for his own, and had also excited suspicions at the Field of the Cloth of Gold; charges were now brought against him by a steward named Knevet whom he had dismissed (detaining, it is said, his property unjustly), and by Sir Gilbert Parke his chancellor and others. By way of precaution Northumberland was arrested and Surrey sent to Ireland; then the Duke himself was summoned from Thornbury to London, and found that all along the road he was watched by armed men at a distance. On arriving in London he tried in vain to see Wolsey, and was presently lodged in the Tower. On May 13 he was arraigned before the Lord

The Duke of Buckingham executed.

High Steward's Court; and the depositions were read and asserted by the witnesses to be true. If so, they certainly amounted to treason according to the ideas of the time; for the Duke had listened to prophecies that he should soon be king, and rewarded them with valuable presents. This appeared to throw a new light on an attempt of his to get the King's sanction to a levy of troops which he thought of making on the Welsh border—perhaps also on some presents which he had made to the King's guardsmen. He was also sworn to have said that the death of the King's children was a judgment for the murder of Lord Warwick, and that, if questioned on the Bulmer affair, he would not hesitate to plunge his dagger into Henry's breast. Of course none of the trials of the time can inspire any real confidence, for the accused had no counsel, and could not cross-examine or bring counter-evidence; and wherever the means of discovering truth were thus neglected it is impossible to believe that 'substantial justice' was generally or even frequently done. The Duke laboured under the farther difficulty that Henry had let it be known before the trial that he had gone through the evidence and considered him guilty. It is said that Buckingham admitted some of the charges while in the Tower; at any rate when condemned he refused to ask for mercy, and on May 17 died as his father had died in 1483. Some of his estates were afterwards given back to his son Lord Henry Stafford, who was also allowed by Edward VI. to succeed to the barony of Stafford, from which his father had taken one of his titles.

While the trial was proceeding, Francis had been pressing on the war in Italy, hoping to secure himself there while Charles was still embarrassed by the revolt of the Spanish cities. The Emperor therefore called for English help according to what was now acknowledged to have been the last year's agreement—namely, that England should help whichever of the two contending parties was first attacked by the other. On the plea that it was necessary to ascertain which was the aggressor, Wolsey was sent by way of Calais to the Netherlands, and his quasi-mediation was made to occupy not less than four months, during which we were preparing for war, and Francis losing instead of gaining ground in Italy. On his return Henry gave him the rich Abbey of St. Albans in reward for his skilful tactics. And it seemed that these would also win him a far higher prize, inasmuch as the news of Pope Leo's death arrived towards the close of the year, and so recent a service to the Emperor was a strong claim on his support. But, in spite of all promises, Charles did very little in his favour, and the choice fell on Adrian of Utrecht, Charles's tutor, who was now enthroned as Adrian VI. It may be mentioned here that in the next Papal election (1523) Charles *did* write strongly in Wolsey's favour, but at the same time sent orders that the courier should be detained till the new Pope was chosen.

Henry's treachery to Francis.

The great French and Spanish war of 1521 was fierce and deadly beyond all precedent, aiming at nothing less than the complete dismemberment of France. When Henry took the Spanish side openly in the following June, Francis was called upon to surrender to the Emperor Burgundy, Champagne, Dauphiné, Languedoc and Provence, and to Henry the Isle of France, Picardy, Normandy, and Guienne; and of the brutalities committed by both invaders of France we may judge by the letters of Lord Surrey to his master, in which he calmly announces that 'the Boulon-

The War of Pavia.

nais is so burned and ravaged that the French have good
reason to be angry.' 'All the country,' he continues, 'that
we have passed through has been burned, and all the
strong places thrown down. When we have burned Dour-
lens, Corby, Ancre, Bray, and the neighbouring country, I
do not see that we can do much more. The Emperor's
Council are willing that Hesdin should be burnt, which
shall be done within three hours.' In 1523 Surrey was
superseded and the army placed under the Duke of Suffolk; it approached within a few miles of Paris, but its
sufferings from the severe winter were terrible, many soldiers being frozen to death, and others losing their fingers
or toes. It was impossible to persevere under such difficulties, and, for the second time in the reign, an
English army went home without orders, having thus
added another to the random and ineffective military
operations which mark the period. The war went on without us, and produced many striking events, one of which
was the capture of Francis I. by the Emperor's generals at
Pavia. After relieving Marseilles from its siege by the
Imperialists in the autumn of 1524, Francis had resolved
on crossing M. Cenis and surprising Milan, which was
defended by only 16,000 of Charles's troops. This he
effected with signal success, the Spanish garrison retreating to the Adda. Instead of pursuing and finish-
ing the war on the spot, the French King occupied himself for three whole months in besieging Pavia on the
Tesino; at the same time detaching 6,000 men to make
a diversion on Naples, and thus leaving his army no more
than equal to the enemy in numbers. In spite of this he
held himself bound in honour to persist in the siege,
because he had declared that he would reduce the place
or die in the attempt. He was therefore attacked in his
position by Charles's generals from the outside, while

Leyva, the governor of the city, made a desperate sally from within. The double shock threw the French army into complete disorder; first its Swiss mercenaries fled, then a well-arranged attack broke its cavalry. Francis himself lost his horse, and narrowly escaped being killed by some Spanish foot soldiers who did not recognise him. His ruin was complete; for ten thousand of his soldiers had fallen, and he himself had to bear a long and bitter captivity in Spain from which he was only released upon intolerably hard conditions.

Among those who fell at Pavia was a leading member of the House of York, Richard de la Pole, the younger brother of the Lord Lincoln who fell at Stoke. Another consequence of the Pavia War was our being engaged in a new struggle with Scotland, to which Francis had again despatched the Duke of Albany (1521) in order to keep up the French interest there. Even Margaret herself now took that side, because Henry had refused to sanction her divorce from Angus, whom she had begun to detest most heartily. So when the King of England demanded Albany's expulsion, he was on the contrary placed at the head of an army of 60,000 men with a strong artillery, and sent to invade England. The old jealousy against his French companions, however, prevented anything important from being done : the Scots failed in the siege of Wark Castle and then retreated. This opened the way for a more conciliatory policy ; Henry tried all means for gaining the affection of the young King his nephew, and even thought for a while of marrying him to his daughter Mary, so as to renew the old scheme of uniting the kingdoms. But such a measure was too wise and wholesome for the times, and it was held to be enough for the present to raise up a party in Scotland which should declare James of full age and capable of governing. This plan

K

succeeded, and in August 1524 James appeared before his nobles with sceptre and crown, and undertook to rule the country 'with the advice of his most beloved mother and the Lords of the Council.' In the following November this step was sanctioned by an Act of the Scottish Parliament, and the hopes of France in that country were for the present at an end.

The wars at this time appear wanton and perverse in themselves, and much more so when we consider how impossible they made expeditions to which Europe was really bound by every tie of honour and interest. Henry VIII., like his father, was the official protector of the Knights of St. John, who had since 1310 constantly made their island of Rhodes the outwork of Christendom in the East. Yet in 1523 he, in common with the other great Powers, allowed them to be besieged by the Sultan Soliman in person without raising a finger to help them. The events of the siege are admirably related by Nicholas Roberts, a member of the Order. The Turks had 150,000 men at least, and the besieged not more than 6,000, so that rest was almost impossible; even the Grand Master, the noble l'Isle Adam, slept as he best might upon the ground. Numbers of huge stone balls were fired into the city from the Turkish mortars, shattering as they fell with an effect like that of shells; breaches were made over and over again, but as often repaired by the skill of the engineer Martinengo. After a while the Turks began a system of mines; yet even when whole bastions were blown into the air the Knights continued to repulse the storming parties. But at length the enemy drove horizontal galleries 150 paces within the walls, and a breach was made which thirty horsemen could enter abreast; then, and not till then, the place surrendered, and was treated not

Turkish conquest of Rhodes.

ungenerously by the conqueror. Transferred by Charles V. in 1525 to the island of Malta, the Order within forty years recovered strength for the equally firm and more fortunate defence against their old enemies of the harbour and walls of Valetta, the capital of their new domain, which they continued to occupy till the island was taken by Napoleon in 1800.

The French war, however useless and ineffective, had of course to be paid for by the people of England; and Wolsey made in 1523 the terrible demand of twenty-six per cent. on real and personal property, and of half a year's income from the clergy. *War taxation in England.* It was estimated that this would produce about 800,000*l.*; but the unwillingness to submit to such taxation was extreme. Wolsey himself came to the House of Commons to argue the point, and Sir Thomas More, who was Speaker, recommended the House to receive him 'with all his pillar and pole-axe bearers.' 'The Cardinal,' he said, 'has been blaming us for not keeping our debates secret; we can turn the tables upon him if he brings his attendants into the House, and runs the risk of *their* making known what passes in it.' When the great minister had made his speech, there was a complete silence. On his asking More for a reply, he was told in the most respectful language that it was the manner of his Grace's faithful Commons to debate matters only among themselves, and that the Speaker, though trusted beyond his deserts by the House, could not venture to declare their views without an express commission from them. Except by this spirited declaration, More does not seem to have displeased the government by his conduct in the debate, and about half the sum demanded was voted by the House. An exemption was given to the northern counties which had borne the burthen of the

Scottish war, and also to the district of Brighthelmstone in Sussex, doubtless because the place had been burned by the French in 1514. Even with these deductions the pressure of the subsidy was simply ruinous, and when in 1525 Wolsey farther proposed to raise what he called an 'Amicable Loan,' England was brought to the verge of a Peasants' War like that which was horrifying Germany in the same year. The Kentishmen complained to Warham that as the subsidy of 1523 was not yet fully paid it was too bad to ask for more money already, and were not mollified by his reminder that 'his Majesty was born in Kent.' They wept, pleaded poverty, and then began to 'speak cursedly'; 'there would be no rest from payments as long as *some one* lived.' Wolsey, it may be remarked, was already unpopular in that county for suppressing Tunbridge Priory and devoting its funds to his new college in Oxford. Strong remonstrances also came from other quarters. The Bishop of Ely wrote to say that there was no ready money in his diocese, and that to procure it people had to sell their cattle at half its value; in Norwich folks tendered their spoons and salt-cellars for want of cash, and there was every appearance that the cloth-makers would have to stop work and dismiss their hands. In an interview with Wolsey, the Lord Mayor of London reminded him of Richard III.'s statute against benevolences, and failed to see the force of his reply that 'he wondered his Lordship should quote the law of a bad King who murdered his nephews, and who, being also an usurper, could not make laws binding a legitimate king.' But the end was that the Cardinal was struck with the arguments alleged, and himself persuaded Henry to allow people to give only what they chose. No one of course came forward, and the benevolence was heard of no more. Though Wolsey might have truly said that it had been no plan of his, yet his loyal silence left its unpopularity to weigh on him; and at the same time the King was not less angry that the scheme had failed than the people were that it had been attempted.

After the battle of Pavia the European war still went on in Italy; hence arose in 1527 one of the most frightful catastrophes of the Middle Ages. For the Constable Bourbon, having deserted his country to take the command of a mixed force belonging to Charles, found himself unable to pay his troops, and was obliged to connive at all their excesses. At last they forced him to attack Rome, and after two repulses made their way into the Leonine City at the back of St. Peter's; as Bourbon himself was killed in the assault (perhaps by a shot from the celebrated sculptor Benvenuto Cellini) even the slight control which he might have exercised was at an end. The Pope and Cardinals just escaped into the Castle of St. Angelo, and then had the gates closed against the crowd of distracted fugitives. For the twelve next days the city suffered the most indescribable horrors; fanatical German Protestants, renegade Italians, and ruthless Spaniards vying with one another in the crimes which they committed, and the unhappy people being tortured by those of each nation in turn to make them produce the valuables of which they had already been robbed by the others. Clement VII., who had been elected Pope in 1523, remained the Emperor's prisoner in Rome till December, when he escaped in disguise to Orvieto. Even there he was far from free or safe, and the next chapters will show the important consequences to England of his quasi-captivity.

Sack of Rome.

CHAPTER XII.

THE EARLY REFORMATION ABROAD. THE DIVORCE. FALL OF WOLSEY.

1521-1530.

THE time was now at hand when differences on religion, which had for many years only slightly influenced English State affairs, were to become all-powerful both in changing the character of the nation and in breaking up society into new party combinations. England was to recall all the memories of former struggle with the Popes, and to consolidate them into a system of permanent revolt. The existing laws against Papal encroachment were neither few nor unimportant. The Constitutions of Clarendon (1164), as long as they were in force, had prohibited appeals to Rome without the royal consent. Edward I.'s outlawry of the clergy and the execution of Archbishop Scrope in 1405 had proved that priests were not inviolable ; and of the three great statutes of Richard II., that of Mortmain (1391) limited the Church's power of acquiring property, that of Provisors (1390) protected our benefices from being filled up by the Pope, and that of Præmunire (1393) vindicated the power of the State to exclude Bulls. Moreover a statute of 1395 forbade the exercise in England of any jurisdiction derogatory to the King's. England too was inclined to the anti-Papal party·on the Continent, and had been represented at the Council of Constance, which exercised the power of deposing Popes ; by no means, however, endorsing its act in murdering John

Old anti-Papal laws.

Hus, the disciple of her own Wiclif, as was shown by the already noticed escape from a furious London mob of the Emperor Sigismund, who had given and broken Hus's safe-conduct. After this, English opposition to Papal claims had flagged for a time; France had sided with the reforming Council of Basle in 1431, and this had been thought a sufficient reason for our taking the other side. Thus was shown the inherent weakness of a mere political opposition in religious matters. It was liable at any moment to collapse, because while the Papal practice was unvarying, the ebbs and flows of State affairs were constantly suggesting fresh combinations which made the help of Rome desirable, and therefore induced kings to purchase it by concessions and by starving Church reform in the manner described in Chapter VI. Public fury might be roused for awhile by some instance of clerical exaction or immorality; but when the burst of feeling had spent itself things were apt to settle down into just their former condition. There was as yet no deep-seated and burning persuasion that such evils sprang from a root of falsehood, and would end only when its last fibres were torn from the soil.

Fortunately for the world, however, some of the best intellects living had now for years been concentrating themselves on religious thought. The simple goodness of John Hus had naturally made a deep impression, which was increased by the unparalleled infamy of his murder; and at the end of the fifteenth century his disciples, under the name of the 'Brothers of Unity,' still formed 200 churches in Bohemia. In 1489 this body decided that 'if God anywhere raised up faithful doctors and reformers of the Church, they, for their part, would make common cause with them;' nor did they fail to keep their promise

Forerunners of the Reformation. Doctrine of Luther.

when the time came. Elsewhere similar associations were formed on semi-catholic principles; as in the Netherlands by the so-called 'Brothers of the Common Lot' (to which belonged Thomas a Kempis, the celebrated author of the 'Imitation of Christ'). These good men lived together in voluntary communities without vows, and devoted themselves to preaching, to the instruction of the young in Latin and Greek, and to the transcription and printing of books. They held that the Bible contains a sound and simple doctrine accessible to all, and evident of itself to any reader without great pains or learned controversy. It is, therefore, they thought, open to all, and should not be forbidden—a doctrine which drew on them the strongest opposition from the Mendicant Friars, who were also aggrieved at their being only half-monks, and accepting the rule of no Order. In England there were still relics here and there of an even exaggerated Lollardism; as in the ten inhabitants of Tenterden who were summoned before Warham in 1511 for maintaining that the elements are mere bread and wine, rejecting baptism, holding confirmation and confession to be needless, and refusing extreme unction, pilgrimages, and saint-worship. Sometimes eminent foreign teachers, though remaining in communion with the Church, aimed at nothing short of a revolution in theology. Such was John of Goch, who about the year 1470 boldly called Thomas Aquinas the 'prince of error,' and was before Erasmus in maintaining that monastic vows are so far from indicating a higher religious standard, that they are tolerable only as supports to those who cannot do their duty without them. With still greater boldness the celebrated Wessel, who died in 1481, had maintained that the 'treasure of good works' has not been left to be distributed by Papal Indulgences on earth, since

Scripture says of the dead that 'their works do follow them.' He had also taught that the Fathers' interpretations of the Bible are not the work of the Holy Spirit; that the monastic state is not favourable to salvation; and that Christ has left no vicegerent on earth. All this shows us how open men's minds had long been to the notion of deeply-seated Church abuses, and how ready the world was for thinkers like Erasmus, especially for those of his works which simplified Bible interpretation. It is highly remarkable that the starting-point of all wholesomer ideas of religion was both in England and abroad that preference for family over monastic life which made Sir Thomas More's household what it was, which dictated, as we have seen, Colet's arrangements for the government of his school, and which formed so large a part of the teaching of Erasmus, Goch, Wessel, and Luther. It was not accident but the very spirit of the time which made the young Luther in his cell at Erfurt dwell with such delight on the history of Hannah and Samuel, and declare that he wanted no more happiness than to be always reading of such fathers, mothers, and children. The notion being once conceived that the very ideal of holiness had been distorted in this main point, many farther steps were easy;. might not other Church maxims be equally groundless, such, for instance, as the power of priestly absolution apart from real change and enlightenment of the soul? And, above all, might it not be true that all the evils and superstitions of the Church had sprung from forgetfulness of the true old religion, that of enthusiasm, the religion of St. Paul and of Augustine, which looked for justification not in anything which we do or can do, but in faith only, a strong and converting faith founded on denial of self and the acceptance of

Christ's redemption? This and this alone, Luther began to think, could give value to the moral life by quickening and spiritualising action. Our deeds are accepted not for anything in themselves, but in proportion as they express and as it were utter this faith. Hence all merely formal modes of obtaining God's favor appeared to Luther anti-Christian; consequently when in 1517 the Pope's agent, Tetzel, ventured to offer Indulgences for sale close to his own parish of Wittemberg, he could not but make his celebrated protest, as Hus had done before him. For the theory of these documents was the very antithesis to that on which he considered all religion to be founded; according to them something of the nature of a spiritual gift might be obtained without *any* spiritual condition whatever. They did not indeed profess to take away sin—this belonged to the Power of the Keys, which was different from that of Indulgence—but they did assert that any one in the outward communion of the Church might, by paying a small sum, and (it was expressly said) without any other condition, obtain participation in all good works done by the Church Militant, and also the relief of departed souls from purgatory. By 1520 Luther, having much cleared and strengthened his views by the study of Greek, had farther come to maintain that both Councils and Fathers might err concerning doctrine, and was expressing his high admiration for Melanchthon, who denied transubstantiation and the sacerdotal theory. He also saw objections to the seven sacraments of the Roman Church, and treated the Pope's infallibility as an arrogant pretension. In that year he also declared against auricular confession and the refusal of the Cup to the laity, published in October his book on the 'Babylonish Captivity' of the Church, and on the 10th of December burned at the gate of Wittemberg the Pope's Bull of condemnation. On April 19th, 1521, he appeared by the Emperor's command before the Diet at Worms, and declined to retract his theological opinions unless convinced out of the Bible; thus creating among the German princes a strong enthusiasm in his favour. He was, indeed, by the single act of Charles placed under the ban of the Empire; yet in spite of much pressure from those who wished to repeat the Constance tragedy by burning the new heretic and throwing his ashes into the Rhine, his safe-conduct was not violated as that of Hus had been. A few weeks later the Elector of Saxony, his own sovereign, had no difficulty in arresting him collusively and concealing him in the safe retreat of the Wartburg, a castle close to Eisenach.

Before the end of 1521 Henry VIII. wrote his book on the Seven Sacraments in answer to Luther's 'Babylonish Captivity,' and for this Pope Leo gave him the title of 'Defender of the Faith.' The King, it seems, considered that the new doctrines were making their way in his own kingdom, and was thus stimulated to authorship. It is certain that Luther's works were read in Oxford and elsewhere at the time; for Archbishop Warham as Chancellor thought it necessary in the same year to order a search for them in the University. Similar enquiries were set on foot in the diocese of Hereford, and Bishop Fisher preached an anti-Lutheran sermon in St. Paul's, at which some German merchants had to do penance for eating meat on Friday. Henry uses against the heresiarch the customary arguments: Was it conceivable that not only Pope Leo, whose character was so high, but all other holy Popes were in error when they enjoined Indulgences? and was the Church to believe that so many teachers, by whom and at whose graves miracles

Henry VIII. Defender of the Faith.

had been done, should be after all in error as to the Papal power, and that a mere 'fraterculus' was born to set them right. Considering the resemblance of these arguments to the after-reasonings of Sir Thomas More there is no reason to doubt the statement that at least one illustrious convert was brought over to a belief in the Pope's supremacy by the very controversialist who was afterwards to behead him for retaining it.

So far as it could be proved by zeal in controversy, Henry's orthodoxy may therefore be considered as beyond question. As he had fought for the Pope in the days of the Holy League, so he argued for him now. But 'all these fences and their strong array' were to be scattered to the winds by one violent temptation. His wife Queen Katherine had for some time been distasteful to him from age and other reasons; and either the remembrance of the secret protest which his father had caused him to make against his betrothal in 1496 or some other evil suggestion brought to his mind the notion that his marriage had been unlawful from the first. It has been maintained that the first hint came in 1526 from the Bishop of Tarbes, who in one of the manifold negotiations for the Princess Mary's marriage had expressed some doubts of her legitimacy. It is not, however, uncharitable to say that dates prove passion and not policy to have suggested the notion. For from the time when the young and beautiful Anne Boleyn appeared at Court in 1522 on her return from France, her father, Sir Thomas Boleyn, had received a shower of honours and profitable employments such as nothing but a strong fancy on the King's part for his daughter would be enough to account for. It is therefore superfluous to discuss Henry's alleged qualms of conscience as to his marriage, and his misgivings that

Beginning of the divorce question.

God had warned him of its unlawfulness by the death of so many of his children in infancy. However strong and even sincere these may have become at last, their first origin is perfectly plain. Wolsey seems first to have realised the King's intentions in 1527; and the Cardinal's manner of seconding them justly earned all the misfortunes which it afterwards brought upon him. He first advised Henry to put away Katherine by his own authority, giving as a reason that she had been married to Arthur *in facie ecclesiæ*, and that after this no more could be said—she could not thenceforward be her brother-in-law's wife, all appearances notwithstanding. As the King thought this plan likely to fail, Wolsey next lent himself to a shameless mockery of law, collusively citing the King to appear before himself as Legate and Warham, and to answer for his misdemeanour in cohabiting with his sister-in-law for eighteen years. The idea seems to have been that this might be enough to make Katherine yield at once; as she never thought of such an act of weakness, the hypocritical procedure came to an end of itself, and it then became necessary to appeal to the Pope, since Katherine certainly would at last. It seemed for many reasons safe to do so, for such a supporter of the Papacy as Henry would surely not be refused. Nor were precedents hard to find either abroad or at home. Both the daughters of Louis XI. had been divorced; and in Scotland Henry's own sister had since 1526 been striving not unsuccessfully to be set free from her husband Lord Angus on the impudent plea that James IV. was not killed at Flodden, but lived till after her second marriage. Moreover the first nobleman at the English Court, the Earl of Suffolk, had, as Mr. Brewer remarks, twice committed bigamy and been three times divorced, his first wife having been his aunt and his last his daughter-in-law. With such instances full in view, what fear could there be of failure?

But Wolsey had neglected to allow for the one decisive circumstance that Pope Clement had been taken prisoner by Charles's army just a month before Henry thought of applying to him, and that, if he decided against the Emperor's aunt, there was every chance of a second sack of Rome. The unhappy pontiff tried to gain time by twice sending dispensations which would not work; and it was only on a third embassy from England that something like an agreement was arrived at. In order that Wolsey might not bear the whole odium of the transaction, Cardinal Campeggio was to act as Papal Commissioner along with him. Even thus much concession was dangerous to the Pope; besides which there was no little fear of disorder in England, where the sound instincts of the people were all for Katherine and passionately against her rival. An unpopular war with Charles was plainly in the air; for Henry had sent him a defiance on hearing of the sack of Rome, and had forced Wolsey once more to transfer the English staple to Calais. All this threw trade into still further disorder, and that just at a time when several harvests had been bad. The cloths of Essex, Kent, Wiltshire, Suffolk, and other counties found no sale. Formidable disturbances again arose in Kent; the rioters declaring that they would seize the Cardinal and place him on the sea in a leaky boat. The continued suppression of small monasteries had added to his unpopularity, as had also the search which he had ordered for Lutheran books; nor was he in high favour even with Henry himself, having offended him, apparently through inadvertence, with regard to a trifling appointment in which Anne Boleyn was interested. There was also difficulty in

Its dangers to England.

finding an opportunity of justifying himself, since Henry, in alarm at finding Anne attacked with the sweating sickness, was hurrying from one house to another in unkingly fear for his own safety.

On arriving in London (October 17, 1528) Campeggio discussed a proposal that the Queen should retire to a religious house, on condition that if no son was born from any other marriage, her daughter should succeed to the throne; but Katherine would not hear of the arrangement. He then intimated that he must report to the Pope before he judged the case; in fact he was being constantly urged by no means to omit this, as the Emperor was advancing on Italy and a false step might be ruinous. *Commission of Campeggio.* Meanwhile Katherine's enemies were plotting against her in many ways; her Flemish advocates were ordered to leave the kingdom before the trial; she was accused of popularising herself and thus causing conspiracies against her husband; attempts were made to get away from her a paper most important to her cause; it was threatened that her daughter should not be allowed to see her; and Mary's establishment was broken up on pretence of economy, while Anne was brought to live in the Palace. All the time Campeggio did not tell even Wolsey what his commission from the Pope really was; but, as this reserve was not generally known, delays were attributed to the minister, and his power began to crumble under him. Things got still worse when seven months passed without any step being taken towards a decision. At length the case took a more definite shape; for Charles being manifestly resolved on supporting his aunt to the uttermost, the Pope was obliged to receive Katherine's protest against her judges, and determined on revoking the cause—that is, on reserving it for his own consideration. It therefore became an object for the promoters of the divorce to get the Legatine Court held in London before the revocation arrived; and it was opened on the 21st of June, 1529. At this session the well-known scene took place; the Queen knelt at Henry's feet, besought him to have pity on her as a poor woman and a stranger born out of his dominions, and urged him to consider her own honour and her daughter's, and that of the Spanish nation and her relatives. Finally she informed him and the assembly that she had appealed directly to the Pope, before whom it was only reasonable that the cause should be decided, without partiality or suspicion: to Rome only would she make her answer. She then left the room, and being thrice summoned in vain to return, was declared 'contumacious.' The next sessions of the Court were for taking evidence; on the 28th the aged Bishop Fisher, the faithful servant of Henry's family for three generations, appeared to maintain that Katherine's marriage was indissoluble, seeing that every defect in its legality had been made good by dispensations which the Pope was perfectly competent to give. He ended by putting in for the information of the Court a book which he had written on the subject. Great was the astonishment at this act of boldness, and at the fervour and eloquence with which the old man pressed his view. The judges replied, lamely enough, that it was not his business to pronounce so decidedly on the cause, as it had not been committed to him; but Henry himself made up for all deficiencies by a reply still extant, which bears unquestionable marks of the royal style. 'I never thought, Judges,' says this document, 'to see the Bishop of Rochester taking upon himself the task of accusing me before your tribunal—an accusation more befitting the malice of a disaffected subject and the unruly passions of a seditious mob than the character and station of a bishop. Why has he kept silence for so many months, and then declared his opinion thus unseasonably? It would have been more dutiful to begin by private admonition, and thus avoid discrediting both the King who is pressing for the divorce and the Pope who has been entertaining the question. And what need was there to talk of maintaining the truth even to the fire, as if any harsh measures had ever been taken, or were likely to be taken, against the Queen's defenders?'

Through the greater part of July the cause dragged on, Campeggio getting constantly more and more unwilling to decide it, because the Emperor's agents were constantly pressing the Pope in opposition to Henry's wishes, and thus keeping him, as he said, 'between the hammer and the anvil.' The 23d of July was at last appointed for the decision; and Henry was present to hear it. To his utter disgust, Campeggio only said that the Roman Courts always had vacation from the end of July to the beginning of October, and that he must therefore adjourn the case till the next term began. As July was not yet over, this of course signified that the sentence, if given in London, would require a farther process at Rome; and it more than implied that the Legatine Court was now sitting for the last time, seeing that the revocation would certainly arrive before October. 'No good ever came of Cardinals in England!' cried Suffolk with an oath. 'You at least should not say so,' rejoined Wolsey quietly, 'for, Cardinal as I am, your head would have fallen on the scaffold but for me!' But in spite of this spirited reply, he knew well that the words just spoken by Campeggio were the signal for his destruction; and it was not long before the tempest was upon him.

L

The attack took the strange form of a prosecution directed against him by royal permission in the Court of King's Bench for having exercised, in violation of the statute of 1395 already referred to, the legatine jurisdiction which Henry had invoked; and this involved a writ of *præmunire* with the forfeiture of all his property to the King. Nor was Henry restrained by any feelings of honour or delicacy from pressing his claim to the uttermost, though the case was much as if Charles I. had of himself broken with Strafford and taken pains to get him prosecuted for the illegal things which they had done and planned together, or George III. punished Lord North for his own obstinate enmity to America. The Cardinal was ordered at once to give up the Great Seal, which passed, much shorn of its power, into the hands of Sir Thomas More; the Dukes of Norfolk and Suffolk, as President and Vice-President of the Council, were to do much of what had been Wolsey's work. His experience of his master induced him to submit at once, and to sign a paper confessing that he had vexed many of the King's subjects by his proceedings as Legate, and deserved to suffer imprisonment at the royal pleasure; he accordingly prayed Henry to take into his hands all his temporal possessions and benefices. His reason for thus abandoning all defence was, as he afterwards explained, that Henry, after once getting possession of his property, would do anything, however harsh, rather than resign it again; consequently, even if he were acquitted on this charge, others would be brought against him, and, if found guilty on any one of them, he would certainly be sentenced to perpetual imprisonment. Having arranged for the delivery to the royal officers of York Place (the modern Whitehall) and all that it contained, the Cardinal went by water to Putney on the way to Esher, to

Fall of Wolsey.

which he had been ordered to withdraw; and thousands of boats thronged the river to see the outward signs of the great minister's fall. At Esher he remained almost destitute for some weeks, paying his servants' wages with money borrowed from his chaplains. But even while thus degraded and impoverished, he was hardly less formidable to his enemies than when his power was at the highest. So well known was his administrative talent, that it hardly required Henry's frequent taunts as to the blundering way in which business was now done to make Norfolk and Suffolk apprehend that on the first great emergency he would be recalled to office and revenge himself on those who had ill-treated him. Accordingly they fretted him continually with small affronts, hoping that he might thus be goaded to some unseemliness of language or action. Day by day he was either informed of some new charge against him or robbed of more property. We read with amazement that, just after a cheering message which Henry sent him at Christmas when he was seriously ill, the Council persuaded the King that a gallery lately erected at Esher would be a suitable ornament for the palace at Westminster, and that accordingly the work was torn away before its owner's face. A Bill was pressed on in Parliament making him incapable of serving the Crown; but it fell through at the prorogation. The next best thing was to banish him as far as possible from Henry's presence; and with this object the Council refused his request to be allowed to retire to Winchester, and insisted that he should go to York, 'the place from which he had his honour.' Winchester was given to Gardiner, except a pension of 1,000*l.* a year for Wolsey. At the same time the courtiers secured for themselves a number of assignments out of his other benefices, and the King tried very hard to secure that his pensions from foreign Powers should for the future be paid to himself. On the 12th of February, 1530, a formal pardon was given him, together with about 6,000*l.* of his property. As soon as the roads were fit for travelling, he started for the north (April 15) by way of Royston, Peterborough, and Southwell, the last a dependency on the see of York. Both on the way and during his short residence at Southwell the goodwill of the gentry towards him was strongly manifested. Sir William Fitzwilliams, whom he had supported in a struggle against the Corporation of London, received him at his house near Peterborough with the most generous affection. In starting from Southwell he had to rise before day to escape from the friendliness of those who wished ' to lodge a great stag or twain ' for his amusement by the way. His first occupation on arriving at his own seat of Cawood Castle was to hold a confirmation of children, which he continued, like Wulstan of old, till he almost dropped with exhaustion. He also succeeded in setting at rest a feud between two neighbouring gentry, expostulating not with them only but with their turbulent retainers. He listened with kindness to the claim of the Dean and Canons that he should not enter the choir of Yorkminster till he was formally installed as Archbishop, but directed that the ceremony should be less magnificent than they had intended—refusing, in particular, to have cloth laid down as usual from the city gate to the cathedral. Of all the trials inflicted on him the hardest to bear was the treatment of his colleges. As he had founded them before the *præmunire*, the Judges held unanimously that they had lapsed to the Crown; therefore the King confiscated the property of that at Ipswich, and seemed inclined to do the same with regard to Cardinal College or Christchurch, Oxford. For this noble foundation Wolsey pleaded in a tone which he had ceased to use for his own sake. About the same time the college authorities, on appealing to the King, were angrily reminded by him that several of their members had been against the divorce; and the Duke of Norfolk told them that their foundation would be dissolved and the buildings pulled down. However they managed to avert the storm (fees to courtiers being, as they said in confidence, a 'chief means' of effecting what they wished), and the King at last consented that Christchurch should retain a portion of its endowments; it was, he said, perhaps with more wisdom than is generally recognised, not for the welfare of the kingdom that it should be completed on the splendid scale planned by the Cardinal. But before this matter was brought to a close its great founder was dead. To understand the last events of his life it is necessary to go back a few weeks. Shortly after leaving Esher he had made a rash attempt, through Du Bellay the French ambassador, to secure the intercession of Francis I. His message to Du Bellay was sent by Agostino, an Italian physician in whom he had great confidence. But this man, having received from Norfolk a bribe of 100*l*. to betray his master, revealed Wolsey's secret mission, which was interpreted into a wish to bring about political changes for his own interest; nor were suspicions wanting that he was urging the Pope to excommunicate Henry unless he parted with Anne. Yet it may be questioned whether, according to the ideas of the time, what he had actually done would not have been held to justify the harshest measures; for the crime of asking for the intercession of a foreign prince was the same for which in 1456 Giacopo Foscari was racked at Venice thirty times in the presence of his aged father the Doge. Intercession meant interference, and, as we shall see in another chapter, was considered a form of aggression.

Cavendish gives a complete account of Wolsey's arrest, which he himself witnessed. It was effected by the young Earl of Northumberland, who had been brought up in his household, but had become his enemy on receiving a reprimand for misconduct in the North. Wolsey was not allowed to see the warrant; it contained, Northumberland said, 'secret matters which were not to be made known to him.' On the next day the prisoner was sent southward under the care of Sir Roger Lascelles, the Earl remaining behind at Cawood to search for papers, and, once more, to take an inventory of his effects. At the end of the third day's journey the party reached Sheffield Park, where Lord Shrewsbury received the Cardinal with great respect, and tried to persuade him that the King would certainly comply with his request and give him a personal hearing. But on learning that Sir W. Kingston, the Lieutenant of the Tower, had come to take charge of him, Wolsey thought the very name so ominous as to outweigh all the Earl's encouragements. 'I perceive, he said, 'more than you can imagine or know ; experience of old hath taught me.' Nor was he more cheered when Kingston told him of the King's belief that he would clear himself of all charges; 'such comfortable words were intended only to bring him into a fool's paradise.' Meantime a dysentery had been coming on, and his strength was failing. Yet he held on for three days longer, and by way of Hardwick, Hall and Nottingham arrived at Leicester Abbey. On the next morning Kingston found him too weak to be questioned, according to orders, about a sum of 1,500*l*. which should have been at Cawood, but had not been found ; Henry being concerned that the money should be 'embezzled away from both of us.' In the course of the same day occurred the celebrated conversation with Sir W. Kingston, containing a character of Henry VIII. of which every true history of the reign must be an expansion. 'He is a prince of royal courage, and hath a princely heart; and rather than he will miss or want part of his appetite, he will hazard the loss of one-half of his kingdom. I assure you I have often kneeled before him in his privy-chamber the space of an hour or two, to persuade him from his will and appetite, but I could never dissuade him.' Sad to relate, Wolsey's last message to his master contained an earnest entreaty 'that he would have a vigilant eye upon this new pernicious sect of Lutherans,' which, if allowed to grow up unheeded, might enact over again in England the horrors of the Hussite war in Bohemia. His whole administration, like that of Richelieu in after-time, had been marked by a scornful neglect of merely theological questions. At this supreme moment worldliness resigned its sway; yet in favour, alas! not of true religion, but of the persecuting spirit. Had he lived longer to carry out such views of the religious life, all England might have had cause to regret the day when he began 'to serve God as faithfully as he had served his King.' He died on the 29th November just as the clock struck eight—the very hour which he had foretold would be his last.

Within a week of Wolsey's condemnation by the Court of King's Bench met the celebrated Reformation Parliament of 1529. Unlike its forerunners in the reign, it was to be carried on in successive sessions till 1536, because, being made up almost entirely of the King's servants, it was ready implicitly to follow his lead against the clerical body, which had as a whole been opposed to the

The first Reforming Parliament. Præmunire against the clergy

divorce. The House of Commons began, evidently according to arrangement, with a petition complaining that Convocation often made, without reference to the Crown or to any civil authority, laws and ordinances against the King's prerogative, as well as vexatious and oppressive to the people. Among the resulting grievances they mentioned the long journeys which had to be made by persons cited to the Archbishops' Courts, the money often charged for the administration of the sacraments, the vexations of summoners and informers, the questions asked in the Church Courts to entrap people into heresy, and the abuse of conferring benefices on children. This paper Henry sent to Archbishop Warham, calling on him for a reply, and at the same time directing Parliament to prepare Bills remedying the grievances of which they complained. After laying the paper before the Bishops, Warham made a singular reply in their name. They made laws, he said, only according to the warrant of Holy Scripture and the Catholic Church, consequently it would be only right that the King should 'temper his own laws into conformity' with these. Although, he continues, 'we may not submit the execution of our duty prescribed to us by God to your Highness's assent, yet we most humbly desire your Grace to show your mind and opinion to us, which we shall most gladly hear and follow, if it shall please God to inspire us to do so.' This meant in brief that the clergy legislated in religious matters, though the civil power might advise them; a view which did not show any profound knowledge of English constitutional precedents. The Archbishop laid down in the later paragraphs of his answer that open penance for sin may rightly be commuted for money where it is desirable to maintain the party's good fame; that severity must be used to repress the beginnings of

Lutheranism in England; that witnesses even of bad
character should be received in such prosecutions if their
tale is likely; that the jurisdiction of the Archbishops
had been exercised for centuries and ought to be so still,
in spite of the inconveniences to those cited out of the
dioceses in which they lived; and that when a quite
young person is appointed to a benefice, its income may
properly be spent for his education. Such an answer
proved that the clerical mind was running in a groove of
its own, and unlikely to understand the statesman's view
of things; especially when it was considered what kind
of a comment upon the Archbishop's principles was
furnished by familiar aspects of Church rule—here an
ignoble squabble about the coverlet of a man just dead,
there an arbitrary increase of tithes, elsewhere a fine of a
few shillings inflicted on a clergyman as sufficient punishment for a grave delinquency; so that, as Warham
himself complains, priests were hooted in the streets
or knocked into the kennel. Obviously, therefore, no
question more required settlement than whether Church
or State law was to be supreme; and this was soon
decided by a stratagem which in a moment turned the
defences of the ecclesiastics—suggested, as it is said, by
Cromwell, a servant of Wolsey's, who after his fall had
become the King's secretary, having earned golden
opinions by his bold defence of his master in Parliament.
Henry suddenly announced that the whole body of the
clergy had subjected themselves to *præmunire*, with its
two consequences of imprisonment and forfeiture of goods,
by acknowledging Wolsey's legatine jurisdiction. They
might reply that they had done so only as all England
had, and as the King had ordered them; indeed it
seems strange that a body of men not wanting in spirit
failed to see that consequences could not easily be en-

forced against them if they showed an even front and stated their case well. As it was, the audacity of the charge seemed to strike Convocation with a kind of panic, and they consented to pay 119,000*l.* as a fine for their misdemeanour. But over and above this they were, under the same penalty, to acknowledge the King's supremacy in Church affairs, which would plainly involve the abandonment of their claim to make canons without his permission. Convocation voted the subsidy on the 24th of January, 1531, and a fortnight later the King was most reluctantly recognised as 'the singular protector and only supreme governor of the English Church, and, as far as the law of Christ permits, its supreme head.' On the 13th of May, 1532, they agreed, for themselves and their successors, to frame no new canons without the royal license; and farther consented that whatever in the existing body of Church law 'appeared not to stand with God's law' should be abrogated by the united action of King and clergy. For the present nothing was expressly said about the power of the Pope, inasmuch as Clement might possibly still decide on the marriage as the King wished.

The act of Convocation was not quite unresisted by the general body of the clergy. As to the fine, they *Resistance of the clergy overruled.* vainly argued that it ought to be paid only by those who had done things really acknowledging the legatine jurisdiction—that is, only by the bishops and superior clergy; and on the other point a protest was numerously signed against any interference with Church liberties or the Pope's authority. At Rome itself the enforced submission of the Church was treated as a revolt on Henry's part; therefore all delays were put aside, and he was informed (May 31, 1531) that the revoked cause would at once be reopened there, and that the Court would proceed to a decision whether he appeared or no. Before the session of 1529-30 ended, Parliament passed Bills for the reduction of the probate duty and the partial abolition of mortuaries—that is, of the offensive perquisites claimed by the clergy on the death of a parishioner. Another Bill was to restrain clerical trading and farming, with pluralities and non-residence; but this was shown to press so hard upon many of the poorer incumbents that it was passed only in a mitigated form. Such was the first session of the celebrated Parliament of 1529, which was to be continued, session after session, till 1536, ready to pass, suspend, or recall measures according to the royal word of command, yet on the whole deserving our gratitude for much of the work which it accomplished. For the evil attending its measures at the time has long been purged away from Church and State; while the good has 'grown with our growth and strengthened with our strength.'

CHAPTER XIII.

MORE AND FISHER.

1531-1535.

As the year 1531 proceeded, things began to appear as if Henry might possibly shake off his ignoble bondage. The insolence of the favourite alienated many of her friends, while others when promoted became far less inclined than before to hazard anything for her. Both her father and her uncle the Duke of Norfolk began to fear the results of popular anger if they sanctioned the marriage. Even some of Henry's agents at Rome, while seeming to press the Pope hard, were privately conjuring him to remain

Appeal to the Universities on the divorce.

firm; the cause, they said, ought to be heard at Rome and decided in favour of Katherine, and Henry would certainly give way if the Pope persisted. The King still saw his wife sometimes, and, curiously enough, used to refer to her when his wardrobe required attention. It seemed more than doubtful whether he would long endure being rated by his mistress for timidity in not putting obstacles aside, and above all for not holding his own in disputes with Katherine on her marriage. Warham was dying and repentant for former concessions; there was therefore no hope of assistance from him. Anne herself appeared to be providing for adversity; she was created Marchioness of Pembroke, and property was settled upon her and the heirs of her body 'whether legitimate or not,' so that it appeared as if she might soon be a mere discarded mistress. She was to go with Henry to meet Francis I. near Calais; but there was a world of difficulty in procuring either English ladies to attend or French ladies of any character to meet her. Indeed any French alliance was in itself as unpopular as ever. Anne would hardly have weathered the storm but for the help she got from Cromwell, who had been in the King's confidence since 1530, and from Cranmer, who succeeded Warham as Archbishop of Canterbury in 1533. Cranmer had been first a tutor in Lord Wiltshire's family, then chaplain to Lord Rochford and to the King; he had also gone abroad on the King's service, and had married the niece of the German reformer Osiander, an act which made him liable to prosecution at any moment. His great claim to Henry's favour had been his scheme of 1530 for coercing the Pope in the divorce question by the opinions of English and foreign Universities. This obtained something like what it desired from the Heads of Houses, Doctors, and Proctors of Oxford, all other resident members having been prudently shut out from the deliberation; the other University yielded somewhat more easily to Cranmer as a Cambridge man. Among the German Protestants Cranmer had little success, in spite of his connection with them; at Paris faintly approving opinion was obtained by Francis's management, and that this might not be cancelled afterwards, the registers of the University were spirited away. The academic bodies under the Emperor's control would of course have no liberty of action; so that the net result of the appeal was meagre in the extreme, and what there was had been obtained either by threats or bribery.

The questions which arose on Cranmer's promotion were, first, whether the Pope would sanction it, and then whether he would issue the bulls for it without the usual payment of annates to the amount of 10,000 ducats. Henry met this difficulty in a characteristic way. Parliament had enacted in 1532 that annates should not be paid in future to Rome; but they had appended to their Bill a provision that it should not come into force before Easter 1533 unless the King ordered that it should do so by letters patent. Henry therefore allowed it to be understood that if Cranmer's business was expedited this unwelcome law might never be enforced; and the Pope, in his ignorance of the new Archbishop's real character, fell helplessly into the snare. Even the Emperor did not see what was coming, in spite of the warning of the acute Chapuys, his ambassador in England, but thought it impossible that Henry should persist so long in a whim; he must surely have made Anne a marchioness in order to get rid of her. The result was that the bulls were passed, and only half the usual fee exacted. Before they arrived, however, the state of the

Cranmer's Court at Dunstable. Popular feeling towards Anne.

Marchioness of Pembroke made a prompt resolution necessary if appearances were to be saved. A public wedding was out of the question; it would at once have stopped Cranmer's bulls and led to an excommunication. The only remedy was that it should be solemnised privately; and with such success was this done, that even now it is not known certainly by what priest it was performed or when—the date, however, was about January 25, 1533. The secret remained an open one for a few weeks, during which with some difficulty an Act of Parliament was passed forbidding appeals to Rome in matrimonial causes, and the Convocation of the clergy was induced by various manœuvres to declare the King's first marriage invalid. On the 10th of May the new Archbishop opened a Court at Dunstable, summoned Katherine to appear, declared her contumacious for not doing so, and then gave sentence that her marriage had been invalid all along. A few days afterwards another session was held, and the King's last marriage declared to be regular. But when Anne went in state to the Tower the people would by no means take off their caps or shout 'God save the Queen;' and when she was first prayed for in a church the congregation went out in a body. Meanwhile Katherine on her enforced journey from Ampthill to Buckden was cheered by crowds of people, who cried 'God bless her' and declared that she was the one true queen. The Princess Mary was equally popular, and owed her quiet succession long after to the still living memories of this time. Anne tried in vain to make Henry punish such disloyalty; her influence was already abating, and within three months he was telling her that she must shut her eyes to his *amourettes*, 'as her betters had done before her.' On the 11th of September the long-expected child was born; but it was a daughter after all, in spite of the predictions of a host of astrologers and wizards who had been consulted. In the midst of the King's disappointment he was mean enough to order that his daughter Mary should come to Hatfield and enter the service of the infant Elizabeth; while Anne with characteristic coarseness declared that she would make Mary act as her lady's maid, and even after a while give petulant orders that she should be beaten if she claimed the title of Princess.

The course taken by the Pope and Emperor was now dangerously serious and dignified. When asked whether he would undertake the deposition of Henry if the Pope pronounced it, Charles replied that he could not give such a pledge upon a mere contingency, but that his Holiness would always find him an obedient son of the Church. *Conditional excommunication of Henry.* The Pope therefore annulled Cramner's acts at Dunstable (July 11, 1533) and declared that Henry would be excommunicated at the end of September if he had not separated from Anne before that time. This was likely to be no *brutum fulmen*, for English discontent was quite prepared to welcome the Emperor, who, as the supreme authority of Europe, might place on the throne either James of Scotland or one of the Pole family, the descendants of George Duke of Clarence, Edward IV.'s brother. Henry had tried to meet the excommunication beforehand by an appeal to a General Council; not only, however, was this clearly against the Papal constitutions, but it annoyed Francis I., who was unwilling to offend the Pope by repeating the very demand for a Council which the Emperor was constantly making. To reinforce his position, he asked the Privy Council in the following December to advise him, first, whether the Pope is superior or inferior to a General Council, and, secondly, whether he has by

God's law more authority than other bishops. Cranmer was the only prelate who gave the negative answer fully and at once; but the replies were on the whole considered sufficient, and orders were issued that all preachers at St. Paul's Cross, as well as the heads of the four Orders of Friars, should declare their assent to this doctrine. The King was farther encouraged by an opportunity which seemed to offer itself of heading a North European League independent of French and Imperial politics. A Lübeck captain named Marcus Meyer, who was charged with piracy for attacking Dutch vessels in English harbours, had the address to persuade him that, as the King of Denmark was just dead, he might get himself chosen as his successor, and then form with Lübeck (as the head of the still powerful Hanseatic League) a combination strong enough to face all enemies. Though this fanciful project came to nothing, it still inspirited Henry at one of the most difficult and cheerless periods of all his life. Thus encouraged, he declared that unless the Pope consented in nine weeks to cancel the sentence of July by declaring his first marriage null and void and his second valid, he would separate England from the Roman obedience altogether. Yet it was most doubtful whether he would be able to carry the people with him; indeed within a few weeks a bold preacher said to his face that the Pope's authority is the highest on earth; and what Hugh Latimer thus dared to tell him openly tens of thousands must have been feeling in their hearts.

The Nun of Kent. Peter's Pence. The congé d'élire.

Henry was now threatened at home by the terrors of superstition. A peasant-girl named Elizabeth Barton had for some years been known as a kind of 'estatica.' She constantly fell into convulsions, during which she uttered words surprising from their persuasive or terrifying power, and also appeared to know events of which she could not have been informed in any natural way. She must evidently be inspired, people thought, either by the spririt of God or by Satan; and as all her utterances were in favour of holiness, the latter could hardly be her case. The rector of Aldington, in which parish she lived, thought it well to make her known to Warham as his diocesan. The Archbishop felt much as St. Bernard did when the sayings of Hildegard were reported to him. He declared that the words which she had spoken came from God, and commended her to the care of Father Bocking of Christchurch, Canterbury, and some other monks. Under their auspices she was 'miraculously' cured of her random and irregular trances; thenceforward they returned upon her at intervals of a fortnight, and on these occasions she was consulted as an inspired person about Church matters of all kinds. Her answers strongly denounced the system of interference with Church privileges, and, when the divorce question arose, she issued 'in the name and by the authority of God' a solemn prohibition to the King, declaring that if he parted from his wife 'he should not reign a month, but should die a villain's death;' and the Pope was similarly threatened if he complied. No punishment, however, was for the time inflicted on her; and she presently entered the priory of St. Sepulchre, Canterbury, and was known as Sister Elizabeth, the Nun of Kent. When Henry was returning from Calais with Anne, she met him on the way with her raven prophecies of evil to come. But the days were at hand when statesmen would hold her inspiration as cheaply as Voltaire himself might have done. A spy of Cromwell's was the first to put him on the track of an important conspiracy in which she was to be an instrument. Cranmer was ordered to

M

examine her, and by feigning to believe, as Warham had believed, in her visions, he obtained a good deal of information. The papers of her accomplices were seized, and it actually appeared that among those who were in correspondence with her was Sir Thomas More, who had resigned the Great Seal (May 16, 1532) from disgust at the anti-Papal measures then passing through Parliament, with Bishop Fisher, the Marchioness of Exeter (who was a strong friend of Mary's), the Countess of Salisbury (Reginald Pole's mother), and many other eminent persons; nothing was, however, found implicating either Katherine or Mary. The juncture was indeed a serious one. A war with Charles was impending, which, if it took place, would ruin English trade. Some fresh measures lately taken for the punishment of Lutheranism and the prohibition of foreign books were beyond measure unpopular; and the feeling for the injured Mary was more passionate than ever. It was not hard to foretell the consequences if at some critical moment a band of fanatical friars, backed by the Nun's inspiration, went abroad among the people to preach that Henry was God-forsaken; especially as every one knew that the fearful Peasant War in Germany had been stirred up by an enthusiast of the Nun's type. Accordingly the Nun was made to read at St. Paul's Cross an acknowledgment of her imposture, and then committed with her accomplices to the Tower to wait for the meeting of Parliament in January 1534. A Bill of Attainder was then brought in against her and the monks who had helped her, and they were executed (April 21). The Bill at first included the names of Sir Thomas More as well as of Bishop Fisher; the House of Lords, however, were of opinion that there was not sufficient evidence against More. Fisher was held to be guilty of misprision of treason (that is, of having countenanced and favoured it), and was committed to the Tower, his only defence being that, though he had really thought the Nun inspired, he had never had the least notion of fulfilling her warnings by conspiracy. With regard to the other persons suspected in various degrees, the risk which they had run and the knowledge that they were liable to be questioned again at any time might perhaps keep them from farther plans against Henry; therefore no steps were taken against them. At the same time Parliament abolished Peter's Pence and all the varieties of payment to the Pope from England; yet intimated that the Act was not irrevocable if his Holiness should consent to the divorce. The mode of appointment to bishoprics was also nakedly and statutably reduced to what had been essentially the established practice. In the case of a vacancy, that is, the Cathedral Chapter was to be admonished by a *congé d'élire* from the Crown to choose, as they regarded the welfare of their souls, a fit and proper person for the see; but at the same time a second document was to be placed in their hands naming the person whom they were to elect, with *præmunire* in case of refusal. On this footing such elections have remained ever since, except in part of Edward VI.'s reign, during which bishops exercised their office on a simple patent from the Crown, as indeed those of the Irish Church did up to its disestablishment in 1869. In the same session Parliament settled the succession of the throne on Elizabeth, as born from the King's only lawful marriage, and enabled him to appoint a Commission consisting of Cranmer, Audley, who had succeeded Sir Thomas More as Chancellor, and the Dukes of Norfolk and Suffolk, which should impose on all English subjects an oath to defend the Act of Succession 'and all the whole contents and effects thereof.'

They then drew up a Bill of forbidden degrees in marriage, in conformity with the book of Leviticus, and, as Blackstone says, on the general principle that marriage is not barred by a relationship more remote than that between uncle and niece. Finally the Parliament declared that on separating from the Pope they 'had not intended to decline or vary from the articles of the Catholic faith of Christendom, or from anything declared in the word of God to be necessary for salvation.'

By the middle of 1534 the discontent against Henry was getting still more dangerous. We can trace almost day by day the steps of conspiracy. On the 9th of July Lord Dacre of the North was indicted before the Peers for treasonable correspondence with the Scots; but they voted his acquittal with a boldness which astonished every one and gave great confidence to the malcontents, as in case of failure they might be able to safeguard one another in the same way. All through September several noblemen were trying to arrange an invasion from Flanders with Chapuys, Charles's ambassador. Lord Darcy promised to raise 8,000 men in aid of it; Lords Dacre and Derby, and even the Duke of Northumberland, the last loyal peer north of the Trent, were prepared to join. Men like the acute Lord Sandys and Dr. Butts, the King's physician, thought that Charles would have no difficulty whatever in conquering the country, which had now scarcely any navy left. Even the courtiers hardly made a secret of their contempt for Anne, paying visits to the Princess Mary under her very eyes. If Mary was sent to the Tower, Sir W. Kingston was ready to take up her cause; while if Henry was once dethroned, he was pretty sure to find that for him there was no prison but the grave. At almost the same time Lord Thomas Fitzgerald,

Northern conspiracies. Rising in Ireland.

who had been made Irish Deputy when his father Lord Kildare was summoned to England, threw up his office on hearing of Kildare's imprisonment (June 11) and immediately plunged into rebellion, calling on Charles for help. 'He was,' he declared, 'of the Pope's sect and band; him he would serve against the King and all his partakers; Henry and all who took his part were accursed.' Sir John White, the governor of Dublin, was unable to defend the city, as the Fitzgeralds, while in power, had stripped it of military stores. Allen, the Archbishop of Dublin, tried to make his way to England for help, but was intercepted and murdered near Clontarf. Dublin Castle was besieged till October, but saved at last by the Earl of Ormond, who made a diversion by attacking the besiegers' homes in Kildare. After much delay, some forces were sent over from England; Lord Kildare's castle of Maynooth, which was supposed to be impregnable, was battered down by Henry's artillery, and by what is called in Irish tradition the 'Pardon of Maynooth' the greater part of its defenders were hanged on the ruins. Lord Thomas was thenceforward a fugitive; yet he was bold enough to stay in Ireland in the hope that Imperial troops might be on the way to help him. As none arrived, he tried in August 1535 to make his peace with Lord Leonard Grey, the new Deputy, who was his relation by marriage. Grey, on his own showing, 'allured him with comfortable words' to surrender, and, it seems too clear, promised that his life should be spared. But the pledge was broken; he remained in prison for about a year, and was then executed with his five uncles, leaving the male part of the family to be represented by one youth whom his friends had concealed.

Instead of really sounding the depths of the conspiracy

against him, Henry seems to have thought in the latter part of 1534 that it would be enough to terrify consciences by the new Act of Succession; if they were firm, honest, and resistant consciences, so much the better for his purpose. His new Commission of Oaths might be made a crucial test of loyalty, if applied not to nobles like Darcy or Northumberland, who would have made any professions without giving up their plans, but to such men as More, Fisher, and the monks of the Charterhouse, who were likely to swear what they meant and mean what they swore. The Carthusian community had a high reputation for holiness. Haughton, its Prior, was known to have warned his penitents against admitting the Royal Supremacy in Church affairs with whatever mental reservation, and it was certain that he would himself refuse the oath. On his doing so, he was prosecuted with two other Priors of his Order; and on the 15th of May, 1535, they suffered the penalty for treason in its fullest horror, giving God thanks, as they passed to the rope and quartering-knife, that they were held worthy to suffer for the truth. Many others of the brotherhood were either executed later on or chained to posts in Newgate and there (by express orders) so starved and otherwise ill-treated that nine out of ten thus imprisoned died within a fortnight.

Death of Fisher and More.

Somewhat earlier than this the first steps had been taken for the trial of Sir Thomas More. On the 13th of April he had been ordered to appear before the Commission of Oaths. As he went to his boat at Chelsea, he closed the garden-gate behind him, that his children might not follow him as usual to the waterside, and whispered after a few minutes to Roper, his son-in-law, 'I thank our Lord, the field is won.' He had overcome all fears, and was ready to meet any consequences. Being called upon to swear to the Act of Succession, he replied by a distinction. Parliament, he said, had complete power to settle the succession to the throne, and he would willingly swear true allegiance to the heir named by it; but to no nullifying of the first marriage, such as the preamble of the Act contained, would he consent to commit himself. He was therefore sent to the Tower, where Bishop Fisher had been ever since his conviction in the Nun's affair. Just then it occurred to the ministers that More's crime, after all, was not capital, as the Act had made it only misprision of treason to refuse the oath. It was therefore thought better to challenge him on the subject of the Royal Supremacy over the Church, as admitted in 1531 and established by Act of Parliament in 1534. Accordingly, Cromwell went to the Tower and called upon him to swear on this point, which he at once refused to do, and thus brought his life within the reach of the law. Cardinal Fisher—for the new Pope, Paul III., had given him this title since his imprisonment, thus incensing Henry far more against him—made the same noble answer, and was within a few days tried, sentenced, and executed (June 22, 1535). More's trial began on the 6th of May; he was prosecuted as having originally dissuaded the King from marrying Anne, as refusing to acknowledge him for Head of the Church, and as having written treasonable letters to Fisher from his prison. To the first charge he replied that a Privy Councillor's honest advice to the King cannot be treasonable; to the second that he kept silence without malice, and only because anything he said would have been misconstrued; to the third that the letters to Fisher were burnt, and that no evidence was offered of their contents, which he declared had no relation to the matter of the charge. Sir R. Rich, the Attorney-General, then swore that the accused, while in prison, had expressly stated to him that Parliament had no power to make any one Head of the Church. 'I never said so,' retorted More, 'nor is it likely that what I concealed from his Majesty I should reveal to one of light tongue and not commendable fame.' After his sentence some attempts were made to bring him to submission by a side wind; but they were all in vain, and he was executed on the 6th of July. His quiet humour both at the foot of the scaffold and just before the axe fell has often excited admiration; yet perhaps less than if it were considered that Sir W. Kingston was his dear friend whom he was anxious to cheer in that supreme moment. Never perhaps was this great man better described than in a passage of the 'Spectator,' which, though not ascribed to Addison, still is serene and pure like him. 'The innocent mirth which had been so conspicuous in his life did not forsake him to the last. His death was of a piece with his life; there was nothing in it new, forced, or affected. He did not look upon the severing of his head from his body as a circumstance which ought to produce any change in the disposition of his mind; and, as he died in a fixed and settled hope of immortality, he thought any unusual degree of concern improper.' His head was savagely set up on London Bridge, stolen from thence by his beloved daughter Margaret Roper, and seen many years afterwards in her coffin close to what had been her heart.

We sometimes meet with men whose turn is so far sceptical, that they sympathise for awhile with the freest enquiry, and lead on others by their apparent acquiescence, while at the same time a deeply-seated and almost physical conservatism rules their heart and conscience, and they are likely at any moment to fall back with unshaken conviction upon argu-

<small>Character of Sir T. More.</small>

ments which they seemed long ago to have outgrown. Such a man was Sir Thomas More; hence towards the end of his life he was intellectually much more like his early patron Cardinal Morton than the Erasmus who had been his delight in early manhood. Now he saw nothing unlikely in the idea that God might work miracles by means of particular images or relics; if more than one place claimed to possess the body of a saint, he thought it enough to reply that part of the body might be in one place, part in another, or that there might be two saints of the same name, or that relics genuine in themselves might have been wrongly styled. It was, he thought, easy to believe that specially beautiful or specially old images might be the channels of great blessing. Forgetting Laurentius Valla's refutation, he boldly appealed to our Lord's portrait sent by Him to Abgarus of Edessa as justifying the use of images in general. Above all arguments he constantly refers to the indefectibility of the Church; any taint of real idolatry would, he thought have falsified our Lord's promise, and therefore nothing that the Church ever did can have this character. And as a corollary to this he always thought it enough to justify any superstition if he could show that it was practised by the Fathers of the first four centuries.

He has been accused as Chancellor of great and even extra-judicial cruelty to Lutherans; and it must be admitted that the peculiar dogmatism of Luther had always been odious to him as putting aside the sounder views of reformation in union with culture which he had learned from Erasmus and Colet. But, on the charge of torturing Protestants out of Court, there is no need to doubt his assertion that only twice did he ever do anything even distantly resembling this: once when he ordered a moderate whipping to a boy who used profane language, and once when he 'cured' a man whose madness took the form of heresy by stripes applied with much vigour. As to the latter case, we must not of course forget that beating and starvation were almost up to our own memory the accepted treatment for insane persons, and that here and there the same notion still survives. It cannot unfortunately be denied that he allowed his jurisdiction to be invoked by the Bishops, and misused it by keeping men in prison when they ought legally to have been released; nor that he was too deeply concerned in the death of Bilney, whose chief heresy was charging the priesthood with immorality, and of Bainham, who held that 'if a Jew or Saracen trusts in God and keeps his law, he is a good Christian man,' and was therefore racked in the Tower by the Chancellor's order. It is impossible not to feel deep sorrow in contrasting More's spirit, as regards persecution, with that of Wolsey, who is said to have found some means to save every heretic brought personally before him, indeed, we find with pleasure that the Tenterden men already mentioned, whom Warham judged in 1511 for denying the chief Roman doctrines, were not executed after all. Even the threatening persecution of 1527 at Oxford (which Dalaber's personal narrative, given by Froude and Maitland, describes with so much life) was ended without bloodshed by the accused persons making a kind of recantation and 'bearing a faggot' at St. Paul's. Yet if More is less humane than Wolsey, he is far above both Audley (his successor in the Chancellorship) and Cranmer. He would not have racked people with his own hands like the former; and would have been incapable of the levity with which Cranmer speaks in 1533 of 'one Frith who looketh to go to the fire for holding concerning the sacrament after the manner of Œcolampadius.' And if we condemn some of his actions, we must remember that the very standard by which we test them was first created by him. He it is who first assigned to human life its true value, maintaining that it ought never to be taken for anything short of murder; because, as he puts it, law has the same right to give a man a dispensation for robbery or adultery as for killing another because he steals. His was the first protest against the perpetual 'paring away' of poor men's wages, and against the constant and increasing sycophancy of judges. Above all he declares that in Utopia any one may be of what religion he will; and that even atheists, although excluded from government because they cannot rule nobly, are still not to be visited with any farther punishment. The least, then, that can be required of a real student of history is, first, that such a man's life, character, opinions, and practice shall all be taken into account in judging of him; and then that it should be considered whether a man of high honour who resolves to die for a noble cause does not thus irresistibly claim that the balance of judgment should be in his favour, even if all his actions cannot be approved.

CHAPTER XIV.

THE DISSOLUTION OF THE MONASTERIES. THE PILGRIMAGE OF GRACE.

1535-1538.

THE death of More and Fisher soon appeared to have been acts not less stupid than wrongful; they were as much against Henry's interest as they should have been against his conscience. From the time of his excommunication he had been wishing to conciliate foreign Protestants, and in the course of 1535 he sent Fox, Bishop of Hereford, to the various reformed States of Germany, in order to counteract the schemes of Francis I. for the re-establishment of Catholic unity there.

The Bull of Deposition drawn up.

But the Germans, while firm in resisting French persuasion, yet valued the learning of the Renaissance, of which More had been such a noble representative, and distrusted the King who was Protestant in nothing but in murdering him and in hating the Pope. Moreover both he and Fisher were considered to have been witnesses, on the whole, to evangelical truth in opposing Anne's marriage. As to foreign sovereigns, Charles V. announced More's death with grave and sincere concern to the English ambassador, who had not yet heard of it; Francis ventured to suggest that banishment might in future cases of the kind be a better punishment than death, and was vehemently rated by Henry for such unfriendly interference in our internal affairs. At Rome, of course, the death of Cardinal Fisher destroyed the last hope of accommodation; so that the Bull of Deposition was at once drawn up, although the influence of both Charles and Francis was used to hinder its publication. By this instrument, had it been published, all officers of the Crown would have been released from their oath of allegiance, the entire nation forbidden under pain of excommunication to acknowledge Henry, and orders given to the clergy to forsake the land, and to the nobles to rise in rebellion, helped by the faithful princes of Europe. Charles V., who had just been achieving some real and undoubted glory by the capture of Tunis from the pirate Barbarossa, and the recovery of 20,000 Christian prisoners there, seemed marked out to execute the Papal sentence; and as in crushing the ruler of Tunis he had deprived Francis of a powerful ally and therefore disposed him to peace in Italy, it was not impossible that both Powers might unite against England.

The death of Katherine, which happened at Kimbolton in January 1536, was a gleam of light among Henry's manifold embarrassments; so much had he wished for it that in the preceding November he had sworn to his Council that his next Parliament should rid him of both her and Mary. This Chapuys reports to the Emperor as having been told him by the Marchioness of Exeter. Anne at first showed signs of great joy at her rival's death; but it was observed a few days later that she seemed to recognise its true effect upon her position. Hitherto Henry had been able to choose only between her and Katherine, but now there were many ladies by whom she might be supplanted. Soon after this her hope of a son was again disappointed, and she saw too clearly that her last hold on her husband was gone; indeed he was already planning to marry Jane Seymour. By Katherine's death the main ground of quarrel with the Emperor had of course been removed; therefore it was not impossible, from his own point of view, for Henry to be reconciled either to him or to the Pope. To show his disposition that way, he censured an untimely sermon of Cranmer's against Imperial usurpations, and was quite willing to help Charles V. against the Turks (with whom Francis, on the contrary, had just been making a commercial treaty); although, adhering, after the fashion of weak men, to a fixed idea, he even then demanded that Charles should allow himself to have been wrong from the first in opposing the marriage with Anne. Seeing that things were taking this direction, Cromwell became convinced that he had been rash in pressing things so far against

Execution of Anne Boleyn.

Rome; and about the middle of April it seems to have struck him that nothing would tend so much to conciliate the Catholic party as the sacrifice of Anne Boleyn, who was detested by them not only because England had broken with the Pope for her sake, but because she had herself showed some Protestant leanings. He is reported, with apparent truth, by Chapuys, as declaring that 'he began to contrive and conspire the said affair' (*il se meist à fantasie et conspira le dict affaire*) against the Queen; and the way in which he managed the prosecution seems strongly to confirm this view of his conduct. For he induced Henry to sign, on the 24th of April, 1536, a commission by which the Lord Chancellor, the Duke of Suffolk, with some other noblemen and any four of the judges, were to enquire, not into anything about Anne, but generally 'into all kinds of treason, by whomsoever committed,' and to try the offenders. Among the Commissioners were the Queen's father the Earl of Wiltshire, and the Duke of Norfolk, her uncle. The Court being thus constituted, a charge against Anne and its evidence were next to be provided. Accordingly, on the 30th of the same month a conversation was reported to Cromwell, as having taken place *on the previous day* between Anne and Mark Smeton, a musician of the household, which indicated improper relations between them. Smeton was immediately arrested, and (with what encouragements or under what threats we know not) confessed adultery with the Queen. At any rate what he said implicated several other young courtiers, particularly Sir Francis Weston, Henry Noreys, and William Brereton; and to these Anne's brother, Lord Rochford, was afterwards added. She was accused of the grossest misconduct with all five, and with having conspired with them to kill the King. It is not desired

here to go into the details of these most revolting trials ;
yet it must be remarked that Anne was said to have
done acts of unchastity at times when from the state of
her health they were all but impossible, and that the
charge of compassing Henry's death is absurd, seeing
that the moment it happened she would have been
exposed defenceless to the whole vengeance of Katherine's
party. Her guilt has been supposed to be proved by the
fact that her father and uncle were among the judges
who recognised it. But to this it is replied that Wiltshire was excused from sitting on her trial, and that
Norfolk had long been hostile to her. Great stress has
also been laid on the dying confessions or non-denials of
Smeton and the other accused persons ; but here, again,
there is uncertainty. They all said on the scaffold that
they had deserved death, but not that they had done the
crime for which they suffered ; and as for Smeton's
earlier confession, may he not have made it to escape
torture, just as in this very year Sebastiano Montecuculi
confessed for the same reason that he had poisoned the
Dauphin of France, who was not poisoned at all? Besides this, the prisoners were simply hanged or beheaded,
none of them suffering the more horrid penalties of
treason ; and it is at least conceivable that they paid for
this remission by not protesting their innocence at last—
caring, as a traveller of the period remarks of Englishmen in general, much more for bodily pain than for death.
Anne was found guilty (May 15) by a jury composed
almost entirely of gentlemen in the King's service. On
the 17th Cranmer held a Court at Lambeth in which he
decided, apparently because of a shameful confession by
Henry, that Anne's marriage was null and void *ab initio*.
It seemed to occur to no one that if she had never been
married, the charge of treasonable adultery fell to the

ground of itself. On the 19th the sword of the Calais headsman freed Henry from his hated wife. People were surprised at his revelries during the trial; he was, perhaps, somewhat elated by seeing how many sovereigns were thinking how to find him a new queen. He chose, however, to 'carve for himself,' and married Jane Seymour on the day after the execution. Against the general expectation, he did not recognise Mary as legitimate. The Duke of Richmond, his favourite child, the son of his early mistress Elizabeth Blount, was now seventeen years old; and as Parliament had allowed him to appoint his successor by will, there was some thought of first legitimating the Duke (as in the case of the Beauforts), and then making him heir to the crown. Authority, both Romish and Protestant, had even suggested the strange notion that he should marry his half-sister Mary, and thus close all controversy. The Protestant Tyndal advised this; and it had been considered as a possibility by Pope Clement VII., until informed by his Council that such a permission was *ultra vires*. Richmond's death, however, in the course of 1536 frustrated all such schemes.

Instead of being diminished by Anne's death, Henry's unpopularity with the Roman party was now increasing daily, for many reasons. One of these was his already mentioned wish to form an anti-Papal league in Northern Europe. The Confession of Augsburg (1530) had now embodied the views of the Lutheran body, and he had held out hopes in 1535 that he might sign it. He had also urged the Bishops to produce a correct translation of the Bible; and, as they hesitated, had employed Miles Coverdale to collect and edit the various portions, perhaps with Tyndal's help. Six copies of the work, when printed, were ordered to be attached to stands in St. Paul's, and one

Henry's Protestant leanings.

to be bought for every church in England and placed in the choir. But what seemed most clearly to define his position was his issuing in 1536 the so-called 'Articles to stablish Christian Quietness' (apparently composed by himself), in which, while on the whole adhering to the Roman doctrine, he yet partially adopted the Protestant expressions about justification, and spoke severely about the Papal corruptions connected with Purgatory and Indulgences. But, above all, he had with a strong hand carried out his plans with regard to the monasteries as a reply to Paul III.'s Bull of Deposition, which he well knew to exist, although it appears, in spite of the assertions of many historians, never to have been published at all. For it has been pointed out that there is no contemporary copy of it in England; that Bishop Burnet printed it for the first time, not from the Records, but from a Roman Bullarium; that Hall and Foxe make no mention of its publication; and that for several years after this it is spoken of by the Romish party only as likely to be published.

The monasteries of England had, almost from a fatal necessity, degenerated from the principles on which they were founded. It may be said in general that decay in such institutions can be hindered only by a system of vigorous inspection and control, combined with authority, such as the Popes had exercised, to break up and remodel them according to the needs of the time. But most of the important English monasteries belonged either to the Cistercian or to one of the great Mendicant Orders; in any case their superiors were foreigners, and, as such, could only with great difficulty exercise any superintendence in England. Thus the rules enforcing labour, study, or mission-work had become relaxed; numbers of servants were kept in the

State of the monasteries.

large foundations to work for the monks; and the inmates had in many cases begun to fret against the law of celibacy to which they were subject. Their position as feudal superiors also from time to time embroiled them with their dependents, so that most violent armed rebellion against their authority was not unknown. Warham, as we have seen, had feebly tried to abate the monastic disorders of his own day; and Wolsey had suppressed a few of the poorer foundations in order to obtain funds for endowing Christchurch. Now the establishment of the Royal Supremacy laid the abbeys open to attack; so in the summer of 1535, just after the death of Sir Thomas More, Cromwell, as the King's vicegerent in ecclesiastical matters, ordered a Visitation of the Universities, the religious houses, and all other spiritual corporations in the kingdom. That there was no thought of any such reform as that which had produced the self-devotion of the Theatines in Italy, or the exertions of the Franciscan body there during the plague of 1528, is plain enough from the character of the Commissioners. These were Drs. Legh, Layton, and Aprice, ecclesiastical lawyers of no great standing, but apt at ferreting out clerical scandals, such as Layton soon began relating to Cromwell with huge gusto and self-gratulation at having found such desirable evidence. Nor was the time allowed for the enquiry a less clear evidence of its intention; this was only four months, after which the Commissioners' report was to be ready for the session of Parliament. As there were more than 1,000 monasteries to be reported on, it was clear that the work could not be got through in the time, especially as each foundation was, as a rule, visited by two of them successively, and there was a schedule of eighty questions to be gone into with each community. Plainly, therefore, the reporters must have adopted very short methods of getting evidence together —indeed they seem to have chiefly aimed at having something to say about each ; and this something, if evil, was generally about the Abbot or Superior, who, as we have seen, had often been appointed by the King, or some other patron, for reasons quite. unconnected with the discipline or welfare of the house.

It would have been well if all the Commissioners' work had been like what they did at Oxford, making very real reforms and carrying off no plunder. At Magdalen, New College, and All Souls they established classical lectures and provided for their support, imposing loss of commons on all resident students who did not attend one of them at least daily. *The Universities visited.* They commanded that no monastic student, under pain of being 'sent down' to his cloister, should be found in any tavern. They also ordered the works of Duns Scotus to be disused—'a shallow way,' says the annalist of Oxford, 'to treat an author so profound that wise men could hardly understand him after thirty years' study.' Accordingly, on a second visit to New College, 'we found,' reports Layton, 'all the great quadrant court full of the leaves of Duns, the wind blowing them into every corner, and Mr. Grenfell, a Buckinghamshire gentleman, gathering them up to trim sewels or blanchers to keep the deer within the wood, thereby to have the better cry with his hounds.' As the agitation in the Church was driving clerks to try for a living through medicine, the Commissioners also ordained that no member of the University should practise it till he had satisfied the Professor of Medicine as to his knowledge.

From Oxford Layton went down into Kent, and on Monday, October the 22d, had the pleasure of detecting the Abbot of Langdon in a breach of morality. On the next day, as it appears, he went on to Canterbury ' to visit the Archbishop's see,' intending, as he says, to be at Faversham by the evening. If so, the late October day must have been well occupied; as, beside the two journeys, there was an anti-Papal sermon by Cranmer at the Cathedral, and an inventory to be taken of the Christchurch valuables. At Faversham the Abbot was found 'too old to visit his domains actively'—he had been in office since 1498—but when called upon in the following March to resign, he quietly replied 'that he was not so far enfeebled, neither in body nor in remembrance, but that he might well accommodate himself to the governance of his poor house and monastery.' On the 5th of November Aprice wrote to Cromwell that the Abbot of Bury St. Edmunds 'delighted much in playing at dice and cards, and spent much money in this and in building for pleasure. He was also fond of staying at the various granges. The monastery, too, was full of false relics; pieces of the true Cross enough to make a cross of, some of the coals with which St. Lawrence was burned,' and the like. Meanwhile Legh had joined Layton for the Visitation of the northern abbeys. At Chicksand they found that two nuns had been ill-conducted. At Leicester they exceptionally commend the authorities of St. Mary's Colleges and Hospital as keeping these well and honestly, and having 300*l.* ready for use in their treasury. 'The monks of Leicester Abbey,' they say, 'are confederate, and will confess nothing '; Layton therefore intends to object against them things which he had heard elsewhere, though not of them. In Yorkshire the Commissioners found instances of disgusting vice, they do not say where; in St. Mary's Abbey at York they 'expect to find much evil disposition both in the Abbot and the convent.' At

Fountains the Abbot, 'a mere fool and idiot,' and said to be grossly immoral, had stolen the sexton's keys, possessed himself of a jewelled cross, and sold it with other valuables to a London jeweller. The Commissioners announce that he has been deposed, but secretly, for fear that the Earl of Cumberland should claim the appointment; Layton recommends for it a monk of the house, called Marmaduke, who will pay 400*l*. for the appointment, and 1,000*l*. of first-fruits.

As not many of the letters sent by the Visitors now survive, there is little to add from this source to the extracts just made. When the visitation of Fountains took place, the meeting of Parliament was at hand, and the Commissioners set about preparing their report, which is said to have been commonly called the 'Black Book,' and to have excited so much anger when read in the House of Commons that all with one voice cried out 'Down with them!' Selden, on the contrary, states that Henry had to threaten the members with death if they did not pass the Act of Suppression; and there is no doubt that the debate upon it was long and bitter. The 'Black Book' itself, if there ever was such a document, has perished; three MSS. however remain, generally called the 'Comperta,' which purport to be extracts from it, and to analyse the confessions made at different monasteries. In some instances the 'Comperta' can be compared with the Visitors' letters, as for instance with regard to Fountains. We have seen what was said of this by Layton, which is far from describing the place as the universal sink of iniquity of which the 'Comperta' speaks. Nor can it well be replied that the original and detailed confessions may have been in writing and therefore different from what the Commissioners received orally; for, if so, some of them would have been still among the Records, which is not the case. According to Burnet's account, the 'Black Book' itself was destroyed by Reginald Pole under Queen Mary; but if it was in Henry's reach at the time of the Pilgrimage of Grace, why did he say nothing of what would have been the best of all proofs that he had done well and not ill in destroying the monasteries? To this it must be added, on the highest authority, that, as a rule, documents discreditable to Romanism were *not* destroyed under Queen Mary.

After all, the Act distinguished the houses that were to be suppressed, not by their greater immorality, but, as Wolsey had done, by their less wealth. 'Parliament had heard from the King,' so said the Act, 'of enormities done in the abbeys; he in turn had learned these from his Commissioners and from other credible witnesses.' It was therefore ordained that those which had an income less than 200*l.* a year should revert to the Crown instead of to the founders' heirs as we might have expected. But Henry was authorised to preserve as many of them as he pleased by letters patent; and out of the 376 then confiscated thirty-seven were refounded in the following August, and remained till the general dissolution. At first a fresh Commission had been formed, in which neighbouring gentlemen were in each case included, to settle which should be preserved; but the reports from this were so uniformly favourable to the abbeys that Henry rudely accused the members of receiving bribes and soon cancelled it. He at the same time placed the remaining monasteries under a rule which aimed at shutting up monks rather than utilising them; and rather than submit to this a number surrendered to him of their own accord.

Such was the celebrated Visitation of the Monasteries. Instead of being made centres of learning and education, they were generally demolished and the materials sold by the courtiers to whom Henry granted them. How far the monks deserved their fate there is little evidence to show. As Church writers of earlier times seldom spared accusations of immorality against the regular clergy, and as these bodies had very little effective visitation, it is natural to suppose that their morals would in some cases be those of a large school or college left to itself. But it is not to be supposed that the Record Office contains a huge 'mystery of iniquity' in documents which escape publication by being too bad for it. It is to be feared that historians will always be reduced, in the absence of sufficient evidence either way, to acquit or condemn these institutions rather by their own notions of the probable than on any quite convincing arguments.

As the year 1536 rolled on, it was plain that the conspiring lords had lost their opportunity. The Emperor, in whose help they trusted, was now most unlikely to send troops either to England or Ireland, as a fresh war with France for Milan had broken out, and by August in this year the sovereigns were engaged in a cross invasion, with the result that Francis fortified himself in Turin, while the Emperor lost 30,000 of his veterans from famine and disease in his attack on Provence. Consequently the Northern peers remained inactive, though sullen; and the conspiracy would probably have died out, had not the commons of the same counties suddenly blazed into an insurrection from motives partly the same as those of the nobles and partly peculiar to themselves. Like their betters they objected to the plebeian advisers of the King, the promotion of Cranmer and other heretics in the Church, the suppression of the monasteries, and a new Statute of Uses which made it very difficult for landowners to throw on their

The Louth rebellion.

estates the charge of providing for their younger children. But as a revolution is seldom really vigorous unless a question of land is at the bottom of it, so to these grievances was added a deep-felt middle-class discontent at the system of enclosures and sheep-feeding which still continued to harass farmers of the old school in a manner which they only half understood but entirely resented.

The town of Louth, in the marshes of East Lincolnshire, is even now somewhat out of the world. The country round it is so intersected with 'cuts,' so liable to inroads of the sea, and so incapable of growing trees, that field-sports are out of the question in it; therefore the resident gentry are few, and a system of small holdings still prevails there, creating, as usual, a most independent spirit in the owners. This was the district where revolt was first to show itself. The nunnery of Legbourne, close to the town, was on the point of suppression, and Heneage, one of the Visitors, was expected with the Chancellor of Lincoln Cathedral on this unpopular errand. On Monday the 2d of October, 1536, he arrived, and a furious riot instantly broke out, from which he took refuge in the church, but was brought back and forced to swear that he would be true to the commons. The book containing Cromwell's commission was torn in pieces, and his servants placed in the stocks. Shortly after this a similar rising began at Horncastle, and was joined by a number of gentry and by the Abbot of Barlings, who appeared with his canons in full armour; there too the celebrated banner of the Five Wounds of Christ was raised for the first time. The unhappy Chancellor fell into the hands of the mob and was murdered; and on the same day there was a rising at Lincoln, and Bishop Longland's palace was plundered. If the nobles had now come forward to head the movement, and strengthened it by the forces at their command, Henry's reign and life might soon have come to an end together. However, Lord Hussey, who had spoken much of rebellion, could not persuade himself to take either side, but remained inactive at Sleaford; and within a week from the outbreak the advanced guard of the royal forces arrived at Stamford. Two days later the Duke of Suffolk with the main body joined them, to hear that the insurrection was already breaking up. In this emergency Henry had shown a really royal firmness—not ill pleased, perhaps, to have nobler occupations than those which had so long enthralled him. To the written demands of the rioters for the dismissal of low counsellors and the like, he replied that the 'rude commons of one·shire, and that one of the most brute and beastly of the whole realm, should not be allowed to rule their prince; his orders were that they should disperse at once, and surrender a hundred of their chief men.' Expecting on this to be delivered up, the leaders thought of cutting their way through and placing themselves in Suffolk's hands. They were, however, allowed to pass without resistance, and the first act of the Pilgrimage of Grace was at an end.

But a far harder trial was to come; for on the 8th of October a much better-organised insurrection burst out in Yorkshire. A paper urging a rebellion for the sake of God's truth had been circulated in that county under the signature of a popular young lawyer named Robert Aske, who had been watching the Lincolnshire events; and on returning home, although he declared that he knew nothing of the paper, he found himself stormily welcomed as leader. Lord Darcy, the chief person in Yorkshire, followed Lord Hussey's example in temporising, and shut himself up

The Yorkshire insurrection.

with a few foreigners in Pontefract Castle, although he had been all along one of the conspiring nobles, and was favourable to the objects proposed by the rebels, who on the 14th of October mustered on Weighton Heath, about eighteen miles east of York; their troops being picked men, well armed and equipped for war. Having summoned Hull in vain, they left half their forces to besiege it, while the rest marched on York and were unhesitatingly welcomed there; the monasteries were cleared and their old inhabitants restored. They then marched to Pontefract, where, after some hesitation, Lord Darcy joined them just when Lord Shrewsbury was at hand with forces for his relief. Soon Hull surrendered, and at length the small castle of Skipton, which still remains entire, was the only strong place in Yorkshire unsubdued; while large rebel reinforcements were arriving from Durham under Lords Latimer and Lumley, and two sons of the Duke of Northumberland had already brought up the standard of St. Cuthbert for a southward march. Even the Archbishop of York, who had been with Lord Darcy at Pontefract, had for the time given in his adhesion. Thirty thousand excellent troops now moved under Aske's command against Doncaster, more than a third of them being mounted and clad in armour. But Henry, mingling prudence with firmness, used a variety of means to break it up, reminding Lord Latimer and others how disgraceful to them it was to be serving under a man of such low rank as Aske, and explaining by means of papers scattered all over the North that a plan of Cromwell's for parish registers had no reference to taxation, and that none of the recent Church measures had been hostile to true religion. When the rebels reached the banks of the Don, they found that he had wisely opposed to them the Duke of Norfolk and Lords Shrewsbury, Rutland, Huntingdon, and Talbot, all men popular in the North, yet evidently resolved to obey the King's orders whatever happened. It was impossible to force Doncaster Bridge in face of their artillery, and twice, when an attack had been planned, a storm made the river too deep to cross, the floods seeming as fatal to the Pilgrimage of Grace as that of the Severn had been to Buckingham's revolt in 1483. Thus Aske was compelled to negotiate; his terms being that all concerned should receive a pardon, and that their Articles of Accommodation should be transmitted to the King. These included restoration of the Pope's authority, and condign punishment for all concerned in overthrowing it, among whom Cromwell, Layton and Legh, and the reforming Bishops were especially named (the penalty suggested for the last being 'fire or such other'), remission of taxes, enforcement of the Acts against enclosure, and a few others. But Henry now began to feel that the game was in his own hands. Aske and Darcy were, he plainly saw, men who wished for revolution only if it could be had without overt acts of rebellion. He therefore detained Aske's messengers for a fortnight, firmly refusing to hold a Parliament till the crisis was over, or even to grant an unreserved pardon. The leaders would, he felt sure, find their scheme of a Northern Parliament impracticable, and be unable to get help in time from the Emperor, or to bring over to them the country south of the Trent. He therefore ordered Norfolk to reoccupy the line of the Don which he had abandoned, and to maintain it at all hazards. Yet as more and more insurgents gradually came in from the North, and the severe weather made it difficult to keep the field against them, Henry was at last induced to relent. On the 2d of December news came that he had granted a full pardon, promised to hold a Parliament at York, and consented to enquire into the question of enclosures. On hearing this Aske instantly threw off his badge with the Five Wounds, and declared that henceforth he would wear no device but the King's. Nor was Henry unfaithful, for the time at least, to his part of the compact. He had before checked and reproved as dishonourable Norfolk's desire to make terms with the intention of breaking them; and he now admitted to his presence the insurgent leaders and explained to them how little reason there had been for the outbreak. One of these was Aske himself; the King said that he took him now for his faithful subject, and wished to hear from him the history of the rebellion. Aske in return warned the King of the dangerous discontent still remaining in Yorkshire, and of the general fear that the pardon would be delusive. In fact early in 1537 partial insurrections, entirely disavowed by the late leaders, were raised by Sir Francis Bigod in Yorkshire, and by Nichol Musgrave in Cumberland. As these were believed to have been instigated by the monks, express and stern orders were sent to put to death any who were taken; and in obedience to these about seventy-four persons were hanged on the walls of Carlisle. Of the Lincolnshire prisoners nineteen with Lord Hussey were executed after trial; and, saddest of all, the new insurrections drew on the death of Aske and his colleagues, who were alleged on slight evidence to have gone against the government in them and thus to have forfeited their pardon. Lady Bulmer was burned alive in Smithfield for a plot to carry off the Duke of Norfolk, the Abbots of Fountains and Jorvaulx were hanged, and, strangely enough, Lancaster Herald, the King's own messenger, who had boldly faced Aske at Pontefract, now shared the same fate because he had disgraced his tabard by kneeling to a rebel in order to dissuade him from his enterprise. In spite of the treasons of the Northern Abbots, their monasteries were not at once confiscated; but their offence was held to be a sufficient reason for claiming possession at any time. There is a curious Lancashire tradition that the Abbot of Whalley had been driven into insurrection by a stratagem of Aske's, who managed to get the great convent-beacon fired, and so made it appear that the signal had been given by the Abbot himself; if this is true, it did not save the unfortunate man's life nor his monastery. Soon the great abbeys of Jorvaulx, Bridlington, and Furness were suppressed, and not long after this Chertsey, Castleacre, Lewes, and Leicester surrendered under the old Act. To these must be added St. Augustine's, Canterbury, the mother of English Christianity, which has been so nobly and happily restored in our own time as a hardworking Missionary College.

The point to which the English Reformation had now advanced doctrinally is indicated by two events. One of these was Henry's passionate refusal to let England be represented at the Council of Mantua, which even Luther had accepted in 1535 on the proposal of the lately elected Pope, Paul III., and his vehement exertions to hinder the German Protestants from attending it, on the ground that it belonged not to the Pope but to princes to summon such assemblies. The other was the publication by authority in 1537 of the 'Institution of a Christian Man,' drawn up chiefly by Cranmer and Bishop Fox, and generally called the 'Bishops' Book.' Its plan was to represent the Christian faith, article by article, not as bare dogmas, but as powerful to influence men's hearts and lives. It is anti-Roman mainly as teaching that, wherever the faith is held, there the Church is, and that no Church has rule over any other; in contrasting strongly the Church militant and its

The 'Bishops' Book.'

admixture of evil with the invisible and unfailing Church unseen ; and in speaking much more of the work of the priesthood and their obedience to civil rule than of inherent powers possessed by them. While in terms admitting seven sacraments, it still defines them much as Protestants would have done. It is curious that it repeatedly prohibits as offensive to God all divination, palmistry, or witchcraft; and an Act of Parliament passed in 1541 throws light on this by showing that a system had grown up of searching by supernatural means for the treasures built up or buried in the ruined monasteries, whose exact position was now forgotten.

On the 20th of October, 1537, the long-wished-for Prince of Wales was at length born, and many regulations were made for watching a life so precious. At the same time the Queen's brother Sir Edward Seymour was made Earl of Hertford, Sir William Fitzwilliams Earl of Southampton, and Sir W. Russell Lord Russell. As if it were fated that the hope of the dynasty was to rest on one son, the Queen, who seemed at first to be doing well, took cold and died in four days. Her virtues and graces have been exaggerated by history; yet Henry's grief was sincere, and proved by his ordering 1,200 masses for her soul and remaining a widower till 1539. The submissions which the Princess Mary had been long offering were now accepted; and, though not acknowledged as legitimate, it was understood that she was placed in the line of succession. About the same time the navy, which was in the utmost decay, was so far restored as to be able to guard our coasts from the secure insolence of pirates. Considering Henry's early predilection for the sea, it is strange to hear of Spaniards and Frenchmen daring to attack one another in our harbours, and of English vessels

Prince Edward born.
Case of Lambert.

being plundered by corsairs within sight of land. However, a small fleet was now fitted out which successfully fought a French plundering squadron in Mount's Bay; single pirates were captured here and there, and our harbours put in a state of defence. The expenses were paid out of the Abbeys; this being the chief national purpose (except indeed the foundation of six new bishoprics) achieved by the many spoliations which went on through 1538 and 1539. One remarkable instance of this was the destruction of the shrine of St. Thomas of Canterbury, from which twenty-six cartloads of treasure were taken; a paragraph added at this time to the unpublished Bill of Deposition gives some credit to the story that St. Thomas himself was summoned to appear (much as the dead Pope Formosus was by his successor) and plead to the charge of treason against Henry II. On the same view of history a friar named Forrest, who had asserted that Becket and Fisher were alike martyrs, was burned in a fire made with the wood of a celebrated Welsh image called 'Derfel Gadarn,' which had been supposed to have power to draw souls out of hell. An exhibition was also made at Court of the mechanism by which the statue of Christ at Boxley had been made to move its head and weep. It really seemed as if the Reformation had taken the 'holding-turn;' such certainly was Latimer's view when he preached Forrest's death-sermon, in the firm belief that the birth of Edward had secured the victory of Protestantism among us and made God, as he expressed it, 'really an English God.' But causes of an opposite tendency were also at work, undivined by the simple-minded Bishop of Worcester. Negotiations had been going on for the King's marriage with the Duchess of Milan, Charles V.'s niece; and this required, from the lady's point of view, a Papal dispensation. Such difficulties *might* possibly be got over by inducing the Emperor to break with the Pope as Henry had done; but there was absolutely no hope of this, unless England could be shown to be orthodox in spite of the schism. Henry was also moved in the same direction by a letter from the Landgrave of Hesse against Anabaptism, which had shocked all Germany in 1535 by its unbridled rule of polygamy and murder at Münster. It is also clear that he felt deeply scandalised at the profanity and mockery of holy things which was getting rife in his own dominions. All these motives made him wish to give some striking proof that his faith was sound; and a suitable opportunity soon occurred. John Lambert, who had been a friend of Tyndal, was condemned in the Archbishop's Court for denying transubstantiation, and appealed to the King. Henry heard the cause in person at Whitehall, showed his animus against the prisoner by taunting him with having two names, forced him to say 'Aye' or 'No' without qualification to the question whether Christ's body is in the sacrament, crushed him with the text 'This is my Body,' and then left him to die, saying that 'the King would be no patron of heretics.' This was evidently no freak or accident, but the sign of a settled policy; the next chapter will show how it was to be carried out, how resisted, and in what the resistance was to end.

CHAPTER XV.

THE YORKIST CONSPIRACY. ANNE OF CLEVES. THE
SIX ARTICLES. THE FALL OF CROMWELL.

1538-1539.

IT seemed fated that revolts against Henry should fail for want of combination. This, as we have seen, had been the case with the conspiracy of the nobles and the two acts of the Pilgrimage of Grace; and now the fourth division of the same general movement was to be managed still more impotently, and to bring still wider ruin on its promoters. Lord Exeter and the Poles. The Six Articles.

The House of York was in 1538 chiefly represented by the Marquis of Exeter, whose mother, Lady Courtenay, was Edward IV.'s daughter, and by Lady Salisbury, who was daughter to George Duke of Clarence, niece to King Edward, and sister to the Earl of Warwick who had perished with Warbeck. The sons of this venerable lady were Lord Montagu, and Arthur, Reginald, and Geoffrey Pole. The Marquis of Exeter had unwillingly joined in the suppression of the Pilgrimage of Grace, yet remained bitterly hostile to Cromwell and the new teaching. Since then he had been complained of as hindering the course of justice in his own county; and now information came from members of his household that he was raising men in Cornwall with the view of getting himself named heir to the Crown, and from a painter at the turbulent Cornish village of St. Kevern that orders had been given for a banner of the Five Wounds. On farther enquiry it appeared that the tenacious Cornishmen had not forgotten Blackheath Field, and still longed to over-

O

throw the Tudor dynasty. That the Poles shared in the plot was presently made too clear by the cowardice of Sir Geoffrey, who, to shield himself, volunteered evidence that his brother Lord Montagu and Lord and Lady Exeter were all in correspondence with Cardinal Reginald Pole. The danger was serious; for other evidence showed that Paul III. was plotting a Spanish conquest of Ireland and had sent Pole to Liège that he might be near enough to hold all the threads of the intrigue together. And, worst of all, the Emperor had for some unexplained purpose collected 200 ships at Antwerp. The strongest measures were therefore adopted; Exeter and Montagu were put on their trial and condemned, not for the conspiracy, which it was better to keep as secret as possible, but as traitors in word; Lady Exeter and Lady Salisbury were attainted and imprisoned in the Tower. On this occasion Henry asked the Judges whether Parliament could attaint without giving any reason; their reply was that the question was dangerous, that Parliament is bound to set an example not of lawlessness, but of justice; yet that if it *did* so deal with any one, his attainder would hold. It might have been expected that being thus attacked by the Pope would have made Henry more Protestant; yet it had not this effect, as he seemed still anxious to prove himself as faithful as any rebel could be to the old religion, undeterred by a danger which after all had not been extreme. He also really hated, as we have seen, the spirit of ribaldry which had set in under pretence of religion. To meet this he first published an earnest and even touching exhortation to decent reverence in externals, and then, after proclaiming an amnesty for past offences against religion, set himself to consider how they might be prevented in future. Even on the principles of our own time some punishment was required to check disorder; for Bible-reading aloud in church had been made an excuse for interrupting the service and abusing its minister, and if a zealous Protestant disliked any church-ceremony, he was not unlikely to rate the clergyman performing it, and to tell him loudly that he 'did nought.' Some were reported as 'common singers against the sacraments and ceremonies,' others as players of interludes railing on the priesthood, others again as mimicking the elevation of the Host with the most odious profanity. To deal with this state of things, a Commission was formed of Cromwell, the two Archbishops, and six Bishops representing various parties; but, as these could not agree on their report, or at any rate did not send it in at once, the Duke of Norfolk moved in the House of Lords that Parliament as a whole should discuss the main points of controversy and settle the law concerning them. The result was an Act imposing by lay authority alone the celebrated 'Six Articles,' the very sound of which was thought certain to daunt the profane. In the first of these transubstantiation, the very antithesis to Protestantism, was again and finally affirmed; any one denying it was to be burned without any chance of saving himself by retraction. In the next four communion in one kind was asserted to be sufficient, the observance of vows of chastity was enjoined, and private masses and auricular confession maintained; whoever twice denied any of these was to suffer death as a felon. All marriages contracted by priests were pronounced void, and the wives were to be dismissed by a certain day. To refuse communion or confession was also felony.

Of course if this Act had been fully enforced, there would have been a persecution worthy of Alva or Torquemada. And for a few days the risk of this appeared considerable—as in the City of London, where the Roman party formed a committee at Mercers' Hall, and denounced not less than 500 of their fellow-citizens as heretics. But the King was not inclined to persecute on this scale; he allowed the accused to be securities for one another, and so dismissed them. Partly from his backwardness and partly from Cromwell's opposition, the Six Articles, though professedly in force for eight years, were really so only at intervals, and when Henry gave permission. As there were four of these short persecutions in the remainder of the reign, some of them specially cruel, and costing on the whole twenty-seven lives, the result of the Act is sufficiently lamentable not to need exaggerations; historians therefore should not have spoken of Gardiner and the Bishops as 'daily sending men to the stake' under it. One of its first consequences was that Cranmer sent his wife abroad, and Latimer and Shaxton were deprived of their sees. At about the same time an Act of Parliament vested the abbey lands in the King and those to whom he granted them, thus establishing, as Mr. Hallam remarks, the wealth of great families like the Russells, who were to be famous in after years, and at last to become the surest barrier against tyranny in England. So was completed the dissolution of the monasteries, which every historian must be glad at last to dismiss; unhappily some of its last scenes were also the ugliest, as when the Abbot of Glastonbury, who had hidden his plate in the hope of better times, was hanged for this crime at the top of the 'Tor' close by, to be seen far and wide across the Somersetshire plain.

In strong contrast with such horrors stands that admission of Wales into the English polity which is the most honourable thing Henry ever did; indeed its effect on

Welsh turbulence has been compared by Burke to the
'calming of the tempest when the "Twins"
are first seen above the horizon.' According *Legislation for Wales.*
to existing laws, no Welshman could buy land
or house in or near any city or town in the Marches, or be
a burgess of any corporate English town, or an apprentice
in any English town whatever. The manufacture and im-
port of armour were forbidden in Wales, and all Welsh
meetings were unlawful, except by special license. The
vernacular poet Glyn Cothi complains bitterly that his
furniture had been confiscated on his presuming to marry
an Englishwoman; had he been English and his wife
Welsh, he would have forfeited all franchises and made
himself a Welshman in the eye of the law. Unlike his
father, Henry VIII. thought much of the Principality in
the latter years of his reign; and it was settled by various
statutes that the English law alone should be current
there, that instead of the despotic jurisdiction of the Lords
Marchers justices of the peace should be established and
hold sessions in each county twice a year, that Welsh-
born subjects should have the same privileges as Englishmen, and that each county and each county town should
send a member to Parliament. As raids into England
might still happen, it was ordered that no ferry-boat
should take any Welshman acrose the Severn by night.
And, by way of complement to this, English disorder was
repressed by the vigour of Roland Lee, the Warden of the
Marches, both in Cheshire, which had long presumed on
its privileges as a County Palatine not subject to the royal
courts by sending bands out to plunder neighbouring
counties, and in Shropshire and Herefordshire, which
used their position on the border for the same purpose.

When Henry's hand was refused by the Duchess of
Milan, Cromwell, finding the Six Articles passed in spite

of him, devised a singularly bold plan for saving Protestantism in England by marrying Henry to some lady who would lead him in that direction. Anne, sister to the Duke of Cleves, seemed well suited for this purpose; for the Duke was a Protestant, and his dominions, which included Juliers, Berg, and part of Hanover, placed him in the closest connection with the Protestant States of Hesse and Saxony, and with Hermann Archbishop of Cologne,

The alliance with Cleves. Fall of Cromwell.

CLEVES, MARK, BERG, JULIERS.

who was already showing the Protestant tendencies which led to his deposition in 1543. He was therefore a most important member of the 'Smalkaldic League' against the Emperor, which had been formed in 1531, and had on the 10th of July, 1536, been enlarged and renewed for ten years, the contingent of troops which each of its members was to supply being also arranged against emergencies. Moreover he had claims on Gelderland,

which, if established, would make his territory like an
open gate for any one wishing to attack the Emperor
either in Holland or Germany, and having France for an
ally. Cromwell therefore threw his whole force into the
negotiation, hoping thus to checkmate the party which
had carried the Six Articles and which wished to see
Charles invade England. On the 27th of December,
1539, the lady landed at Deal; on the 31st Henry met her
at Rochester and found her lamentably unlike Holbein's
portrait, quite devoid of accomplishments, knowing no
language but her own, and much marked with the small-
pox. His consternation was extreme; he could hardly
utter a word, and forgot to take from his pocket the
present which he had prepared. Foreigners in those
days were sometimes half surprised and more than half
amused at our caring so much for female beauty; and
Henry was as English in this point as his father had
been. Hardly would he have submitted to such an
infliction even for a cherished purpose of his own, much
less for one with which he only half sympathised. Could
not a pre-contract be made out? No, the lady was very
decidedly free; and after all it would not do to throw
the Duke into the alliance between Charles and Francis,
which was now assuming the most threatening appearance, Charles being actually on a visit to the French
Court and ominously refusing all enquiry into the treatment of Englishmen in Spain by the Inquisition. So the
marriage took place on the 6th of January, 1540, hateful
though it was to the bridegroom, and unpopular because
of the risk from it to Flemish trade. For the next
five months a life-and-death struggle went on between
the two religious parties. Cromwell seemed for a while
to be scoring at all points. He was created Earl of
Essex on the 17th of April, and afterwards a Knight of

the Garter, and succeeded in imprisoning some of his antagonists or driving them from the Council. It was expected every day that Gardiner would be sent to the Tower. The minister also carried the attainder of some priests, once of Queen Katherine's household, who had been 'contumacious' ever since; and succeeded in checking the action of the Six Articles, and in abolishing many rights of sanctuary. But all the time his main scheme was collapsing miserably. He could not persuade Francis to join the league of Protestant Germany, and its members in alarm made their peace with Charles for the time. This was the opportunity for which Cromwell's enemies had been waiting; now their charges, carefully gathered for years, might securely be hurled at him. On the 10th of June Henry allowed him to be arrested at the Council-table, the other members loudly proclaiming him a traitor and tearing the ribbon of the Garter from his neck. He was immediately attainted on eight charges, the substance of which was that he had planned to crush the nobles of England, and to form a confederacy of heretics in the country by means of which he might raise a rebellion. He was truly or falsely sworn to have said that, if the King and realm varied from his opinions, he would fight against them sword in hand, and that, if he lived a year or two, he would bring matters to such a state, that the King would have no power to change it even if he desired. Events then rushed on with lightning speed. The attainder was passed by acclamation about the 19th of June; on the 1st of July Norfolk and the new government carried a Bill for the better observance of the Six Articles; on the 7th the King's late marriage was brought before Convocation and annulled on the wonderful plea that it had been 'extorted under compulsion by external causes;' on the

12th an Act of Parliament was carried to the same effect, and Anne of Cleves, intending to remain in England, was endowed with 3,000*l*. a year and the grotesque title of the 'King's Sister.' On the 28th Cromwell laid his head on the block, and two days later Barnes, Garrett, and Jerome, who had rashly put themselves forward as opponents of Gardiner, were sent to the stake as gainsayers of the Six Articles ; the priests attainted by Cromwell being hanged at the same place and time for denying the Supremacy. Soon after this, Parliament, which had in the previous year given to Henry's proclamations the force of laws (thus going near to establish a kind of Turkish despotism in the State), did nearly the same in Church matters by enabling a committee of the Archbishops, Bishops, and certain doctors of divinity acting with the King's sanction (that is, the King himself) to declare absolutely the judgment of the English Church on all questions of theology, whether raised here or on the Continent, and to enforce it by pains and penalties.

In April of this year, James V. of Scotland, on his way back from France, stopped for a short time off Scarborough and boldly received a deputation of Yorkshire gentlemen asking for the help against Henry which he was well disposed to grant. *The Reformation in Scotland.* After 1524 he had soon begun drifting back towards the French alliance. True the negotiations for his marriage with Mary were more than once renewed, but neither side would take the first step—the Scottish statesmen declaring that a lasting peace would be easy after the marriage, and Henry wishing for a reliable treaty before it. Till Margaret's divorce from Angus was granted in 1528, and she was allowed to marry a new favourite, Lord Methuen, she had been quite resolved 'to seek for help wherever she could find it ;'

and as none came from Henry, this meant that she would appeal to France. Therefore two political parties became clearly defined; that of Lords Angus, Lennox, Murray, Glencairn, and Sir George Douglas, who were prepared to go all lengths for the English connection, being opposed to Methuen, Arran, and James and David Beton, successive Archbishops of St. Andrew's, who were in the French interest. From 1528 forward the beginnings of the Reformation in England made the Scots anti-reformers, inclined to ally themselves with our enemies still more closely, and to mark their religious zeal by persecution. Thus Patrick Hamilton, the protomartyr of the Scottish Reformation, was burned in that year ' for denying pilgrimage, purgatory, prayer to the saints, and such trifles,' says Knox; and for some time there was an exodus from Scotland of gentlemen and clerks escaping with their lives from charges of reading the Bible in English, and asking Lord Dacre for relief when they were across the Border. James, as time went on, was heard to boast that he was to be made Duke of York, not by his uncle, but by the Emperor; and when Henry went to York to have an interview with him, the rash young man was induced by the bribes of the Church party to break his engagement, thus giving up the chance of seeing how widely different from his own kingdom was that which might fall to him as Henry's son-in-law, and which his grandson was at length to inherit. As the Catholic partisans were quite determined to stop the English negotiations altogether, they also induced James to marry Magdalen, the beautiful, but delicate daughter of Francis I., who died within a few months from the change of climate. It was in bringing home his bride that he received the Scarborough deputation, and heard how they were ' robbed and murdered' and how much they longed for him to come and 'have all.' On arriving at Leith he bade farther defiance to England by prosecuting some of Angus's relations and supporters; his sister, Lady Glamis, a woman of great beauty and intelligence, was burned alive for treason, as Lady Bulmer had been in England. After Magdalen's death, Henry renewed his advances; but found James fatally resolved on a second French wife, Mary of Guise, the widow of the Duc de Longueville, whom he married in June 1538. Henry meanwhile was preparing two deadly blows against his recreant nephew. The first of these was an attempt to get him kidnapped while hunting on the Border. A paper still remains in which the English Council remark that they find in the scheme 'many difficulties, above all the risk of a struggle in which James might be killed, and the infamy thence arising.' They admit that the proposer, Sir Robert Wharton, an English commander on the Border, may have had a 'good meaning' in proposing it, but think that he ought to be strictly charged to carry it no farther, and not to communicate it to any living creature. The second scheme bore a still more threatening aspect; for Henry ordered that search should be made by Lee, the Archbishop of York, for all ancient records of homage paid by Scotland to England, manifestly intending to take up this old quarrel where Edward II. had been compelled to leave it. He also allowed his Parliament in an address to him to call James an 'usurper of the kingdom which rightly belonged to his Majesty.'

Thus the two parties were bent on a war which might have wrecked the fortunes of both countries. Fortunately neither possessed organising power sufficient for a great enterprise; and though each side was well inclined to push on with reckless haste, material of war was

Solway Moss. Death of James V. Attempts at Union.

almost entirely wanting. The Duke of Norfolk was ordered to advance with 30,000 men by Berwick to the Lothians, but provisions soon failed him, and he was obliged to disband his troops for fear of starvation On this James vindictively insisted on crossing the Eske and ravaging Cumberland ; but the nobles told him that they had done their feudal duty in defending Scotland, and had no idea of going any farther. Maddened at their refusal, he declared that they were all traitors, and not obscurely hinted that he should sweep off a hundred of them by proscription. Meanwhile he called for volunteers, who were to meet at Lochmaben and receive their orders there ; and about 10,000 men obeyed the summons. It was only when they were already in England that they found they were to be commanded, not by the King in person, but by Oliver Sinclair, a most unpopular Court-favourite. This produced a commotion in the army, in the midst of which they were suddenly charged by a few hundreds of English Border horsemen. Imagining that Norfolk was upon them, they actually turned and fled homewards ; but, missing the way, most of them reached the Solway when the tide was up, and were either drowned in attempting to cross it or taken prisoners on the English side. The King had remained at Caerlaverock Castle during the expedition ; he now returned in the deepest dejection to Falkland, with bad news dogging him at every step and his health daily drooping more and more. His two infant sons had both died shortly before, and Mary of Guise was expecting her third confinement at Edinburgh. On the 7th of December, 1542, the news came of the birth of another Mary, so soon to be known by the fated name ' Queen of Scots.' 'It came with a lass and it will go with a lass,' said the hapless father, in allusion to the throne coming to the Stewarts by a daughter of Bruce ; and a week latter he died, leaving the government in the hands of the Earl of Arran, the head of the Hamiltons, who claimed it because of his father's marriage with James III.'s sister, which made him next of kin to the infant Queen. The new Regent at once imprisoned the leaders of the French party, and wrote to Henry a letter of appeal, asking indulgence for the baby kinswoman who, by a calamity which seemed to bring back the days of Flodden, was now the hope of her country. Henry replied by offering to marry his son to the infant, and strongly endeavouring to win over the prisoners of Solway Moss to his plan, which was that Mary should at once be sent to England for education, that Edinburgh, Stirling, and Dumbarton should receive English garrisons, and that Cardinal Beton, the great enemy of England, should be transferred to an English prison. The Scots on their part were willing to accept of the marriage, but only on the absurd condition that, if ever the two crowns were on one head, an independent Regency of Scotland should for the time belong of right to the Arran family. Henry's other conditions would, they declared, be resisted by every man, woman, and child in Scotland. After much uncertainty, a treaty was at last signed at Greenwich (July 1, 1543) providing for an alliance between the countries during the life of the two sovereigns, and one year more ; the Queen was now to be allowed to stay with her mother till the age of ten. In case the crowns were united, the liberties of Scotland were fully guaranteed ; if the infant Mary ever became a childless widow, she was to resume possession of her kingdom in peace. The settlement seemed hopeful, yet the bond was torn up almost before it was drawn by the audacity of Cardinal Beton, who carried off Mary from Linlithgow to Stirling Castle, where she was in the power of his partisans; and on this even Arran himself, unable any longer to stem the torrent of popular longing for independence, joined the Romish party, cancelled the Greenwich treaty, withdrew a recently granted permission to read the Bible, and announced that heretics would be prosecuted according to Church law. Though the murder of Beton in 1546 at St. Andrews (to which Henry, as Mr. Burton has fully shown, was accessory before the fact) seemed likely to help towards union with England, yet it had the opposite effect; for in the year after the Cardinal's death many of the most vigorous spirits of the English party (including John Knox), after holding St. Andrews for a time, were captured by a French army and sent as prisoners to France, leaving no one who could supply their place. It was little comfort that an English force under Lords Lisle and Hertford captured and burned Leith and Edinburgh in the following year, besides wasting Fifeshire, which seldom suffered in such wars. The burning of 243 villages and 192 towns was not the way to produce kinder feelings in Scotland, or make the people more content to accept real union.

Ireland had also had its own disorders after the death of Lord Thomas Fitzgerald in 1537. Lord Leonard Grey, his captor, was ordered to put down resistance to English authority in the West. To this task he bravely addressed himself, storming various castles on the Shannon, and, above all, capturing 'Brene's Bridge' over that river near Limerick, which was so strongly fortified with marble works that artillery could make no impression on it, while the ramparts themselves could be approached only across two broken arches which had to be spanned with scaling-ladders. But the tide of victory was almost immediately checked by want of money; and it was too clear that the

Lord Leonard Grey in Ireland.

Irish government was farther than ever from the chance of paying its own way. Stung by this disappointment, Lord Leonard was thenceforward at constant variance with his Council, whom he treated most harshly and overbearingly; while on service he disgusted his best officers by requiring the impossible and disgracing them if they refused to attempt it. The Dublin Parliament now ventured on throwing out a Bill for the dissolution of the Irish monasteries; and enmity to England daily produced the same effects as in Scotland, making the people more and more ardent partisans of Rome. At this juncture Cromwell's fall began to be expected; and Grey, who was intimate with the Duke of Norfolk, thought that he might further a reaction in Ireland, such as his leader was accomplishing at home. He therefore favoured the bishops most opposed to the Reformation, and went so far as to entrust many important charges to the ever-rebellious Fitzgerald family—with which, as we have seen, he was connected by marriage—and to maintain a bishop made by the Pope, whose appointment he was expressly ordered to disallow. All this, too, was during the perilous times when the fear of the Emperor's invading Ireland was not yet at an end. He then made a progress through the rebellious districts, and reported to Henry that his reception had been most excellent. But even he himself soon discovered that he had been deceived; his new friends were manifestly conspiring to promote the foreign invasion, and in October, 1539, he had to attack and defeat the rebellious chiefs on the borders of Ulster. After this he reconciled himself with Ormond and the loyalist nobles whom he had offended, and asked for a few weeks' leave of absence from his government. This was allowed, but his *locum tenens*, Sir W. Brereton, soon informed Henry of new insurrections, the direct effects of Grey's wrongheadedness. The King sent the Deputy to the Tower, and ordered the chief members of the Irish Council to come over and give their evidence against him. It was sworn that Grey had abused those who spoke ill of Cardinal Pole, that he had taken bribes from Irish chiefs, had connived at their attacks on the more loyal, and had released from prison, untried, men who had been committed for treason. Above all the incredible charge was hinted, though not expressly made against him, that he had left behind him in the West some of the King's guns, with the intention that they should be found and used by the invaders. In hope of mercy, Grey pleaded guilty to his actual indictment, and was executed on the 28th of June, 1540. St. Leger, his successor in office, carried out the suppression of the monasteries, and by judicious distribution of the spoils managed to procure for the home-government a certain respite from Irish troubles.

The King within a few days of his release from Anne of Cleves married Katherine Howard, another niece of the Duke of Norfolk, a fascinating girl of nineteen, for whose perfections he was strongly inclined to have a special service of thanksgiving drawn up. The poor creature had, however, young as she was, dishonoured herself before marriage, and now felt obliged, as Queen, to give appointments about her person by way of hush-money to the very men who ought to have kept farthest from her. All her terrible secrets soon came out; and to Cranmer was entrusted the commission of telling Henry how he had been deceived. The only chance of life which remained to Katherine was that she should make the common 'pre-contract' excuse; but, with a truthfulness which went far to redeem her errors, she refused to make

Katherine Howard. Death of Lady Salisbury.

any such statement, and was attainted in Parliament for high treason, and beheaded on the 12th of February, 1542; with her suffered Lady Rochford, who had before done much to ruin her sister-in-law Anne Boleyn. On the 27th of May in the preceding year the noble old Countess of Salisbury, almost the only remaining Plantagenet, was accused for continuing, or being supposed to continue, a treasonable correspondence with her son Cardinal Pole. She loudly asserted her innocence on the scaffold, refusing to kneel at the block, and telling the executioner that he might get her head as he could—a proceeding which was considered strangely presumptuous and undutiful. Somewhat more to Henry's credit was the execution of Lord Dacre of the South, with three companions, for having caused the death of a gamekeeper while engaged, by way of a frolic, in shooting deer in a neighbour's park without leave asked. Thus sternly was the principle vindicated that homicide is murder if done in the course of an action otherwise illegal; yet true equity would have inflicted death only on the person who actually struck the fatal blow.

CHAPTER XVI.

HENRY'S LAST FRENCH WAR. CLOSE AND RESULTS OF THE REIGN.

1541.

SELDOM has royal ambition exposed Europe to such deadly peril and suffering as when in the latter part of Francis I.'s reign he joined with the Turks. Even at the moment when he gave up his sword at Pavia, he ordered a servant instantly to take his ring to the Sultan as an appeal for

Charles V. fails at Algiers.

P

help. And in the times which followed his liberation from captivity he constantly used the Turkish alliance for the purposes of his ambition, inducing Sultan Soliman to attack Austria and Hungary and to send his corsairs to all the seaboard of the Empire, while he himself, with a child's pertinacity, tried once more for Milan. Charles V., on the contrary, though his difficulties both from France and from the Protestant States of Germany were immense, still carried on a determined war against the Porte. He had always intended to make his conquest of Tunis in 1535 the stepping-stone to Algiers, which was a more important focus of piracy, and nearer his Spanish dominions. To carry out this plan, he sent thither a magnificent fleet and army in October, 1541, in spite of all warning that it was too late in the year for such an expedition. The result was that a storm came on before the troops could land their material, and half the ships and men were miserably lost. Francis, overjoyed at his rival's defeat, forthwith arranged attacks upon him from Constantinople and Venice on the one side, and from Denmark, Sweden, and the German Protestant League on the other. The scheme was detestable on many grounds; for it gave a fresh spur to Soliman, who had in the previous July overthrown the combined forces of Austria and Hungary and occupied the latter country; besides which Francis was fully purposed to atone for his alliance with Mohammedans and Protestants abroad by the most horrid of religious persecutions at home. His military plan was that in the summer of 1543 the Turkish fleets should ravage all Charles's Italian seaboard, while he himself should invade the Emperor's dominions by the open gates of Gelderland and Cleves.

But by this time Henry, vexed indeed at some French backslidings in money matters and at their support of his enemies in Scotland, but also acting at last upon reasons of sound European policy, had agreed with the Emperor that Francis must be compelled to break his present alliance with the Turks and to repay to Charles and the Diet the money spent by them on the earlier Turkish wars which he had occasioned. *Henry joins Charles against Francis and the Turks.* The first-fruits of this combination were the rejection, already related, of the Greenwich Treaty by the French party in Scotland, and the final breaking down of the scheme of union. The war began at once; and Charles, with Gardiner attending him as English commissioner, stormed the city of Düren, massacred its inhabitants, and forced the Duke of Cleves to beg for mercy. About 10,000 Englishmen joined their great ally at the siege of Landrécies, which had been taken and fortified as a place of arms by the French earlier in the year. The politic Charles expressed the utmost admiration for his confederates, declaring that he would live and die with them, and they should be his guards. While the siege went on, the French fleet in the Mediterranean was actually co-operating with the Algerine pirate Barbarossa in an attack on Nice, the last possession which Francis had left to the Duke of Savoy. This alliance, however, was ultimately fatal to Francis's plans; for it excited such horror in Germany that Charles was able at the Diet of Spires to proclaim war anew in the name of the whole Empire against the *two* enemies of Christendom, whose fleets, he said, were at that moment riding side by side in a Provençal harbour. The Diet voted 24,000 men and an universal poll-tax. Henry on his part persisted in the war in order to weaken French influence on Scotland. He had now reinforced his army up to 30,000 men, and had also 25,000 Germans under his command. With these he agreed to march on Paris from the north, while the Emperor reached it by the valley of the Marne. Fortunately for France this scheme was not carried out. Henry, whose many wars had taught him little generalship, stopped to besiege Boulogne, which held out till September 14, and thus by its steadiness made Henry miss the rendezvous. Finding that he could not make head alone against the French, Charles fell back on Soissons, and, breaking his engagement not to make a separate peace, signed the treaty of Crépy, by which Francis agreed to abandon the Turks, to help in the recovery of Hungary from them, and to join Charles in his suspended struggle with Protestantism. The Emperor wanted, in fact, one thing above all others, the defeat and dispersion of the Smalkaldic League, which had become much stronger and more dangerous by the accession of Denmark. Indeed he was not wrong in supposing that events were now deciding the future of religion in Europe. Up to this time there had been hope that the Protestants might rejoin Rome, and in 1541 the most evangelical members of the Papal Church had held a conference at Ratisbon to bring this about. But it had failed, and its Italian members had either decided to become Protestants or contented themselves with adhering to Catholicism as it was. As this kind of conciliation had become impossible, Pope Paul III. resolved to reform the Church of Rome on her own principles, and with Jesuitism and the Inquisition for her mainstays. For this purpose he gave notice that the first session of the long-expected Council would be held on March 15, 1545, at Trent in the Tyrol. To this the Protestants were not to be admitted, even if they still desired it; indeed one of the first resolutions of the Council was for the sterner war against them which led to their defeat at Mühlberg in 1547.

Francis on his side was equally determined to put down heresy in his own dominions; indeed, as soon as the peace of Crépy made Protestant allies needless, he seized the opportunity to murder 3,000 inoffensive Vaudois. But he was quite equally anxious to revenge himself for the fright which England had given him by the invasion of France; therefore, collecting in Normandy a fleet of 235 vessels of all sizes, he directed part of them to convey a force to Scotland, and the rest to make a descent at the nearest point of England, while his land army blockaded the Castle of Boulogne. As in the case of the Armada long afterwards, an untoward accident marked the starting; for the King's cooks set fire by carelessness to the largest vessel of the fleet, on board which he was giving an entertaiment. On the 18th of July, 1545, the ships were off the Isle of Wight. Our fleet, of only sixty ships, being not strong enough to defend the Solent, ran for the shelter of the batteries, and a calm ensuing, was in great danger from the enemy's galleys, which could fire at the ships without suffering in return, as their oars enabled them to move about quickly and thus baffle the English aim. Presently a breeze sprang up, and we advanced again; but one large vessel, the 'Mary Rose,' was either sunk, as French accounts will have it, by their fire, or, according to our own, lost—as the 'Eurydice' was in our own memory—by heeling over too far, so that the sea came through her lower-deck ports. Annebaut, the French admiral, then proposed to run up and bombard Portsmouth; but the pilots declared it impossible either to carry the fleet through the obstacles, or, if this were done, to anchor in such a tideway. He then landed

French attack on Portsmouth.

several bodies of men on the Isle of Wight, with the intention of holding and fortifying several points in it; but the Act of 1487 had long ago restored its population, and the militia under Sir Edward Bellingham were able to frustrate all such attempts. Finding he could make no impression, Annebaut then ran over to France, discharged most of his land forces, and, returning to the English coast, made a descent at Seaford, which the Sussex militia dealt with, and seemed on the point of fighting with Lords Lisle and Surrey off Shoreham. But the hot August weather spoiled his provisions and bred disease in his still crowded vessels; his chance was over, and he was obliged to retreat to Havre. Though the French pressed with all vigour the siege of Boulogne, or rather of the old citadel on the heights whose picturesque ramparts still remain, yet Sir Edward Poynings held out for the whole winter of 1545, with typhus ravaging both armies, and in the next June Henry agreed to surrender the place in eight years for a ransom of 5,000,000 francs. In the treaty of peace Scotland was included, so that French influence still remained supreme there.

Next came, as usual, the difficulty of finding the million and a half which the war had cost. A Benevolence had been raised for it in 1545—it was then that Alderman Rock, on refusing his quota, was ordered off for service as a private soldier on the Scottish Border. This had produced about 60,000*l*., and the remains of a subsidy were still available; the balance was now provided by a debasement of the currency—of all modes of taxation the one which creates most distress, by throwing all contracts into disorder, reducing the value of fixed wages and incomes, and making recovery impossible by driving good money out

The currency debased.

of circulation. Yet Henry by a succession of tamperings reduced the quantity of silver in an ounce of coin first to half an ounce, and later to six pennyweights nearly— the regular quantity being rather more than eighteen pennyweights. The evil therefore was a growing one; nor was it remedied till the first year of Elizabeth, when the coinage was at length restored by the means so graphically described by Mr. Froude.

Peace was concluded with France on the 5th of June, 1546; a trifling quarrel had all but plunged us meantime into a war with the Emperor. For an English captain, when ill-treated and robbed by the Inquisition in Spain, had retaliated on the first Spanish vessel which he met at sea. Henry refused to surrender the man, as he had been wronged first; therefore Charles put an embargo on English vessels in his ports, and we in turn seized two Spanish treasure-ships in the Channel. Fortunately wiser counsels at last prevailed, and no war followed.

Before the end of the French conflict Lord Surrey had been deeply vexed at finding himself superseded in the command by Lord Hertford; and, the King's death being shortly expected, he seems to have made known without the least caution his views on the situation. 'In case of God taking his Majesty to himself,' the proper guardian for the young Prince Edward would, he declared, be his father, the Duke of Norfolk. Others bore witness that he had said —not indeed to them, but to others—that when the King died he, Surrey, would deal sharply with the low-born Privy Councillors. Another charge was, considering the ideas of the time, a very serious one indeed. The Duchess, Surrey's mother, was a daughter of the late Duke of Buckingham; hence, as we have seen, Surrey could claim royal descent, and he had some time before

Execution of Lord Surrey.

applied to the Heralds' College to be allowed to quarter the royal arms on the first instead of the second division of his shield, which only the family of the reigning king were entitled to do. It must be recollected that Henry had in 1528 ordered a heraldic visitation of the country which was to be repeated every thirty years; and such an assumption as Surrey's was an offence which had been severely dealt with in the case of Edward Hastings, who was imprisoned for sixteen years for not submitting his coat to the judgment of a Court Military. Moreover the precise alteration made by Surrey had both precedent and explanation in the case of Edward III., who symbolised his claim to the throne of France by transferring the lilies from the second to the first quarter of his shield. No doubt, therefore, such a change was constructively treasonable; and the notion of degrees in treason or of any punishment for it short of death never seems to have found its way into the absolute logic of Henry's mind. Another charge against Lord Surrey was that he 'delighted to converse with foreigners and conform his behaviour to theirs'—an unkindly one, surely, to bring against the poet who had done so much to infuse Italian grace into the rugged forms of English poetry. His own sister, the widowed Duchess of Richmond, contributed to his ruin by confessing, when questioned by the Council, that Surrey had urged her to use her personal attractions to captivate her father-in-law; but Henry's state of health since Richmond's death in 1536 suggests that there must have been some misunderstanding here. On these charges (or some of them) Surrey was tried at the Guildhall, condemned, and executed; the Duke, his father, was attainted in Parliament, and saved only by Henry's death a few hours before the time appointed for him to go the way of More and Cromwell. Considering that the evidence in these cases was chiefly hearsay, we may hope that they tended to produce the Act which immediately afterwards made it capital to bring anonymous charges of treason without afterwards coming forward to prove them.

Of the second persecution under the Six Articles the date is unknown; five persons perished in it. The next was in 1543, when Filmer, Testwood, and Peerson were burned under Windsor Castle for unseemly jesting on religion, and Merbeck, the Church musician to whom the manner of intoning our services is mainly due, narrowly escaped the same fate—it is said for making a Concordance of the New Testament. 'Poor innocents!' Henry had exclaimed, on hearing how the men died; and in the same spirit he now interfered to protect the deposed Bishop Latimer, and a physician named Huick who appealed to him. In 1546 the fourth and last persecution took place, when Lascelles, a gentleman of the Bedchamber, a priest named Belemian, and Adams, a tailor, suffered for the still unpardonable offence of denying transubstantiation. But their fame has been eclipsed by that of Anne Ascue, a young and beautiful woman who was accused on the same point. With the consequences full in view, this heroine wrote, as an account of her belief, 'The bread is but a remembrance of His death, or a sacrament of thanksgiving for it.' It gives a thrill of anger even now to hear that the Lord Chancellor and Solicitor-General tortured her again and again to find out who favored her. She was burned, and the place watched all night, to hinder her friends from doing reverence to her ashes and arrest them if they tried. A little earlier than this an Act of Parliament had placed in Henry's hands the 'chantries' of the kingdom

Henry's last persecutions; his last foundations.

—that is, the innumerable foundations for private masses in cathedrals and other churches—and with them the 'colleges and hospitals,' requesting him to take the property 'for his wars and the maintenance of his dignity.' At the Universities Henry used the power thus given him to compel the surrender of several Cambridge halls and to found Trinity College out of their collective property; its larger endowments, however, are due not to him but to Queen Mary. In the same spirit Henry left to the citizens of London the ancient Priory of St. Bartholomew to be a hospital for the poor.

Within a few days of the death of Katherine Howard the King married Katherine Parr, the widow of the Lord Latimer who had been engaged in the Pilgrimage of Grace and pardoned after it. This lady was a most kind stepmother to all his children, and a first-rate nurse to himself. Her Cambridge correspondents called her 'Regina doctissima,' and their admiration is justified by her book of devotion called the 'Lamentacion of a Sinner.' She was inclined to Protestantism, her almoner being Miles Coverdale; is said to have interceded for Merbeck, and certainly contributed much to the conviction for perjury of Dr. London, who, after distinguishing himself in the Visitation of the Monasteries, had undertaken the congenial task of forging evidences in cases of heresy. This made Chancellor Wriothesley and Bishop Gardiner her bitter enemies; and, according to Lord Herbert of Cherbury, they succeeded in inducing the King to have articles of heresy drawn out against her, as having received forbidden books from her sister, Lady Herbert. Henry, it appears, had been annoyed by her pressing him strongly to allow the general use of the translated Bible, and therefore gave his consent to the articles; Wriothesley, however, accidentally dropped

Katherine Parr.

the paper containing them, and thus it came to Katherine's knowledge. She at first gave herself up for lost, but presently succeeded in persuading her husband that, if she had ever spoken to him on theology, it was in order to be herself instructed. It is supposed that the torture of Anne Ascue was intended to elicit evidence against the Queen; but if so, it failed signally of its purpose.

On Friday the 28th of January, 1547, Norfolk was to die at nine in the morning; but when that time struck Henry had been dead eight hours, and the Duke was safe. Late on the preceding evening the King had been told that his end was near; on which he characteristically said that as his physicians had condemned him, their work was over, and he wanted no more interference from them. He would send for no one but Cranmer, and put this off so long that when the Archbishop arrived he could only press his hand as a sign that he looked for mercy through Christ. He desired to be buried at Windsor in the same tomb with Queen Jane; and, like his father, ordered that masses should be said there 'perpetually while the world shall endure.' Finally with unwavering faith he asked for the intercession of the Blessed Virgin and the Saints. During his absence at Boulogne in 1544 Queen Katherine had been his Regent; but, to her great disappointment, she found the power given by Henry's will to a Council of Regency headed by Cranmer. As Parliament had in 1536 allowed the King to dispose of the crown by will, he placed first Mary and then Elizabeth in succession after Edward, on condition that they married only with the royal consent. Foreseeing in all probability the marriage which so very soon took place between Katherine and Sir Thomas Seymour, the lover from whom he had taken her, he allowed her only a moderate provision.

Death of Henry.

At his death Henry left the Church still under the Six Articles, though procedure according to them had on purpose been made more difficult. Its position had also been defined by the 'Necessary Doctrine and Erudition of a Christian Man' (generally called the 'King's Book'), which was printed for the first time in 1544, having been accepted by Parliament in the previous year. Many of its statements are, as we might expect, more Roman in tone than those of its predecessor, the 'Bishops' Book.' But fortunately for the Church there had grown up besides these formularies something of far better omen for the future. Erasmus had adopted in the years from 1516 to 1535 the bold course of publishing successive editions of the Greek Testament based upon, in great part, though not entirely, the evidence of MSS.; this was in effect a declaration that St. Jerome's Latin translation, generally called the Vulgate, had not really the final and conclusive authority ascribed to it by the Roman Church. His Paraphrases also set the good example of explaining all passages with their full context, instead of taking a verse here and there and drawing random inferences from it, in the manner of which we have seen an example in the discussions on the exemption of the clergy from the civil Courts. Moreover, the Bible had, as we have seen, been twice translated, and though Tyndal suffered martyrdom at Vilvorde, and the circulation of his English Bible was fenced about with many restrictions and sometimes nearly stopped, it had still been publicly declared to be 'the only touchstone of true learning.' The Lord's Prayer and the Ten Commandments had been taught in English since 1539; in 1543 and 1544 English litanies were used by authority, and Cranmer also translated the Te Deum and other hymns 'in order that all

Henry's influence on the Church.

such as were ignorant of any strange or foreign speech might have what to pray in their own familiar and acquainted tongue with fruit and understanding. Thus everything was ready for the great work of Edward's first years, the drawing up of the Book of Common Prayer in a form like that which we still have, though in some points nearer to that now used by the Episcopal Churches in Scotland and America. Roman Catholic writers have constantly assumed not only that these formularies are heretical, but that the effect of Henry's ordinances has been to enslave the Church of England to the State. The former of these points can hardly be discussed in a work like the present. On the latter it will be enough to remark once more that at the time it was absolutely necessary to check the use by the clergy of their independent powers. It deeply concerned the very being of religion in England that priests should neither kill their parishioners for Christ's sake, nor plot against their property, nor claim immunity from crime as a privilege of their order; hardly anything, indeed, could be more violent and therefore more anti-Christian than their attempts to compel belief by penalties. It cannot be doubted that Henry's Parliament did rightly in depriving them of powers so much misused; nor has anything since occurred to make us wish the changes undone. It has been well that the sturdy sense of Parliament should have to be persuaded before religious changes could be made; well, too, at least in times when the people have cared for religion, that bishops should be chosen, not according to the narrow standard of purely clerical electors, but by a Minister of the Crown who, with every reason both of feeling and interest to select wise and practical men for the office, can also resist currents of temporary Church feeling and in some degree see events as history will see them. Under no other institutions, perhaps, would the Church, by losing step by step all compulsory powers, have been so wholesomely trained and so perpetually encouraged to rely on persuasion only, thus gaining a strength which she never could have dreamed of in her masterful days. And although agitation has sometimes been created in our own time by the sentences of certain civil Courts in Church questions, yet such judgments have been generally acquiesced in when the immediate stir has been over, and found not in any way to lower the Church or to fetter her development. It would be hard to point to any one good thing desired by the Church which has been hindered by her relations to the State, or to any evil thing to which they have given a longer life. If uncorrected abuses still exist, we may be sure that they remain so because members of the Church have not yet made up their minds that they are intolerable, and not because, the law being what it is, such things must needs live on to vex us however much we may dislike them.

The laws affecting religion occupy so large a space in this reign that those on civil matters are apt to escape notice, though many of them well deserve to be remembered. Such were those affecting beggars, who, if really impotent, were to have written leave to ask alms in a specified district; if 'whole and mighty in body' were to be whipped the first time they begged and sent home to their own parish, where by another law the overseers were bound to employ them. If any such person offended a second time, the gristle of his ear was to be cut off, besides a whipping; and for a third offence he was to die as an enemy of the commonwealth. On the same principle of hatred to people with no visible livelihood all Gypsies were in 1530 sent out of the country.

Civil laws of Henry VIII.

Another kind of poverty which the age would not tolerate was that of the 'poor and broken bankrupt;' it was held that 'the crime and its name were both of foreign growth,' and the surrender of all the insolvent's property would never give him a discharge till the last farthing was paid. An Act of 1546 repealed the old laws of usury, allowing interest to be charged up to 10 per cent.

New felonies were created under Henry VIII. as quickly and easily as when Burke made his celebrated protest against them. It became felony to cut dykes in Norfolk or the Isle of Ely, to sell horses to Scotchmen, to poach fish between six in the evening and six in the morning, to come masked into a royal park in order to kill deer, to steal young hawks or peacocks, or to burn any frame of timber prepared for building a house. New treasons were still more profusely invented, going far beyond the old definition of Edward III., which almost limited the crime to the three cases of levying war against the King, compassing his death, or adhering to his enemies. For Henry's Parliament declared at different times that those were traitors who 'took, judged, or *believed*' the marriages with Katherine of Aragon or Anne of Cleves to have been valid, who impugned the marriage with Anne Boleyn, who called the King a heretic, schismatic, or usurper, who married any of the King's family without his permission, who married the King himself without revealing past lapses, or who disobeyed any royal proclamation and then escaped from the kingdom. Lastly, in one peculiar case such a law was *ex post facto*. A cook named Rouse had tried to poison his master, the Bishop of Rochester, and caused the death of two persons; such acts were therefore made treasonable by a general law, which mentioned him by name and sentenced him to be boiled to death.

If from the laws against crime we pass on to the manner in which the Courts administered them, it is too plain that hardly any sound principles of justice were known or thought of. Else how could it have been that hardly any prisoners of state were ever acquitted? Experience has taught us that evidence is generally worthless unless cross-examined, but rarely indeed had an accused person any such chance then; not to mention that the bad habit of prosecuting, not for the crime, but for just so much as would bring the accused under the letter of the law, must have destroyed the chances of showing discrepancy in the evidence which there would have been if the witnesses had been forced to state all they knew. Of course a government which so administers justice must be cynically indifferent to one of its prime duties, that of showing unmistakably to all men, even to the culprit himself, that if the law strikes him it is because he has thoroughly deserved it. Not all Englishmen of the time had Cromwell's Italian unscrupulousness—learned, as he himself said, from Macchiavelli—as to the means by which his ends were to be accomplished; but it is not the less true that such outrages on justice introduced into the national temper a mixture of cruelty and hypocrisy which it took centuries to eradicate.

Trials under Henry VIII.

The barrenness of the last reign in the field of literature still continued, as is natural in a time when religious controversy fills all men's minds; indeed popular poetry was far better represented in Scotland, which the Reformation had hardly yet reached, by the really beautiful poems of Dunbar and Gawaine Douglas, the translator of Vergil, than by anything which England had to show at the same time. In Dunbar's 'Timor mortis conturbat me,' we see here and there

Poetry of the period.

that Shakspere has been beforehand with us in admiring
him, as in the graceful stanza—

> I see that Makars (poets) amang the lave
> Plays here their pageants, syne goes to grave,
> Spared is not their faculty.
> *Timor mortis conturbat me.*

He fully deserves to be called, as he is by Professor
Morley, the best English poet since the days of Chaucer;
his charming ' Without gladness avails no treasure ' is
even alone sufficient to prove this. Gawaine Douglas, who
was Bishop of Dunkeld under Margaret of Scotland,
manages skilfully enough in his ' King Heart' a stanza
something like Ariosto's; and his allegorical treatment
seems to have given many hints to Spenser. Sir David
Lindsay's verse, as Walter Scott said, 'still has charms;'
his poem of 'Jock-up-aland' ends with a fervent prayer
that James V. may be strong enough to 'ding those
mony kings a' doon' who are making Scotland so miserable; and when James freed himself from his guardians,
Sir David was not backward in poetically teaching him
the real meaning of liberty. In England the palm of
satiric verse (it can hardly be called poetry) was borne by
Skelton, who left off mocking at the great Cardinal only
when obliged in 1528 to take sanctuary at Westminster
and thus avoid his vengeance. His 'Colin Clout' is on
the need of reformation in Church and State; in 'Speak,
Parrot,' and 'Why come ye not to Court?' he makes his
bitterest attacks on Wolsey; and in 'Phylyppe Sparrow'
he describes with much humour a tender-hearted nun's
grief for her lost pet. With Sir Thomas Wyatt and the
Earl of Surrey began the refined imitation of Italian
poetic forms; in their hands verse seemed to become
suddenly modern. They introduced the sonnet in English,

Q

and Wyatt at least shows in his 'Renouncing of Love' that he has gained from Petrarca a real sense of its capabilities; he also in his poem on the 'Courtier's Life' employs Dante's *terza rima*. Surrey, too, was an inventor in poetry; to him is due the first English blank verse, as used in a translation from the Æneid. His sonnets, though far less melodious than Milton's, yet have the descriptions of personal character of which the later poet makes such noble use; this may be seen in Surrey's sonnets on the fair Geraldine and on his faithful follower Richard Clere.

The drama was at this time very much in the rough, though it is almost surprising to see how much Shakspere condescends to borrow from the humours of Udall's 'Ralph Roister Doister,' which was probably written in this reign. Heywood was also celebrated at the time for interludes, one of the best being 'The Four P's,' a dialogue between Pardoner, Palmer, Ponticary, and Pedlar. The honour of English prose was still sustained chiefly by Sir Thomas More's History of Edward V. and by the 'Utopia.' Theologians, however, did much to establish purity of style, especially when they wished to be simple in order to instruct the common people. Cranmer's 'Institution of a Christian Man' is really excellent from its direct and winning expression; and though Hugh Latimer did not much conform to any art canons, yet few Englishmen have ever equalled him in the power of downright preaching, especially on semi-political subjects. Above all, of course, the Bible had been beautiful in Tyndal's translation, and was gradually advancing to that perfection which has won the hearts of Revisers in the present day.

The stage and prose.

Scientific study could hardly be said to exist as yet; men were far more curious to know the Latin and Greek names of natural objects, as Erasmus recommended, than to investigate their properties. Hardly any scientific works appear to have been sold by an Oxford bookseller whose trade diary from 1520 onwards has been preserved. It has been already noted that Linacre, the most truly scientific man of the reign, did not describe the most remarkable diseases of his own time; indeed he aimed, perhaps wisely, at restoring medicine through the works of the ancients rather than by direct observation, and devoted himself almost entirely to translations from Galen. The science of the day had not yet broken its connection with the occult sciences; even the earnest and severe Paul III., Pope as he was, never held a consistory or entered upon anything important without consulting the stars. Henry VIII., as we have seen, questioned soothsayers about the sex of his future children with the same faith which afterwards made Charles I. send 500*l.* to an astrologer when he was planning his escape from Hampton Court; he also invited to England the celebrated Cornelius Agrippa, whose reputation for magical knowledge was high. Alchemy was in great vogue at Paris, where hundreds of adepts were following each his own system; in England it was less popular, inasmuch as the celebrated Dee, afterwards so favoured by Elizabeth, had to leave Cambridge on beginning to study it. The belief in witchcraft was shown in England by the statute of 1541 already referred to; but only after Popes had been fulminating against it for fifty years and prosecutions had long been innumerable in France, Germany, and Italy. It is remarkable that the statute made it penal, not in itself, but only if it aimed at destroying life.

It is always difficult clearly to discern the every-day character and feeling of a people in times long past. Yet we are not quite without hints what Englishmen were like in

the sixteenth century. The kindliness and sobriety displayed here in times of pestilence have been
noticed above. Akin to the same temper was
the general submission to established authority, even when, without the support of any standing
army or organised police, it was carrying the most violent
changes. Even in the worst times a hundred yeomen
of the guard were enough to secure Henry's person.
Probably the real reason for this obedience was the
same dread of renewing civil war which afterwards made
England endure without rebelling the many misdoings
of Charles II. Of the social temper of our countrymen
in those days there are curiously opposite accounts. A
French traveller complains of their hatred for all foreigners, especially his countrymen; of the bad names
which they call them, and of the way in which they break
their word. A German, on the other hand, cannot say
enough of English politeness to the aged and to those
whom they consider learned; of their 'incredible courtesy
and friendliness of speech,' of the beauty of the ladies,
who, he says, 'never heretic (*ketzern*) their faces with
paint,' and, strangest of all, of the wondrous comfort,
civility, and respect which travellers received in English
inns. Of course the relations of English commerce to
Germany and France, as described above, may throw
much light on these contradictions in statement. Pleasant
would it be to look into the interior of more families, and
see whether there were many in England where the love
of father and daughter was as profound as that between
Sir Thomas More and Margaret Roper; and into more
meetings of heretics to search for affection like that
between Dalaber and Garret in 1528. 'I besought Garret,' says Dalaber, 'that he for the tender mercies of God
would not refuse me; saying that I trusted verily that he
which had begun this in me would not forsake me, but

<small>Character of the middle classes.</small>

give me grace to continue therein unto the end. When
he heard me say so, he kissed me, the tears trickling from
his eyes, and said to me, " The Lord God Almighty
grant you so to do ; and from henceforth forever take me
for your father, and I will take you for my son in Christ." '
We need not enquire whether the new beliefs (or indeed
the old ones) made men brave ; those who were first to conceive novelties or who had first to defend old things might
be bewildered by their position, but soon there grew up
in both a courage which literally seemed to think nothing
of the fire. A slight forcing of language might have saved
Lambert's life ; Forrest certainly need not have expressed
any opinion about Cardinal Fisher's death. Yet both
these men determinedly spoke out in spite of the terrors
which lay before them, and would not have varied their
mode of statement by a hair's-breadth to save their life.
Some of the reforming party have been blamed for a flip-
pancy and abusiveness before their judges which made it
more difficult to show them any indulgence ; nor can the
charge be altogether denied. But then it is beyond most
men to die like Latimer, with no harsh word to his perse-
cutors, or like More, with a wish that ' he and they might
find mercy together in a better world.' Even if some
came short of this, their tongue-violences may be con-
doned, since they were quite as willing to die for their
cause as to rail at its enemies.

Here, then, this brief summary of two reigns must
end ; it will be for abler hands, with the help of the fresh
material which every year now accumulates, to trace the
gradual expulsion from our political system of the bad
elements of Tudor despotism. To this Henry VIII., in
spite of all appearances, contributed both negatively and
positively. Negatively because his striking personality
dignified in a manner the violences which he committed
and the extravagances which he forced his Parliament

to enact; so that subsequent kings of less imposing character were likely to fail in attempting the like. Could his modes of government have been established, they would have been hardly less than a Turkish despotism; but they lived only in the unregulated and despotic spirit which they were intended to gratify, drooped and flagged when he was gone, and by no means uprooted from the minds of Englishmen the remembrance of their ancient liberties. And he also most unwittingly, but still really, gave our freedom more than one kind of positive help. For his rough and violent hand broke down superstitions, which, though we now regard them tenderly, we should have been sure to denounce if we had lived at the time. He raised up out of the spoils of the monasteries the great and strong middle class which was at length to curb his successors. Above all, his way of referring constantly to Parliament, because he found it servile, and bringing such a variety of affairs under its cognisance, had at least the effect of keeping its powers well in mind against the time when some fortunate election might send up to Westminster a body of members with principles worth having and a strong determination to make them good against all opposition. He trained Parliament to register his edicts; but the very fact that they had to do so proved their inherent right to dispute them if they would. Therefore when, as Burke says, new times brought with them new modes of tyranny, it was a light thing for Parliament to use against Elizabeth's monopolies, or James's claim that the sea-coast was his own, or Charles's demand for ship-money, the power which had been technically acknowledged in so many various forms and as applying to affairs so important.

Effect of Henry VIII.'s institutions.

In these two ways, then, the institutions of Henry VIII. have favoured English freedom.

INDEX.

ABE

ABERGAVENNY, Lord, 139
  Adrian VI., Pope, 143
Agrippa, Cornelius, 243
Albany, the Duke of, 130, 145
Alexander VI., Pope, 53
Alfonso of Naples, 81
André, Bernard, 22
Angus, Lord, 130
Anne Boleyn, 156, 171, 189
Anne Duchess of Bourbon, 17, 34, 121
Anne Duchess of Bretagne, 34, 37, 59
Anne of Cleves, 214
Arran, the Earl of, 218, 220
Arthur, Prince, 54
Ascue, Anne, 233
Aske, Robert, 201
Audley, Chancellor, 179, 233
Aurispa, 82
Ayala, Don Pedro de, 54

BARBAROSSA, 188, 227
  Barklay, 92
Bartons, the, 47, 109
Barton, Elizabeth, 176
Bell, Dr. John, 126
Beton, Cardinal, 221
Bothwell, Ramsay, Lord, 46
Bourbon, the Constable, 149
Bourchier, Sir T., 18
Bray, Sir Reginald, 48
Brooke, Lord, 38
Buckingham, the Duke of, 106, 140
Bulmer, Lady, 204

CABOT, John, 77
  Cabot, Sebastian, 77, 111
Campeggio, Cardinal, 133
Catesby, 20

EXE

Chapuys, 189, 190
Charles V., the Emperor, 5, 137, 175, 188, 225
Charles VIII., 8, 35, 51
Charles the Bold, 7
Chrysoloras, Manuel, 82
Clarence, George Duke of, 30
Clement VII., Pope, 149, 158, 192
Cleves, the Duke of, 214, 227
Clifford, the Shepherd Lord, 23
Colet, Dean, 83, 85, 96, 110
Columbus, 76
Commines, Philipe de, 8, 11, 17, 41
Conquest, title from, 21
Cordova, Gonzalo de, 59
Council, the Privy, 11, 72
Cranmer, Archbishop, 172, 186, 191
Cromwell, Lord, 169, 183, 213, 215
Crusades projected, 56, 106, 132
Curzon, Sir Robert, 60

DACRE, Lord (of the North), 131, 180, 218
Dacre, Lord (of the South), 225
Dalaber, 244
Darcy, Lord, 180, 201
Daubeny, Lord, 48
Dee, Dr., 242
Deposition, Bull of, 193
Dorset, Marquis of, 114
Douglas, Gawaine, 240
Dudley, Edmund, 63, 104
Dudley, Sir John (Lord Lisle), 222, 230

EDWARD IV., 12, 29
  Elizabeth, Queen, 22, 33, 62, 99
Empson, Richard, 63, 104
Exeter, the Marquis of, 209

FER

FERDINAND, of Aragon, 5, 41, 114, 135
Fisher, Cardinal, 89, 106, 155, 160, 178, 183
Fitzgerald, Lord Thomas, 180
Forrest, 207, 245
Fox, Bishop, 28, 88
Francis, Duke of Bretagne, 17, 34
Francis I., 121, 133, 139, 225
Fraternity of St. George, 69
Frederic III., Emperor, 9, 41
Frederic, King of Naples, 59
Frith, 186

GALLICAN Liberties, 55
Gardiner, Bishop, 163, 216, 234
Glamis, Lady, 219
Glyn Cothi, 213
Goch, John of, 152
Granada, capture of, 39
Grey, Lord Leonard, 181, 222
Grocyn, William, 83

HAMILTON, Patrick, 218
Haughton, 182
Hawes, 92
Henry IV., 10
Henry V., 10
Henry VI., 14, 62, 99
Henry VII., his descent, 13; his title, 14
Henry VIII., character of, 102, 167
Henry III. of Castile, 3
Henry IV. of Castile, 4
Hertford, the Earl of, 206
Heywood, 242
Howard, Sir E., 108
Howard, Sir T. (see Duke of Norfolk)
Hungerford, Sir Walter, 18
Hus, John, 151
Hussey, Lord, 201, 204

INTERCURSUS MAGNUS, the, 50, 74
Intercursus Malus, the, 61
Isabella of Castile, 5, 55, 57

JAMES III. of Scotland, 38
James IV. of Scotland, 64, 108, 118, 157

MOR

James V. of Scotland, 217
John II. (of Castile), 4
Juana, Queen of Spain, 55, 61
Julius II., Pope, 62, 112

KATHERINE of France, 14
Katherine Roet, 14
Katherine of Aragon, 54, 104, 156, 189
Katherine Howard, 224
Katherine Parr, 234
Kildare, Lord, 31, 47, 66
Kingston, Sir William, 167, 180

LAMBERT, John, 208
Landois, 17
Latimer, Hugh, 129, 207, 233
Latimer, Lord, 202
Lee, Bishop Roland, 213
Lennox, Lady, 131
Leo X., Pope, 120, 143, 154
Lilly, William, 90
Linacre, 25, 83, 243
Lincoln, the Earl of, 31
L'Isle, Adam, 147
Lollardism, 152
Louis XI., 6, 72
Louis XII., 58, 111
Lovel, Lord, 32
Luna, Alvaro de, 4
Luther, Martin, 141, 153

MACCHIAVELLI, 2
Magdalen, Queen of Scotland, 218
Margaret, Queen of Scotland, 54, 62, 130, 145
Margaret, the Lady, 15, 105
Margaret of Burgundy, 30, 31, 43, 60
Margaret of Savoy, 35, 37, 62, 112
Margaret Roper, 184
Martyr, Peter (d'Angheria), 79
Mary, Queen of France, 121
Mary of Guise, 217
Mary, Queen of Scots, 220
Maximilian, the Emperor, 45, 112, 117, 137
Merbeck, 234
Merchant Adventurers, the, 49
Meyer, Marcus, 176
More, Sir T., 83, 84, 123, 147, 178, 182.

MOR

Morton, Cardinal, 17, 28, 36, 94, 98
Mountjoy, Lord, 86, 137

NORFOLK, the Duke of (Sir T. Howard), 109, 117, 141, 202, 211, 220, 231.
Northumberland, the Duke of, 38
Northumberland, the Earl of, 166

OXFORD, John Earl of, 23, 72

PAUL III., Pope, 183, 228, 243
Petrarca, 81
Philip, the Archduke, 45, 61
Philip II. of Spain, 6
Poggio Bracciolini, 81
Pole, Cardinal, 210
Pole, Sir Geoffrey, 210
Politian, 82
Poynings, Sir Edward, 43, 67
Præmunire, 150, 162, 169

RHYS AP THOMAS, 18, 24
Richard III., 16, 17
Richard Duke of York, 30
Rochford, Lady, 225
Rochford, Lord, 190
Rock, Alderman, 230

SALISBURY, the Countess of, 22, 178, 210, 225
Scheiner, Cardinal, 134
Schwartz, Martin, 31
Seymour, Jane, Queen of England, 2(6
Sigismund, the Emperor, 151
Simnel, Lambert, 31
Skelton, 241
Staffords, the rebellion of, 29

YOR

Stanley, James, Bishop of Ely, 86
Stanley, Lord, 16, 19
Stanley, Sir William, 19, 45
Steelyard, the, 44
Strange, Lord, 18
Strode, 124
Suffolk, Charles, 121, 157, 161, 201
Suffolk, Edmund Duke of, 60
Supremacy, the Royal, 170
Surrey, Henry Earl of, 231
Sweating Sickness, the, 25

TEROUENNE and Tournay, 117
Torture in England, 12
Tudor, Edmund, 16
Tudor, Jasper, 16
Tunstall, Bishop, 123, 135
Tyndal, William, 192, 236, 242

UDALL, 242
'Utopia,' the, 85, 93

VALLA, Lorenzo, 84
Vasco de Gama, 74, 75
Venice, dominions of, 112

WARBECK, Perkin, 42, 49
Warham, Archbishop, 43, 105, 157, 168, 172
Warwick, the Countess of, 22
Warwick, the Earl of, 21
Waterford, 46
Wessel, 152
Wolsey, Cardinal, 123, 137, 147, 157, 161
Worde, Wynkyn de, 91, 92
Wyatt, Sir Thomas, 241

YORK, Richard Duke of, 30

"The volumes contain the ripe results of the studies of men who are authorities in their respective fields."—THE NATION.

EPOCHS OF HISTORY

EPOCHS OF ANCIENT HISTORY	EPOCHS OF MODERN HISTORY
Eleven volumes, 16mo, each $1.00.	Eighteen volumes, 16mo, each $1.00.

The Epoch volumes have most successfully borne the test of experience, and are universally acknowledged to be the best series of historical manuals in existence. They are admirably adapted in form and matter to the needs of colleges, schools, reading circles, and private classes. Attention is called to them as giving the utmost satisfaction as class hand-books.

NOAH PORTER, *President of Yale College.*

"The 'Epochs of History' have been prepared with knowledge and artistic skill to meet the wants of a large number of readers. To the young they furnish an outline or compendium. To those who are older they present a convenient sketch of the heads of the knowledge which they have already acquired. The outlines are by no means destitute of spirit, and may be used with great profit for family reading, and in select classes or reading clubs."

CHARLES KENDALL ADAMS, *President of Cornell University.*

"A series of concise and carefully prepared volumes on special eras of history. Each is also complete in itself, and has no especial connection with the other members of the series. The works are all written by authors selected by the editor on account of some especial qualifications for a portrayal of the period they respectively describe. The volumes form an excellent collection, especially adapted to the wants of a general reader."

The Publishers will supply these volumes to teachers at SPECIAL NET RATES, and would solicit correspondence concerning terms for examination and introduction copies.

CHARLES SCRIBNER'S SONS, Publishers
743-745 Broadway, New York

THE GREAT SUCCESS OF THE SERIES

is the best proof of its general popularity, and the excellence of the various volumes is further attested by their having been adopted as text-books in many of our leading educational institutions. The publishers beg to call attention to the following list comprising some of the most prominent institutions using volumes of the series:

Smith College, Northampton, Mass.
Univ. of Vermont, Burlington, Vt.
Yale Univ., New Haven, Conn.
Harvard Univ., Cambridge, Mass.
Bellewood Sem., Anchorage, Ky.
Vanderbilt Univ., Nashville, Tenn.
State Univ., Minneapolis, Minn.
Christian Coll., Columbia, Mo.
Adelphi Acad., Brooklyn, N. Y.
Earlham Coll., Richmond, Ind.
Granger Place School, Canandaigua, N. Y.
Salt Lake Acad., Salt Lake City, Utah.
Beloit Col., Beloit, Wis.
Logan Female Coll., Russellville, Ky.
No. West Univ., Evanston, Ill.
State Normal School, Baltimore, Md.
Hamilton Coll., Clinton, N. Y.
Doane Coll., Crete, Neb.
Princeton College, Princeton, N. J.
Williams Coll., Williamstown, Mass.
Cornell Univ., Ithaca, N. Y.
Illinois Coll., Jacksonville, Ill.

Univ. of South, Sewaunee, Tenn.
Wesleyan Univ., Mt. Pleasant, Ia.
Univ. of Cal., Berkeley, Cal.
So. Car. Coll., Columbia, S. C.
Amsterdam Acad., Amsterdam, N. Y.
Carleton Coll., Northfield, Minn.
Wesleyan Univ., Middletown, Mass.
Albion Coll., Albion, Mich.
Dartmouth Coll., Hanover, N. H.
Wilmington Coll., Wilmington, O.
Madison Univ., Hamilton, N. Y.
Syracuse Univ., Syracuse, N. Y.
Univ. of Wis., Madison, Wis.
Union Coll., Schenectady, N. Y.
Norwich Free Acad., Norwich, Conn.
Greenwich Acad., Greenwich, Conn.
Univ. of Neb., Lincoln, Neb.
Kalamazoo Coll., Kalamazoo, Mich.
Olivet Coll., Olivet, Mich.
Amherst Coll., Amherst, Mass.
Ohio State Univ., Columbus, O.
Free Schools, Oswego, N. Y.

Bishop J. F. HURST, *ex-President of Drew Theol. Sem.*

"It appears to me that the idea of Morris in his Epochs is strictly in harmony with the philosophy of history—namely, that great movements should be treated not according to narrow geographical and national limits and distinction, but universally, according to their place in the general life of the world. The historical Maps and the copious Indices are welcome additions to the volumes."

EPOCHS OF ANCIENT HISTORY.

A SERIES OF BOOKS NARRATING THE HISTORY OF GREECE AND ROME, AND OF THEIR RELATIONS TO OTHER COUNTRIES AT SUCCESSIVE EPOCHS.

Edited by

Rev. G. W. Cox and Charles Sankey, M.A.

Eleven volumes, 16mo, with 41 Maps and Plans. Sold separately. Price per vol., $1.00.
The Set, Roxburgh style, gilt top, in box, $11.00.

TROY—ITS LEGEND, HISTORY, AND LITERATURE. By S. G. W. Benjamin.

"The task of the author has been to gather into a clear and very readable narrative all that is known of legendary, historical, and geographical Troy, and to tell the story of Homer, and weigh and compare the different theories in the Homeric controversy. The work is well done. His book is altogether candid, and is a very valuable and entertaining compendium."—*Hartford Courant.*

"As a monograph on Troy, covering all sides of the question, it is of great value, and supplies a long vacant place in our fund of classical knowledge."—*N. Y. Christian Advocate.*

THE GREEKS AND THE PERSIANS. By Rev G. W. Cox.

"It covers the ground in a perfectly satisfactory way. The work is clear, succinct, and readable."—*New York Independent.*

"Marked by thorough and comprehensive scholarship and by a skillful style."—*Congregationalist.*

"It would be hard to find a more creditable book. The author's prefatory remarks upon the origin and growth of Greek civilization are alone worth the price of the volume."
—*Christian Union.*

THE ATHENIAN EMPIRE—From the Flight of Xerxes to the Fall of Athens. By Rev. G. W. Cox.

"Mr. Cox writes in such a way as to bring before the reader everything which is important to be known or learned; and his narrative cannot fail to give a good idea of the men and deeds with which he is concerned."—*The Churchman.*

"Mr. Cox has done his work with the honesty of a true student. It shows persevering scholarship and a desire to get at the truth."—*New York Herald.*

THE SPARTAN AND THEBAN SUPREMACIES. By Charles Sankey, M.A.

"This volume covers the period between the disasters of Athens at the close of the Pelopenesian war and the rise of Macedon. It is a very striking and instructive picture of the political life of the Grecian commonwealth at that time."—*The Churchman.*

"It is singularly interesting to read, and in respect to arrangement, maps, etc., is all that can be desired."—*Boston Congregationalist.*

THE MACEDONIAN EMPIRE—Its Rise and Culmination to Death of Alexander the Great. By A. M. Curteis, M.A.

"A good and satisfactory history of a very important period. The maps are excellent, and the story is lucidly and vigorously told."—*The Nation.*

"The same compressive style and yet completeness of detail that have characterized the previous issues in this delightful series, are found in this volume. Certainly the art of conciseness in writing was never carried to a higher or more effective point."—*Boston Saturday Evening Gazette.*

*** *The above five volumes give a connected and complete history of Greece from the earliest times to the death of Alexander.*

EARLY ROME—From the Foundation of the City to its Destruction by the Gauls. By W. IHNE, Ph.D.

"Those who want to know the truth instead of the traditions that used to be learned of our fathers, will find in the work entertainment, careful scholarship, and sound sense."—*Cincinnati Times.*

"The book is excellently well done. The views are those of a learned and able man, and they are presented in this volume with great force and clearness."—*The Nation.*

ROME AND CARTHAGE—The Punic Wars. By R. BOSWORTH SMITH.

"By blending the account of Rome and Carthage the accomplished author presents a succinct and vivid picture of two great cities and people which leaves a deep impression. The story is full of intrinsic interest, and was never better told."—*Christian Union.*

"The volume is one of rare interest and value."—*Chicago Interior.*

"An admirably condensed history of Carthage, from its establishment by the adventurous Phœnician traders to its sad and disastrous fall."—*New York Herald.*

THE GRACCHI, MARIUS, AND SULLA. By A. H. BEESLEY.

"A concise and scholarly historical sketch, descriptive of the decay of the Roman Republic, and the events which paved the way for the advent of the conquering Cæsar. It is an excellent account of the leaders and legislation of the republic."—*Boston Post.*

"It is prepared in succinct but comprehensive style, and is an excellent book for reading and reference."—*New York Observer.*

"No better condensed account of the two Gracchi and the turbulent careers of Marius and Sulla has yet appeared."—*New York Independent.*

THE ROMAN TRIUMVIRATES. By the Very Rev. CHARLES MERIVALE, D.D.

"In brevity, clear and scholarly treatment of the subject, and the convenience of map, index, and side notes, the volume is a model."—*New York Tribune.*

"An admirable presentation, and in style vigorous and picturesque."—*Hartford Courant.*

THE EARLY EMPIRE—From the Assassination of Julius Cæsar to the Assassination of Domitian. By Rev. W. WOLFE CAPES, M.A.

"It is written with great clearness and simplicity of style, and is as attractive an account as has ever been given in brief of one of the most interesting periods of Roman History."—*Boston Saturday Evening Gazette.*

"It is a clear, well-proportioned, and trustworthy performance, and well deserves to be studied."—*Christian at Work.*

THE AGE OF THE ANTONINES—The Roman Empire of the Second Century. By Rev. W. WOLFE CAPES, M.A.

"The Roman Empire during the second century is the broad subject discussed in this book, and discussed with learning and intelligence."—*New York Independent.*

"The writer's diction is clear and elegant, and his narration is free from any touch of pedantry. In the treatment of its prolific and interesting theme, and in its general plan, the book is a model of works of its class."—*New York Herald.*

"We are glad to commend it. It is written clearly, and with care and accuracy. It is also in such neat and compact form as to be the more attractive."—*Congregationalist.*

⁎ *The above six volumes give the History of Rome from the founding of the City to the death of Marcus Aurelius Antoninus.*

EPOCHS OF MODERN HISTORY.

A SERIES OF BOOKS NARRATING THE HISTORY OF ENGLAND AND EUROPE AT SUCCESSIVE EPOCHS SUBSEQUENT TO THE CHRISTIAN ERA.

Edited by

EDWARD E. MORRIS.

Eighteen volumes, 16mo, with 74 Maps, Plans, and Tables. Sold separately. Price per vol., $1.00.
The Set, Roxburgh style, gilt top, in box, $18.00.

THE BEGINNING OF THE MIDDLE AGES—England and Europe in the Ninth Century. By the Very Rev. R. W. CHURCH, M.A.

"A remarkably thoughtful and satisfactory discussion of the causes and results of the vast changes which came upon Europe during the period discussed. The book is adapted to be exceedingly serviceable."—*Chicago Standard.*

"At once readable and valuable. It is comprehensive and yet gives the details of a period most interesting to the student of history."—*Herald and Presbyter.*

"It is written with a clearness and vividness of statement which make it the pleasantest reading. It represents a great deal of patient research, and is careful and scholarly."—*Boston Journal.*

THE NORMANS IN EUROPE—The Feudal System and England under the Norman Kings. By Rev. A. H. JOHNSON, M.A.

"Its pictures of the Normans in their home, of the Scandinavian exodus, the conquest of England, and Norman administration, are full of vigor and cannot fail of holding the reader's attention."—*Episcopal Register.*

"The style of the author is vigorous and animated, and he has given a valuable sketch of the origin and progress of the great Northern movement that has shaped the history of modern Europe."—*Boston Transcript.*

THE CRUSADES. By Rev. G. W. Cox.

"To be warmly commended for important qualities. The author shows conscientious fidelity to the materials, and such skill in the use of them, that, as a result, the reader has before him a narrative related in a style that makes it truly fascinating."—*Congregationalist.*

"It is written in a pure and flowing style, and its arrangement and treatment of subject are exceptional."—*Christian Intelligencer.*

THE EARLY PLANTAGENETS—Their Relation to the History of Europe; The Foundation and Growth of Constitutional Government. By Rev. W. STUBBS, M.A.

"Nothing could be desired more clear, succinct, and well arranged. All parts of the book are well done. It may be pronounced the best existing brief history of the constitution for this, its most important period."—*The Nation.*

"Prof. Stubbs has presented leading events with such fairness and wisdom as are seldom found. He is remarkably clear and satisfactory."—*The Churchman.*

EDWARD III. By Rev. W. WARBURTON, M.A.

"The author has done his work well, and we commend it as containing in small space all essential matter."—*New York Independent.*

"Events and movements are admirably condensed by the author, and presented in such attractive form as to entertain as well as instruct."—*Chicago Interior.*

THE HOUSES OF LANCASTER AND YORK —The Conquest and Loss of France. By JAMES GAIRDNER.

"Prepared in a most careful and thorough manner, and ought to be read by every student."—*New York Times.*

"It leaves nothing to be desired as regards compactness, accuracy, and excellence of literary execution."—*Boston Journal.*

THE ERA OF THE PROTESTANT REVOLUTION. By FREDERIC SEEBOHM. With Notes, on Books in English relating to the Reformation, by Prof. GEORGE P. FISHER, D.D.

"For an impartial record of the civil and ecclesiastical changes about four hundred years ago, we cannot commend a better manual."—*Sunday-School Times.*

"All that could be desired, as well in execution as in plan. The narrative is animated, and the selection and grouping of events skillful and effective."—*The Nation.*

THE EARLY TUDORS—Henry VII., Henry VIII. By Rev. C. E. MOBERLEY, M.A., late Master in Rugby School.

"Is concise, scholarly, and accurate. On the epoch of which it treats, we know of no work which equals it."—*N. Y. Observer.*

"A marvel of clear and succinct brevity and good historical judgment. There is hardly a better book of its kind to be named."—*New York Independent.*

THE AGE OF ELIZABETH. By Rev. M. CREIGHTON, M.A.

"Clear and compact in style ; careful in their facts, and just in interpretation of them. It sheds much light on the progress of the Reformation and the origin of the Popish reaction during Queen Elizabeth's reign ; also, the relation of Jesuitism to the latter."—*Presbyterian Review.*

"A clear, concise, and just story of an era crowded with events of interest and importance."—*New York World.*

THE THIRTY YEARS' WAR—1618-1648. By SAMUEL RAWSON GARDINER.

"As a manual it will prove of the greatest practical value, while to the general reader it will afford a clear and interesting account of events. We know of no more spirited and attractive recital of the great era."—*Boston Saturday Evening Gazette.*

"The thrilling story of those times has never been told so vividly or succinctly as in this volume."—*Episcopal Register.*

EPOCHS OF MODERN HISTORY.

THE PURITAN REVOLUTION; and the First Two Stuarts, 1603-1660. By SAMUEL RAWSON GARDINER.

" The narrative is condensed and brief, yet sufficiently comprehensive to give an adequate view of the events related."
—*Chicago Standard.*

" Mr. Gardiner uses his researches in an admirably clear and fair way."—*Congregationalist.*

" The sketch is concise, but clear and perfectly intelligible."
—*Hartford Courant.*

THE ENGLISH RESTORATION AND LOUIS XIV., from the Peace of Westphalia to the Peace of Nimwegen. By OSMUND AIRY, M.A.

" It is crisply and admirably written. An immense amount of information is conveyed and with great clearness, the arrangement of the subjects showing great skill and a thorough command of the complicated theme."—*Boston Saturday Evening Gazette.*

"The author writes with fairness and discrimination, and has given a clear and intelligible presentation of the time."—*New York Evangelist.*

THE FALL OF THE STUARTS; and Western Europe. By Rev. EDWARD HALE, M.A.

" A valuable compend to the general reader and scholar."
—*Providence Journal.*

"It will be found of great value. It is a very graphic account of the history of Europe during the 17th century, and is admirably adapted for the use of students."—*Boston Saturday Evening Gazette.*

"An admirable handbook for the student."—*The Churchman.*

THE AGE OF ANNE. By EDWARD E. MORRIS, M.A.

" The author's arrangement of the material is remarkably clear, his selection and adjustment of the facts judicious, his historical judgment fair and candid, while the style wins by its simple elegance."—*Chicago Standard.*

"An excellent compendium of the history of an important period."—*The Watchman.*

THE EARLY HANOVERIANS—Europe from the Peace of Utrecht to the Peace of Aix-la-Chapelle. By EDWARD E. MORRIS, M.A.

"Masterly, condensed, and vigorous, this is one of the books which it is a delight to read at odd moments; which are broad and suggestive, and at the same time condensed in treatment."—*Christian Advocate.*

"A remarkably clear and readable summary of the salient points of interest. The maps and tables, no less than the author's style and treatment of the subject, entitle the volume to the highest claims of recognition."—*Boston Daily Advertiser.*

FREDERICK THE GREAT, AND THE SEVEN YEARS' WAR. By F. W. LONGMAN.

"The subject is most important, and the author has treated it in a way which is both scholarly and entertaining."—*The Churchman.*

"Admirably adapted to interest school boys, and older heads will find it pleasant reading."—*New York Tribune.*

THE FRENCH REVOLUTION, AND FIRST EMPIRE. By WILLIAM O'CONNOR MORRIS. With Appendix by ANDREW D. WHITE, LL.D., ex-President of Cornell University.

"We have long needed a simple compendium of this period, and we have here one which is brief enough to be easily run through with, and yet particular enough to make entertaining reading."—*New York Evening Post.*

"The author has well accomplished his difficult task of sketching in miniature the grand and crowded drama of the French Revolution and the Napoleonic Empire, showing himself to be no servile compiler, but capable of judicious and independent criticism."—*Springfield Republican.*

THE EPOCH OF REFORM—1830-1850. By JUSTIN MCCARTHY.

"Mr. McCarthy knows the period of which he writes thoroughly, and the result is a narrative that is at once entertaining and trustworthy."—*New York Examiner.*

"The narrative is clear and comprehensive, and told with abundant knowledge and grasp of the subject."—*Boston Courier.*

IMPORTANT HISTORICAL WORKS.

THE DAWN OF HISTORY. An Introduction to Pre-Historic Study. New and Enlarged Edition. Edited by C. F. KEARY. 12mo, cloth, $1.25.

This work treats successively of the earliest traces of man; of language, its growth, and the story it tells of the pre-historic users of it; of early social life, the religions, mythologies, and folk-tales, and of the history of writing. The present edition contains about one hundred pages of new matter, embodying the results of the latest researches.

"A fascinating manual. In its way, the work is a model of what a popular scientific work should be."—*Boston Sat. Eve. Gazette.*

THE ORIGIN OF NATIONS. By Professor GEORGE RAWLINSON, M.A. 12mo, with maps, $1.00.

The first part of this book discusses the antiquity of civilization in Egypt and the other early nations of the East. The second part is an examination of the ethnology of Genesis, showing its accordance with the latest results of modern ethnographical science.

"A work of genuine scholarly excellence, and a useful offset to a great deal of the superficial current literature on such subjects."—*Congregationalist.*

MANUAL OF MYTHOLOGY. For the Use of Schools, Art Students, and General Readers. Founded on the Works of Petiscus, Preller, and Welcker. By ALEXANDER S. MURRAY, Department of Greek and Roman Antiquities, British Museum. With 45 Plates. Reprinted from the Second Revised London Edition. Crown 8vo, $1.75.

"It has been acknowledged the best work on the subject to be found in a concise form, and as it embodies the results of the latest researches and discoveries in ancient mythologies, it is superior for school and general purposes as a handbook to any of the so-called standard works."—*Cleveland Herald.*

"Whether as a manual for reference, a text-book for school use, or for the general reader, the book will be found very valuable and interesting."—*Boston Journal.*

IMPORTANT HISTORICAL WORKS.

THE HISTORY OF ROME, from the Earliest Time to the Period of Its Decline. By Dr. THEODOR MOMMSEN. Translated by W. P. DICKSON, D.D., LL.D. Reprinted from the Revised London Edition. Four volumes, crown 8vo. Price per set, $8.00.

"A work of the very highest merit; its learning is exact and profound; its narrative full of genius and skill; its descriptions of men are admirably vivid."—*London Times.*

"Since the days of Niebuhr, no work on Roman History has appeared that combines so much to attract, instruct, and charm the reader. Its style—a rare quality in a German author—is vigorous, spirited, and animated."—Dr. SCHMITZ.

THE PROVINCES OF THE ROMAN EMPIRE. From Cæsar to Diocletian. By THEODOR MOMMSEN. Translated by WILLIAM P. DICKSON, D.D., LL.D. With maps. Two vols., 8vo, $6.00.

"The author draws the wonderfully rich and varied picture of the conquest and administration of that great circle of peoples and lands which formed the empire of Rome outside of Italy, their agriculture, trade, and manufactures, their artistic and scientific life, through all degrees of civilization, with such detail and completeness as could have come from no other hand than that of this great master of historical research."—Prof. W. A. PACKARD, Princeton College.

THE HISTORY OF THE ROMAN REPUBLIC.
Abridged from the History by Professor THEODOR MOMMSEN, by C. BRYANS and F. J. R. HENDY. 12mo, $1.75.

"It is a genuine boon that the essential parts of Mommsen's Rome are thus brought within the easy reach of all, and the abridgment seems to me to preserve unusually well the glow and movement of the original."—Prof. TRACY PECK, Yale University.

"The condensation has been accurately and judiciously effected. I heartily commend the volume as the most adequate embodiment, in a single volume, of the main results of modern historical research in the field of Roman affairs."—Prof. HENRY M. BAIRD, University of City of New York.

THE HISTORY OF GREECE. By Prof. Dr.
Ernst Curtius. Translated by Adolphus William Ward, M.A., Fellow of St. Peter's College, Cambridge, Prof. of History in Owen's College, Manchester. Five volumes, crown 8vo. Price per set, $10.00.

"We cannot express our opinion of Dr. Curtius' book better than by saying that it may be fitly ranked with Theodor Mommsen's great work."—*London Spectator.*

"As an introduction to the study of Grecian history, no previous work is comparable to the present for vivacity and picturesque beauty, while in sound learning and accuracy of statement it is not inferior to the elaborate productions which enrich the literature of the age."—*N. Y. Daily Tribune.*

CÆSAR: a Sketch. By James Anthony Froude,
M.A. 12mo, gilt top, $1.50.

"This book is a most fascinating biography and is by far the best account of Julius Cæsar to be found in the English language."—*The London Standard.*

"He combines into a compact and nervous narrative all that is known of the personal, social, political, and military life of Cæsar; and with his sketch of Cæsar includes other brilliant sketches of the great man, his friends, or rivals, who contemporaneously with him formed the principal figures in the Roman world."—*Harper's Monthly.*

CICERO. Life of Marcus Tullius Cicero. By
William Forsyth, M.A., Q.C. 20 Engravings. New Edition. 2 vols., crown 8vo, in one, gilt top, $2.50.

The author has not only given us the most complete and well-balanced account of the life of Cicero ever published; he has drawn an accurate and graphic picture of domestic life among the best classes of the Romans, one which the reader of general literature, as well as the student, may peruse with pleasure and profit.

"A scholar without pedantry, and a Christian without cant, Mr. Forsyth seems to have seized with praiseworthy tact the precise attitude which it behooves a biographer to take when narrating the life, the personal life of Cicero. Mr. Forsyth produces what we venture to say will become one of the classics of English biographical literature, and will be welcomed by readers of all ages and both sexes, of all professions and of no profession at all."—*London Quarterly.*

VALUABLE WORKS ON CLASSICAL LITERATURE.

THE HISTORY OF ROMAN LITERATURE.
From the Earliest Period to the Death of Marcus Aurelius. With Chronological Tables, etc., for the use of Students. By C. T. CRUTTWELL, M.A. Crown 8vo, $2.50.

Mr. Cruttwell's book is written throughout from a purely literary point of view, and the aim has been to avoid tedious and trivial details. The result is a volume not only suited for the student, but remarkably readable for all who possess any interest in the subject.

" Mr. Cruttwell has given us a genuine history of Roman literature, not merely a descriptive list of authors and their productions, but a well elaborated portrayal of the successive stages in the intellectual development of the Romans and the various forms of expression which these took in literature."—*N. Y. Nation.*

UNIFORM WITH THE ABOVE.

A HISTORY OF GREEK LITERATURE.
From the Earliest Period of Demosthenes. By FRANK BYRON JEVONS, M.A., Tutor in the University of Durham. Crown 8vo, $2.50.

The author goes into detail with sufficient fullness to make the history complete, but he never loses sight of the commanding lines along which the Greek mind moved, and a clear understanding of which is necessary to every intelligent student of universal literature.

"It is beyond all question the best history of Greek literature that has hitherto been published."—*London Spectator.*

"With such a book as this within reach there is no reason why any intelligent English reader may not get a thorough and comprehensive insight into the spirit of Greek literature, of its historic development, and of its successive and chief masterpieces, which are here so finely characterized, analyzed, and criticised."—*Chicago Advance.*

TRANSLATIONS OF PLATO.

THE DIALOGUES OF PLATO. Translated into English, with Analysis and Introductions. By B. JOWETT, M.A., Master of Balliol College, Oxford. A new and cheaper edition. Four vols., crown 8vo, per set, $8.00.

"The present work of Professor Jowett will be welcomed with profound interest, as the only adequate endeavor to transport the most precious monument of Grecian thought among the familiar treasures of English literature. The noble reputation of Professor Jowett, both as a thinker and a scholar, is a valid guaranty for the excellence of his performance."—*New York Tribune.*

SOCRATES. A Translation of the Apology, Crito, and parts of the Phædo of Plato. Containing the Defence of Socrates at his Trial, his Conversation in Prison, with his Thoughts on the Future Life, and an Account of his Death. With an Introduction by Professor W. W. Goodwin, of Harvard College. 12mo, cloth, $1.00: paper, 50 cents.

TALKS WITH SOCRATES ABOUT LIFE. Translations from the Gorgias and the Republic of Plato. 12mo, cloth, $1.00; paper, 50 cents.

A DAY IN ATHENS WITH SOCRATES. Translations from the Protagoras and the Republic of Plato. Being conversations between Socrates and other Greeks on Virtue and Justice. 12mo, cloth, $1.00; paper, 50 cents.

"Eminent scholars, men of much Latin and more Greek, attest the skill and truth with which the versions are made; we can confidently speak of their English grace and clearness. They seem a 'model of style,' because they are without manner and perfectly simple."—W. D. HOWELLS.

"We do not remember any translation of a Greek author which is a better specimen of idiomatic English than this, or a more faithful rendering of the real spirit of the original into English as good and as simple as the Greek."—*New York Evening Post.*

CHARLES SCRIBNER'S SONS,
743 and 745 Broadway, New York.

www.ingramcontent.com/pod-product-compliance
Lightning Source LLC
Chambersburg PA
CBHW032107230426
43672CB00009B/1662